Harnessing Chatbots for Effective Language Teaching

Rubén González Vallejo
University of Malaga, Spain

IGI Global
Scientific Publishing
Publishing Tomorrow's Research Today

Published in the United States of America by
IGI Global Scientific Publishing
701 East Chocolate Avenue
Hershey, PA, 17033, USA
Tel: 717-533-8845
Fax: 717-533-7115
Website: https://www.igi-global.com E-mail: cust@igi-global.com

Library of Congress Cataloging-in-Publication Data

Names: GonzaÌlez Vallejo, RubeÌn, 1991- editor
Title: Harnessing chatbots for effective language teaching / edited by: RubeÌn GonzaÌlez Vallejo.
Description: Hershey : IGI Global Scientific Publishing, 2025. | Includes bibliographical references and index. | Summary: "The book explores the intersection between artificial intelligence (AI) and language education, offering a comprehensive guide for educators, researchers, and technology enthusiasts interested in leveraging AI to enhance language teaching methodologies and learning outcomes. Aimed at language teachers, academics, EdTech developers, and policymakers, the book addresses key topics such as the introduction of AI technologies in language teaching, AI-powered learning tools, and how these technologies can personalize instruction to meet individual students' needs, thus improving engagement and effectiveness"-- Provided by publisher.
Identifiers: LCCN 2025001371 (print) | LCCN 2025001372 (ebook) | ISBN 9798369399743 hardcover | ISBN 9798369399750 paperback | ISBN 9798369399767 ebook
Subjects: LCSH: Language and languages--Study and teaching--Technological innovations | Artificial intelligence--Educational applications | Chatbots | LCGFT: Essays
Classification: LCC P53.855 .H38 2025 (print) | LCC P53.855 (ebook) | DDC 418.0078/635--dc23/eng/20250509
LC record available at https://lccn.loc.gov/2025001371
LC ebook record available at https://lccn.loc.gov/2025001372

British Cataloguing in Publication Data
A Cataloguing in Publication record for this book is available from the British Library.

Table of Contents

Detailed Table of Contents

The integration of chatbots into Metaverse-based classrooms offers new opportunities to enhance learning experiences through AI-driven, interactive, and personalized interactions. As educational institutions increasingly explore virtual environments, chatbots can provide real-time assistance, facilitate collaboration, and support adaptive learning in immersive settings. This paper explores the synergy between chatbots and the Metaverse, highlighting their potential to revolutionize education by improving student engagement, accessibility, and inclusivity. However, challenges such as technological limitations, data privacy concerns, and the quality of chatbot interactions remain. The paper also discusses the future potential of chatbots in virtual classrooms, with advancements in AI, VR, and accessibility promising further innovations. By addressing existing challenges, chatbots in the Metaverse can become valuable tools, fostering more dynamic, inclusive, and personalized educational experiences.

This chapter explores the role of gamification in language-learning chatbots, examining its core elements, advanced features, benefits, and challenges. Gamification, which integrates game mechanics such as points, badges, and leaderboards, enhances learner motivation, engagement, and retention. By analyzing key theoretical foundations, including Self-Determination Theory, the chapter discusses how gamification fosters intrinsic and extrinsic motivation in language learners. Case studies of successful applications such as Duolingo, Babbel, and Mondly demonstrate the effectiveness of these gamified systems in real-world settings. Additionally, the chapter highlights challenges such as learner diversity, content overload, and the balance between intrinsic and extrinsic motivation. Finally, future trends, including the integration of AI, NLP, augmented reality, and social learning, promise to revolutionize the gamified language-learning experience. This comprehensive analysis underscores the transformative potential of gamification in language education.

This chapter explores the integration of Adaptive AI in Metaverse language education, examining how AI-driven platforms and immersive virtual environments are revolutionizing language learning. By combining artificial intelligence, augmented reality (AR), and virtual reality (VR), the Metaverse offers personalized and interactive experiences tailored to individual learning needs. This chapter covers the evolution of language learning technologies, the potential benefits and features of Adaptive AI, and how it enhances language acquisition within the Metaverse. It also addresses key ethical concerns, challenges such as data privacy, accessibility, and AI biases, and the future trajectory of this educational approach. The future promises even more sophisticated learning environments, with emotionally intelligent AI tutors, real-time translation, and multilingual communication tools. This emerging paradigm reshapes how languages are learned globally, fostering accessibility and cross-cultural understanding.

This chapter examines the metaverse's transformational potential in education, highlighting its ability to improve immersive learning experiences via sophisticated technologies like virtual reality (VR) and augmented reality (AR). It examines how these technologies may provide realistic simulations, enabling students to participate in interactive learning settings that enhance their comprehension and retention of knowledge. The chapter emphasizes the significance of personalized learning paths supported by data analytics and artificial intelligence, which provide customized educational experiences that address specific student requirements. Furthermore, it analyzes novel evaluation techniques that enhance critical thinking and problem-

Preface

In recent years, artificial intelligence has rapidly transformed the landscape of education, offering innovative solutions to enhance language learning. Among these advancements, chatbots have emerged as powerful tools capable of providing personalized, interactive, and adaptive learning experiences. This edited volume, *Harnessing Chatbots for Effective Language Teaching*, brings together a diverse range of perspectives exploring how chatbots can be integrated into various educational frameworks, from metaverse-based classrooms to task-based language teaching methodologies. By examining the intersection of AI, gamification, adaptive learning, and immersive virtual environments, this book provides educators, researchers, and policymakers with critical insights into the evolving role of technology in language education.

The chapters in this collection present cutting-edge research and case studies from leading academics and practitioners across the globe. They address key questions about the efficacy of chatbots in fostering learner engagement, supporting autonomous learning, and enhancing communicative competence in different linguistic and cultural contexts. Furthermore, this volume delves into the technical and pedagogical challenges that arise when implementing AI-driven tools in language education, including ethical concerns, data privacy, and the balance between automation and human interaction. By critically analyzing both the opportunities and limitations of chatbots, the contributing authors offer valuable perspectives on the future trajectory of AI in language learning.

As the editor of this volume, I am grateful to the scholars who have contributed their expertise and research to this endeavor. Their work not only reflects the latest advancements in AI-driven education but also underscores the importance of continuous innovation in pedagogical practices. This book serves as both a theoretical and practical guide for educators looking to harness the power of chatbots to create more dynamic, inclusive, and effective language learning experiences.

Chapter 1. Integrating Chatbots Into Metaverse-Based Classrooms

Rohit Yadav, Mohit Yadav, Xuan-Hoa Nghiem

This chapter explores the integration of chatbots within Metaverse-based classrooms, highlighting their potential to revolutionize education by offering AI-driven, interactive, and personalized learning experiences. It delves into how chatbots can enhance student engagement, collaboration, and adaptive learning in immersive virtual environments. The authors examine the challenges of technological limitations, data privacy, and the quality of chatbot interactions. By presenting current and future applications of chatbots in virtual classrooms, the chapter offers insights into how these tools can support dynamic and inclusive educational experiences, despite the ongoing challenges.

Chapter 2. Gamification Elements in Language-Learning Chatbots

Rohit Yadav, Xuan-Hoa Nghiem, Mo Yadav

This chapter investigates the role of gamification in enhancing language-learning chatbots. By incorporating elements such as points, badges, and leaderboards, gamification fosters motivation, engagement, and retention in learners. The authors examine the theoretical foundations of gamification, including Self-Determination Theory, and analyze its impact on both intrinsic and extrinsic motivation. Drawing from case studies like Duolingo and Babbel, the chapter also highlights the challenges of balancing game mechanics with educational content, suggesting that future trends involving AI, NLP, augmented reality, and social learning will further transform language education.

Chapter 3. Adaptive AI in Metaverse Language Education

Rohit Yadav, Xuan-Hoa Nghiem, Mohit Yadav

In this chapter, the authors explore the synergy between Adaptive AI and Metaverse-based language education. They investigate how AI-driven platforms combined with augmented and virtual reality create personalized, immersive learning experiences. The chapter discusses the evolution of language learning technologies and the potential benefits of Adaptive AI, including real-time translation and multilingual communication. Ethical concerns, accessibility, and AI biases are also addressed, along with the future possibilities of emotionally intelligent AI tutors and more sophisticated learning environments that support cross-cultural understanding and global language acquisition.

Chapter 4. The Future of Education in the Metaverse: Immersive, Interactive, and Collaborative Learning

Andi Asrifan, Nurul Aini, Khristianto Khristianto

This chapter explores the transformative potential of the Metaverse in education, focusing on the use of virtual reality (VR) and augmented reality (AR) technologies to create immersive and interactive learning environments. It discusses how these technologies can simulate realistic experiences that enhance student comprehension and retention. The authors highlight the role of personalized learning paths supported by AI and data analytics, offering tailored educational experiences. Furthermore, the chapter examines novel evaluation techniques and collaborative tools that foster critical thinking and teamwork, envisioning a future where education is more engaging, accessible, and effective.

Chapter 5. Integrating AI Into Task-Based Language Teaching: Large Language Models in the Designing of Web Quests

Pinelopi Krystalli, Panagiotis Arvanitis

This chapter advocates for the integration of AI, particularly large language models (LLMs), into task-based language teaching through the design of webquests. By promoting active, research-oriented tasks, webquests enhance learners' motivation, critical thinking, and digital literacy. The authors explore how LLMs, such as ChatGPT and Gemini, can be leveraged to tailor webquests to various language proficiency levels, fostering both linguistic and digital competencies. The chapter also provides a practical framework for educators, offering guidance on how to integrate these AI tools effectively into language teaching while extending learning beyond the classroom.

Chapter 6. Smart Education Sentiment Analysis Combining CNN and ANN for Deeper Insights From Student Feedback

Usha Rani

This chapter presents an advanced methodology for sentiment analysis of student feedback, combining Convolutional Neural Networks (CNN) and Artificial Neural Networks (ANN) to gain deeper insights into student experiences. It discusses the use of AI in analyzing feedback related to teaching quality, course content, and campus facilities, offering a more nuanced understanding of student sentiment. The chapter emphasizes the importance of preprocessing data, aspect extraction, and sentiment classification, demonstrating how AI can be used to improve the responsiveness of educational institutions to student needs.

Chapter 7. Exploring the Impact of AI Tools on Student Engagement, Learning Outcomes, and Wellbeing: A Multivariate Analysis

Usha Rani

In this chapter, the author investigates the impact of AI tools on student engagement and satisfaction through a sophisticated data analysis framework that includes Multivariate Adaptive Regression Splines (MARS) and Convolutional Neural Networks (CNN). By analyzing complex, nonlinear relationships among various factors influencing student wellbeing, the study provides a comprehensive look at the effectiveness of AI tools in enhancing student outcomes. The chapter offers a deeper understanding of how AI technologies can influence student emotions, satisfaction, and engagement, highlighting the evolving role of AI in improving the overall student experience.

CONCLUSION

The integration of chatbots into language education is not merely a technological trend; it represents a paradigm shift in how we approach teaching and learning. As we move toward increasingly digital and interconnected learning environments, the role of AI-driven tools will continue to expand, reshaping traditional methodologies and redefining the teacher-student dynamic. This volume highlights the importance of adaptability and critical reflection in embracing these new technologies, ensuring that they serve as meaningful enhancements rather than mere replacements for traditional educational practices.

It is my hope that this book inspires further research and innovation in the field of AI-assisted language learning. By fostering interdisciplinary collaboration and bridging the gap between technology and pedagogy, we can unlock the full potential of chatbots as facilitators of linguistic and cognitive development. The insights shared within these pages contribute to a growing discourse on the ethical and practical implications of AI in education, ultimately guiding us toward more effective, engaging, and equitable learning experiences.

I would like to extend my heartfelt appreciation to the contributors, reviewers, and publishers who have made this volume possible. Their dedication and commitment to advancing knowledge in the field of language education and artificial intelligence have been instrumental in bringing this project to fruition. I invite readers to explore the chapters that follow, engaging critically with the ideas presented and considering the transformative potential of chatbots in shaping the future of language learning.

Rubén González Vallejo

University of Malaga, Spain

Chapter 1
Integrating Chatbots Into Metaverse-Based Classroom

Rohit Yadav
https://orcid.org/0000-0002-7573-8005
IILM University, Greater Noida, India

Mohit Yadav
https://orcid.org/0000-0002-9341-2527
O.P. Jindal Global University, India

Xuan-Hoa Nghiem
https://orcid.org/0000-0003-2292-0257
International School, Vietnam National University, Hanoi, Vietnam

ABSTRACT

The integration of chatbots into Metaverse-based classrooms offers new opportunities to enhance learning experiences through AI-driven, interactive, and personalized interactions. As educational institutions increasingly explore virtual environments, chatbots can provide real-time assistance, facilitate collaboration, and support adaptive learning in immersive settings. This paper explores the synergy between chatbots and the Metaverse, highlighting their potential to revolutionize education

DOI: 10.4018/979-8-3693-9974-3.ch001

by improving student engagement, accessibility, and inclusivity. However, challenges such as technological limitations, data privacy concerns, and the quality of chatbot interactions remain. The paper also discusses the future potential of chatbots in virtual classrooms, with advancements in AI, VR, and accessibility promising further innovations. By addressing existing challenges, chatbots in the Metaverse can become valuable tools, fostering more dynamic, inclusive, and personalized educational experiences.

1. INTRODUCTION

The rapid advancement in the Metaverse has brought a revolution in various fields, one of which is education. The Metaverse, an immersive virtual environment where users interact with each other through avatars and digital representations, provides a new arena for the strengthening of learning experiences (Cummings & Bailenson, 2016). In education, the Metaverse provides more engaging, collaborative, and interactive experiences compared to traditional classroom settings, thereby breaking down geographical barriers and offering personalized learning opportunities (Dede, 2020). As the Metaverse continues to evolve, educational institutions are increasingly exploring its potential to create a more dynamic and participatory learning environment.

At the same time, the role of artificial intelligence (AI) in education is becoming more prominent. One of the most common AI-driven tools used in contemporary classrooms is a chatbot: a software application that can mimic conversation with users through text or voice-based interactions (Shawar & Atwell, 2007). Chatbots may be used in several ways: instant feedback for students, performing administrative tasks for them, and providing personalized learning experiences. In this regard, their ability to create engaging real-time interactions perfectly fits the concept of the Metaverse as something immersive and interactive.

With the use of chatbots, students in a classroom based in the Metaverse can better fill the gap between technology and pedagogy since intelligent support can be offered anytime to support student learning. However, with the integration of virtual classrooms and chatbots, there will be an environment where students receive the right amount of attention, in real-time, in an immersive, flexible, and engaging setting that is conducing to learning. However, despite this potential, there are many challenges with integrating these chatbots into the Metaverse. Some of these problems include data privacy, the accuracy of AI models, and how inclusive it can be to let all learners benefit the same from this technology implementation (Bower et al., 2020).

This chapter focuses on the inclusion of chatbots in the Metaverse-based classrooms: focusing on educational benefits, challenges, and design requirements to carry out the same well. With such an endeavor, this chapter tries to project how such an interplay of AI and immersive virtual environments might modify the nature of learning experiences for the learner and the educator alike.

2. THE METAVERSE IN EDUCATION

The Metaverse is often referred to as the shared virtual space that has been enabled collectively. Currently, it is slowly becoming an important field to be considered within the education world. It refers to a vast number of connected virtual worlds that can easily be accessed through different devices and usually through immersion technologies like virtual reality and augmented reality (Steed et al., 2021). It means that the Metaverse gives opportunities to learners who can experience this new form of education that isn't confined or limited to being in a single, traditional physical classroom. Students can learn experientially with spatial interaction, immersion in a 3D environment, to enhance the quality and accessibility of education (Vasalou et al., 2020).

One of the important benefits of Metaverse application in education is its ability to provide real-world experience in a controlled, immersive, and risk-free virtual environment. For example, students can conduct complicated experiments about science, historical recreations or virtual field trips. Some experience with maximum immersion and engagement that traditional classroom settings cannot be compared to (Bailenson, 2018). These virtual environments permit active learning wherein the students are not just mere recipients of information but can also interact with the environment and the fellow learners meaningfully. It has been stated that active involvement will lead to better retention and better understanding of complex subjects (Dede, 2020).

The Metaverse also offers a highly personalized and learner-centered approach to education. It can accommodate students with unique learning styles since the virtual experiences allow for self-paced learning, instant feedback, and adaptive content. For instance, a student is not grasping a concept-a set of extra resources or interactivity simulation tailored to improve one's knowledge could be availed (Mikropoulos & Natsis, 2011). This flexibility makes Metaverse an excellent learning environment because it can assimilate learners of all types, from people with disability to those who have the problem of accessing traditional classrooms for one reason or another.

The social aspect of the Metaverse will also play a crucial role in its educational capacity. The virtual classrooms allow students across borders and cultures to co-operate effectively. This promotes global learning communities where students can work on virtual projects together, share knowledge, and participate in discussions that will build on their knowledge and create better communication skills (Bailenson, 2018). Here, educators could transition to a more facilitative role, enabling students to go through immersions as they help them in social learning and critical thinking.

However, despite the promise that the Metaverse holds for education, it must be noted that the challenges in implementing it are immense. One of the most significant barriers remains the access to technology, especially VR headsets and fast internet, for most students and institutions worldwide (Dede, 2020). At a deeper level, teachers are also expected to be trained in depth on how to effectively interact with all these new technologies as they work to transform the way they teach to this new medium (Steed et al., 2021). However, at this level, Metaverse offers an interesting opportunity and really presents transformative opportunities both for teaching and learning in the digital era.

3. CHATBOTS AND EDUCATION

Recently, AI-powered chatbots have been found to be applied in educational contexts and are continuously being adopted. They offer real-time support to the involved students and teachers. Essentially, chatbots are considered a product of interactive applications. Through their interfaces, this application can happen in both text or voice media. In this case, NLP is required to ensure that the user queries are understood and responded to as well (Shawar & Atwell, 2007). Chatbots can play a host of roles within educational settings. They can act as administrative assistance or academic support, which has the benefits of scalability and efficiency that traditional approaches cannot offer. Virtual teaching assistants is one of the most important roles that chatbots play in education. These AI-driven systems can respond to student inquiries, clarify doubts, and provide resources or explanations on demand, thereby extending the teacher's reach and ensuring that students have access to learning support 24/7 (Huang et al., 2020). It reduces the burden of administrative tasks on the instructors by automating routine tasks such as answering frequently asked questions about course materials, assignment deadlines, or grading policies, freeing up time for interactive teaching and more student engagement (Fryer, 2017). As such, it could well be particularly important in big classes, where individualized attention is often a logistically infeasible dream.

In addition to supporting teachers, chatbots can enhance the learning experience for students by providing immediate feedback and personalized learning pathways. Through conversational interactions, chatbots can assess student progress, identify areas where students are struggling, and offer customized learning resources tailored to individual needs (Baker et al., 2020). For example, if a student is not getting the point of a particular concept, the teacher can give additional clarification, exercises, or video tutorials to make it more understandable. This flexibility in real-time adaptation helps to establish a more learner-centered environment that promotes active learning and better retention (Shawar & Atwell, 2007).

Chatbots also provide a platform for collaborative learning since they can be used for peer-to-peer communication and discussion in virtual or hybrid classrooms. AI algorithms allow chatbots to encourage students to conduct group projects, assist them in doing collaborative tasks, or even prompt them to share their insights with their classmates (Bower et al., 2020). Thus, chatbots mediate these interactions for deeper engagement and sharing of ideas to enhance the learning process. In addition, chatbots can be a non-judgmental thing or entity that encourages shy or introverted students to ask questions in discussions that they may avoid in face-to-face settings.

The second advantage offered by the use of chatbots is the possibility of gathering and analyzing data on the performance and behavior of students. This will prove really useful in furnishing insights regarding learning patterns. Data-driven insights will help monitor students' progression in real-time, learning gaps can be discovered, and intervention is put into action where it is necessary (Baker et al., 2020). In addition to this, educators will also be provided with insights by chatbots about how efficient course materials are and teaching methods, thereby affording them scope for continuous improvement and a dynamic learning environment.

Despite their promises, the use of chatbots in education does not come without a host of problems. A common problem here is the use of complex AI algorithms that have a capacity for context and nuances when students engage each other-a tough task indeed, especially where cognitive understanding has to be profound or emotional intelligence involved (Fryer, 2017). Furthermore, institutions will have issues on data privacy and security since they will be handling extensive personal and academic data (Baker et al., 2020). However, the future of education will be written even further with the advancement of AI technology using chatbots that provide scalable effective solutions both for students and instructors.

4. SYNERGY BETWEEN THE CHATBOTS AND THE METAVERSE

The introduction of chatbots in the Metaverse brings about a synergy that can aptly revolutionize the delivery of education in virtual environments. The Metaverse will be an ultimate platform for such dynamic educational assistants from chatbots, with an immersive 3D world or interactive virtual spaces, offering student learning experiences to be far broader than what possible classroom settings have to offer in this regard, according to research by Steed et al., 2021. As students wander through these virtual environments, chatbots can enrich the experience by offering contextual guidance, personalized feedback, and interactive learning that make Metaverse not only an educational space but also highly immersive.

Chatbots in Metaverse can be an interactive guide, always assisting students to navigate through vast digital campuses, find resources to learn with, or tell how to use virtual tools and equipment. These bots would immediately respond to student inquiries, thus allowing for a seamless, continuous flow of learning even in any time outside class hours. Persistent, 24/7 availability is especially useful for the Metaverse because students can wish to engage with educational content at any time, regardless of time zone or location (Bower et al., 2020). With these chatbots embedded into virtual environments, students are supported on-demand while discovering virtual museums or working on collaborative projects or observing live events while in a virtual classroom.

Most importantly, an integration of these chatbots into the Metaverse can offer much more personalized experiences in learning: advanced AI-charged chatbots can adapt according to the learning needs, choices, and progresses of individual learners. In the Metaverse, for example, if a student is not grasping a concept in a virtual science experiment or historical simulation, the chatbot may offer personalized help with suggestions of tools or offer interactive simulations to further support the student's understanding (Baker et al., 2020). This type of personalized support can help establish conditions that are conducive to learning and consequently maximize motivation and learning outcomes.

The Metaverse further allows students to engage in social and collaborative learning, and the role of chatbots is vital in facilitating such interactions. Within a virtual classroom, chatbots can facilitate group activities by assigning roles, moderating discussions, and guiding students through collaborative tasks. In such social learning scenarios, chatbots can prompt students to contribute their thoughts, ask questions, or even suggest topics for discussion, ensuring that all participants are involved. Moreover, the chatbots could foster peer-to-peer interactions that would allow the students to share knowledge, work together, and learn from one another's experiences, thus bringing the social interactions of a traditional classroom into the virtual world (Vasalou et al., 2020).

The support which a chatbot can offer for students to social-emotional well-being goes beyond academic assistance. They are in a good position to offer emotional support to help the student relax and give room for other mental activities as relaxation. Chatbots can be a non-judgmental, approachable point of contact that makes it easier for students to ask for help and engage with the learning process in a low-pressure setting in virtual environments where students feel isolated or overwhelmed (Bower et al., 2020).

Moreover, integrating chatbots into the Metaverse can help bridge the gap between the virtual and physical worlds. For instance, a chatbot may help transition the students back into a regular classroom after having been immersed in an interactive virtual field trip through the use of summaries, quizzes, and discussions for reinforcement purposes. Another area is the fact that from student interactions through the Metaverse, chatbots can use it to provide time-related analytics as well as reviews of educators relating to student progresses, engagement rates, and so forth, thereby making an inter-actively response environment for educating students and professors through continuous interaction in real time with feedback (Huang et al., 2020).

While the synergy between chatbots and the Metaverse offers many promising possibilities, it is important to recognize the challenges that come with such integration. For instance, ensuring the accuracy and effectiveness of chatbot responses in such complex, immersive environments requires advanced AI algorithms and extensive data training. Integration also has to consider aspects that include ensuring data privacy, as well as the safeguarding of biases that will appear in models of AI (Baker et al., 2020). However, despite the challenges involved, the potential for the integration of chatbots and the Metaverse is spectacular enough to redefine how learning is experienced that is personalized, accessible, and interactive.

5. METAVERSE CLASSROOM: DESIGNING CHATBOTS

To design effective chatbots for the Metaverse classroom, one must have a profound understanding of the technological infrastructure of the Metaverse and the needs of learners within these immersive virtual environments. Unlike traditional chatbots, which are usually designed to work in text-based interfaces, Metaverse-specific chatbots must be able to function smoothly within 3D spaces, utilizing rich multimedia and interactive elements to guide and engage students (Steed et al., 2021). Design considerations include user experience, contextual relevance, adaptability, and integration with the virtual tools and resources of the Metaverse.

One of the significant concerns in designing such chatbots for the Metaverse classroom is that they are extremely interactive and context-aware. In an interactive and engaging environment like the Metaverse, a chatbot must be able to identify the user's context-whether it is a specific virtual room, an activity currently under way, or some current learning progress of a student-and respond appropriately (Baker et al., 2020). This implies that chatbots must be provided with sophisticated NLP algorithms and machine learning models that can interpret a wide range of user inputs, including questions, commands, and even non-verbal cues from avatars. Moreover, chatbots must be able to integrate multimedia elements such as visual aids, videos, and interactive simulations to support the learning process. For instance, a chatbot in an online biology lab might provide the learner with step-by-step instructions on how to carry out an experiment, display diagrams, or even simulate biological processes in real time (Bower et al., 2020).

Another crucial design principle is personalization. Every learner comes into the virtual classroom with unique needs, preferences, and learning styles, so the chatbot must adapt to these differences. Using AI-driven models, a chatbot can monitor student improvement over time, better recognize areas of difficulty, and provide students with tailored interventions on learning. For example, in virtual history tours, when a student stumbles on a particular concept, the chatbot could present additional resources or quizzes or commit to revisiting that particular subject via an interactive simulation (Shawar & Atwell, 2007). This level of personalization will keep students interested and ensure that their learning experiences are aligned with their individual pace and interests.

In the Metaverse, chatbots also have to facilitate social learning and interaction. Virtual classrooms are often designed to promote collaboration, group discussions, and peer-to-peer learning, and chatbots can play a pivotal role in mediating these interactions. For instance, it can be able to assign duties in group work, give feedback in real time during group discussions, or even propose how to work effectively with others in a virtual environment. They can facilitate virtual classrooms where they help guide students through aspects of the virtual classroom, assist them in locating resources, or even encourage asking questions and participating with others (Vasalou et al., 2020). A chatbot may also facilitate discussions, ensure that all students have a say, and that the discussion is kept on track.

Accessibility and inclusivity must also be top of the list for a chatbot designed for the Metaverse. Virtual environments, though very promising, pose many challenges to students with disabilities. For example, visually impaired students may not navigate 3D spaces well or read text-heavy instructions. Accordingly, the Metaverse chatbots need to be fitted with accessibility features such as voice recognition, screen reader compatibility, and gesture-based controls. This way, all students can use the virtual classroom and be able to connect with their peers and instructors once more in a quality learning experience. AI models have to be trained to account for different modes of communication, such as voice commands, facial expressions, and body language, so that no student will be omitted from learning (Baker et al., 2020). This would encourage inclusivity from the point of view of chatbots, as they are integrated into a metaverse classroom, to contribute toward a fairer education environment in the Metaverse.

Data privacy and ethical consideration are also called for while integrating chatbots in the classroom of Metaverse. As data collected and processed by these chatbots for determining student behavior, preferences, and performance are significant, privacy protection must be properly implemented in designing these applications. Chatbots must be transparent about the data they collect, with students being given clear information about what data is being collected and how it will be used. Moreover, mechanisms should be implemented to ensure that the AI models deployed in the chatbots are bias-free and allow for equal opportunities for interaction by all learners. Ethical considerations also extend to ensuring that chatbots are not used to replace human teachers but rather to augment and support the educational experience, allowing educators to focus on more complex, creative, and personalized aspects of teaching (Fryer, 2017).

It is very important that designs of chatbots are continually updated and revised through feedback from both students and educators. Because the Metaverse environment is very dynamic, it will be crucial that chatbots evolve with the change in tools, technologies, and teaching methods. Updates must occur regularly with continuous user testing so that the evolution of chatbots keeps up with the changes within the Metaverse environment to keep up with educational goals.

6. BENEFITS OF CHATBOTS IN A METAVERSE-BASED CLASSROOM

The inclusion of chatbots in Metaverse-based classrooms can provide numerous benefits to both the student and educator that can help change the way they learn and teach. It can integrate the immersive nature of the Metaverse with the efficiency and interactivity of chatbots, which would help in enriching educational experiences to be more personalized, accessible, and engaging for learning.

One of the most significant advantages of chatbots in Metaverse-based classrooms is the ability to provide personalized, on-demand support. Unlike traditional classroom settings, where students may have to wait for scheduled office hours or rely on peer support, chatbots can provide immediate assistance anytime, anywhere. This is a great value-add in a virtual learning environment, where students may be working at different rates and need individual attention. Whether students are reviewing content, interacting with simulations, or working on assignments, chatbots provide individualized feedback and clarifications and additional learning resources for a more adaptive and learner-centered approach to education (Huang et al., 2020). This assures better comprehension of the topics, increases retention, and eliminates frustration among a student who may require special attention.

Chatbots are also scalable, which is almost impossible to be accomplished in an ordinary classroom. Since it will not be possible for a teacher teaching a big class to attend each student in a class, the chats can fill the gap in scaling for a Metaverse-based classroom. With these AI-based assistants, the ability to help multiple students by answering a broad category of questions without overloading the instructor is possible. This leaves instructors free to manage the deeper aspects of learning, such as facilitating group discussions or encouraging critical thinking, where the chatbots can handle routine questions (Bower et al., 2020). This scalable model makes the process highly efficient while allowing no student to fall behind; regardless of how big the classes are.

Furthermore, chatbots in the Metaverse foster more interactive and involving learning. While students are thoroughly engaged in various simulations, virtual labs, or other interactive sessions in the Metaverse, they get real-time support and instant feedback from these chatbots on those activities. For example, in a virtual history simulation, a chatbot could provide contextual information, suggest points of interest, or answer questions related to the historical setting, enriching the experience and helping students connect with the material on a deeper level (Baker et al., 2020). That is, multimedia elements like videos, 3D models, or interactive activities can be seamlessly integrated, which makes the learning experience more dynamic and captivating, increasing student engagement and motivation.

Another aspect on which integration of Metaverse-based chatbots has a significant positive impact is the social aspect of learning. Collaborative learning is a key component of the Metaverse, where students can work together on projects, discuss ideas, and share knowledge in real-time, regardless of geographic location. Chatbots can play a pivotal role in facilitating these social interactions by organizing group activities, promoting peer-to-peer communication, and ensuring that all students are actively involved. For example, chatbots can assign tasks in collaborative projects, initiate discussions, or give gentle reminders to keep the group on track. This helps create a more cohesive and interactive learning environment, where students are encouraged to share ideas and learn from each other (Vasalou et al., 2020). Chatbots also serve as a means of mediating discussions among students, making sure that all students have their say, especially those who would not speak out in a typical classroom.

The other significant advantage of chatbots is that they can collect and analyze data regarding the performance and engagement of students. These chatbots can track student progress in real-time, determine trends, identify areas of struggle, and offer insights into learning behaviors. For educators, this data can be invaluable for assessing student needs, adjusting teaching strategies, and identifying students who may require additional support. For instance, if a student consistently struggles with certain concepts or does not engage with specific aspects of the Metaverse classroom, the chatbot can alert the instructor, prompting timely interventions (Shawar & Atwell, 2007). This data-driven approach will lead to more informed decision-making and enhance the quality of education in general.

Furthermore, the constant feedback from the chatbots will help in promoting self-regulated learning. In the Metaverse classroom, students can take greater ownership of their learning, exploring virtual environments, participating in simulations, and engaging with resources independently. Through feedback on their progress, recommendations of areas requiring improvement, and guidance to reflect upon one's learning process, chatbots can provide incentives for further growth. Ongoing reflection and feedback foster a growth mindset, where students view challenges as opportunities for learning and continually improve themselves (Baker et al., 2020). The interactive and immediate feedback from chatbots serve to keep students constantly engaged and mindful of their progress.

Finally, chatbots make the learning environment more inclusive by providing personalized support to students with diverse needs. For example, students with learning disabilities, language barriers, or other challenges can benefit from the adaptability of chatbots, which can provide instructions in various formats, such as text, audio, or visual cues. This will also be a fair avenue for accessing equal learning in the Metaverse among all the learners, ensuring equity in educational inclusivity. Based on its adaptation to all these learning preferences and styles, there is bound to be customized support from a chatbot toward attaining inclusiveness in an education experience (Bower et al., 2020).

7. CHALLENGES AND LIMITATIONS

Although the incorporation of chatbots in Metaverse-based classrooms offers numerous advantages, there are also challenges and limitations to this integration. These concerns need to be surmounted so that the various tools of chatbots bring about better education and do not deter students from learning. A number of the most critical challenges include technology limitations, degradation in the quality of interaction, data privacy and security issues, lack of accessibility, and overreliance on AI.

Another serious issue is the technological infrastructure that chatbots will need in order to support them inside Metaverse. Metaverse itself is still under development as a platform, with multiple tools, virtual spaces, and applications of vastly different quality and not entirely cross-compatible. The virtual environment must be deeply integrated with a chatbot for it to work properly. Such integration may sometimes require sophisticated AI and NLP models for the interpretation of student queries and the delivery of contextually appropriate responses. This heavily requires enough computing power, robust networking capabilities, and software development resources, which may not be readily available in all educational settings (Bower et al., 2020). In addition, with the Metaverse continuing to develop and shift, sustaining such chatbots that might easily be knowledgeable of new virtual spaces, user interfaces, and technologies is probably going to be a challenge the developers will face in the future.

Another limitation is the depth and quality of interactions that a chatbot can present. Although chatbots have made significant advancements in natural language processing and machine learning, sometimes they cannot comprehend the subtle nuances of human communication, especially when the context is complex or ambiguous (Shawar & Atwell, 2007). For example, the emotional tone of a conversation can be very difficult to get, and vague or poorly structured queries are frequently misinterpreted, which might be frustrating for the students who get misunderstood. This can be particularly problematic in a learning environment where the emotional connection between student and instructor, or student and learning assistant, plays a critical role in motivation and engagement. Moreover, chatbots may not always offer the most accurate or insightful responses, especially when dealing with complex subject matter that requires human expertise or judgment (Baker et al., 2020).

Data privacy and security concerns form another significant barrier in the process of deploying a chatbot for educational purposes. Chatbots learn a lot of data about how students behave and what they want, which can then be applied to personalize their learning experience. However, there is also an element of that data being hacked or misused. The Metaverse itself, being a shared and immersive virtual environment, has also brought other dangers related to sharing and storing sensitive information (Steed et al., 2021). It is also an obligation for the educational institutions that the chatbot complies with the privacy laws, like the Family Educational Rights and Privacy Act in the United States, and data stored properly. Transparency is a must, and the relevant data about what is being gathered and how it is going to be utilized must be shared with students. It is imperative to safeguard the students against AI-related biases that may emerge in a chatbot program, thus ensuring the equitable and just treatment of every student (Baker et al., 2020).

The other challenge is in ensuring that chatbots are accessible to all students, especially the ones with disabilities. On one hand, the Metaverse offers tremendous possibility for immersive, interactive learning while on the other hand, for students with disabilities in terms of visual, auditory, cognitive or physical impairments, it will pose accessibility problems. For example, virtual environments may not be designed to have accessibility for the visually impaired such that they would not be able to navigate around or interact with content. On the other hand, students who are deaf will find voice-based chatbot interactions challenging. Furthermore, making the chatbot inclusive of all students, irrespective of ability, calls for close attention to how it should be accessible by the use of screen readers, closed captions, voice-to-text functionality, and alternative interaction modalities (Huang et al., 2020). In the absence of these features, the chatbots will, in the course of it, alienate the students and, therefore, result in unequal learning.

Another risk is that students become too dependent on the chatbots for answers, which would defeat the purpose of developing critical thinking and problem-solving skills. While the chatbots are designed to provide support and guidance, they should not replace the instructor's role or be the only source of learning. Over-reliance on chatbots can diminish students' desire to engage in higher-level cognitive processes such as critical thinking, self-reflection, and collaborative problem-solving. The use of chatbots should be supplemented and not replace educational exchange in the learning process. Chatbots supplement in-person or virtual teaching: They offer more resources to support students with their questions and problems but do not replace interaction in person or the exploration of subjects in depth (Fryer, 2017).

Finally, the tendency of chatbots to propagate biases is another challenge. AI systems, including chatbots, are trained on massive datasets that can have inherent biases or reflect the inequalities in the society. The biases can take many forms, such as biased responses or unfair treatment of some student groups. For example, assume that the AI of a chatbot learns from biased sources; in return, it provides less relevant and even misleading details to the underprivileged communities in schools. Developing such a program requires the careful monitoring and testing of these programs for their level of fairness with no implicit tendency to enforce any stereotype or racism (Shawar & Atwell, 2007). Without proper oversight, AI systems within educational settings are likely to be contributing unintentionally to unequal outcomes in education.

8. FUTURE OF CHATBOTS IN THE METAVERSE CLASSROOM

The future of chatbots within the Metaverse classroom is enormous, with numerous emerging trends and developments that promise to revolutionize the way we think about education. As the Metaverse will continue to expand and grow in popularity, such advanced AI chatbots will even more significantly become integral parts in advancing not only student experience but also functionality of virtual learning environments. There is a lot of potential for better adapted learning experiences in the Metaverse classroom because the integration with emerging technology is highly organic.

The advancement of conversational AI into future directions offers an exciting perspective; the most thrilling part about that is enabling more natural, intuitive interaction through a chatbot for students. Improvement in the field of natural language processing means better comprehension in literal meaning while using NLP and contextual sense along with a specific emotional tone as well as other nuances to get communicated better through the help of chatbots. This will make it more human-like, allowing the chatbots to provide empathetic responses, give personalized advice, and have meaningful conversations that almost feel like a dialogue with a human instructor. Such advancements in the sophistication of chatbots can bridge the gap between virtual assistants and human educators, making learning environments more dynamic and responsive (Baker et al., 2020).

Another significant development for chatbots in the Metaverse would be their integration with other emerging technologies, including virtual reality (VR), augmented reality (AR), and machine learning. As immersive technologies will soon dominate the education sector, the chatbots will no longer act as sources of information or guides but will participate in the learning process. For example, in history class that is taught through VR, the information regarding historical events might be available through a chatbot which interacts with students by moving them through history scenarios, conducting real-time quizzes, or even figures in history to be role-played with students. These immersive experiences together with interactions via a chatbot could ensure experiential and hands-on learning, engaging the students more intensely and profoundly for better understanding to be achieved (Vasalou et al., 2020). The synergetic convergence of chatbots and VR/AR might unlock the potential in the development of hyper-personalized learning experiences that take account of the preferences, needs, and behaviors of individual learners.

As AI technology advances, chatbots will be able to provide more data-driven insights and predictive analytics to optimize both the student and educator experience. These chatbots could track performance, predict areas of struggle, and proactively offer personalized content, resources, or learning pathways. Educators would also be able to use the data to optimize their teaching by identifying trends of student engagement and adjusting lessons in real-time for maximum learning outcome. Combining AI's capabilities to process big data with the immersive capabilities of the Metaverse, chatbots will become part of the design of truly personalized learning journeys. This predictive capability will allow for more targeted interventions, helping ensure that each student receives the support they need at the right moment, leading to improved retention and achievement (Huang et al., 2020).

Finally, the future of chatbots in the Metaverse classroom will depend on the increase in emphasis placed on inclusiveness and accessibility. As educational institutions continue to expand their capacity for students with special needs, there will be much that chatbots can do in ensuring equal opportunity for education access. Future chatbots may feature multilingual capability, which enables them to work with students coming from different linguistic backgrounds. They can include a wide variety of accessibility features, from gesture-based controls and voice recognition to AI-driven assistive technologies so that all students with disabilities are able to participate in the content and fully join in virtual classroom activities. This is because, in conjunction with such adaptive chatbot features, the Metaverse can potentially provide a highly inclusive learning environment that may remove all barriers to education for students of different abilities and needs (Bower et al., 2020).

The use of chatbots in education will continue to evolve, focusing more strongly on ethical considerations and the development of responsible AI. Issues such as data privacy, bias, and transparency will only increase in importance as it becomes more integrated into the learning process. Rigorous oversight will be needed to ensure that the Metaverse classroom understands how AI systems develop and implement them in ways that are ethical and responsible-and better yet, so that they treat all students fairly, bring bias-free equality, and don't breach sensitive student data. Careful attention to these issues can facilitate the success of chatbots in education to prompt fairness, transparency, and trust, which can thus encourage a high level of adoption and acceptance in this context (Shawar & Atwell, 2007).

Last but not least: by that stage, the teachers and the students are expected to have gotten over being insensitive toward adopting the presence of chatbots within the Metaverse, which makes it even likely for them to become agents other than a mere assistant for educational matters within a class; for example, to generate some education-related content: build tailored lesson plans, interactive simulation, or curated learning experience in a virtual space. This ability to understand trends and patterns and learn from past experiences would make them capable of predicting learning gaps, recommending potentially new avenues of exploration, or even creating potentially new forms of assessment and feedback, radically changing how instructors plan and implement instruction within virtual environments (Fryer, 2017).

AI Fairness, Ethical Concerns, and Privacy Issues in Metaverse-Based Learning

Whereas metaverse-based learning is increasingly reliant on AI-driven chatbots, fairness, ethical factors, and concerns regarding privacy are paramount. A major concern is AI fairness, whereby biased training data lead to discriminatory learning results, and particular groups of students are discriminated against (Baker & Hawn, 2021). For instance, language-oriented AI algorithms may lag behind non-native English speakers when they are trained largely on Western-centric data, leading to potential exclusion in an immersive learning environment. Ethical considerations also arise regarding the transparency and accountability of AI-based tutors. There is controversy regarding how much feedback chatbots can provide, especially in areas where emotional intelligence and cultural sensitivity are at issue (Zawacki-Richter et al., 2022).

Privacy concerns arise due to the vast amounts of information collected in metaverse classrooms. As opposed to the traditional digital learning environments, the metaverse records biometric, behavioral, and even emotional information through interactions, eye tracking, and movement sensors (Chaudhary et al., 2023). Without robust data protection legislation and security measures, students' personal information may be vulnerable to exploitation. Regulatory compliance such as with the General Data Protection Regulation (GDPR) and the Family Educational Rights and Privacy Act (FERPA) is vital to safeguarding students' data as well as AI-based educational system trustworthiness.

Case Studies

Various educational institutions and ed-tech companies have pioneered the adoption of AI chatbots in metaverse classrooms both in the realm of benefits as well as setbacks of such adoption. A notable case study is Stanford University's "AI Tutor in Virtual Reality Classrooms" initiative, where chatbots are employed to offer students real-time feedback and adaptive learning paths (Smith & Johnson, 2023). This use case proved that students who utilized AI tutors in VR environments had a 15% higher concept retention compared to traditional online learning environments.

Nevertheless, concerns over student overdependence on AI and lack of individual human interaction were raised.

The second practical use is the "EduVerse" platform, a metaverse educational environment for K-12 students with chatbot tutors to assist interactive learning sessions (Lee & Kim, 2022). The platform incorporates AI-driven avatars that respond to students' queries and personalize based on individualized learning trajectories. EduVerse has been successful in enhancing the engagement of students, especially those facing challenges with traditional learning. Nonetheless, privacy issues have been highlighted as a result of the large-scale data collection practices necessary to tailor the learning experience.

Effectiveness of Chatbot Integration: User Data and Feedback

The success of chatbot integration for metaverse-classroom environments has been evaluated through empirical studies and user feedback. A study by Patel et al. (2023) contrasted student engagement in AI-supported metaverse learning with traditional e-learning platforms. The study revealed that 78% of the students stated that chatbot-supported learning in the metaverse was more engaging and interactive, attributing enhanced real-time feedback and gamified learning processes. Nevertheless, 22% of students complained about the lack of personal touch in AI feedback, preferring human teachers for more sophisticated discussions.

Furthermore, a University of Tokyo study found that metaverse classroom tutors using AI significantly enhanced student motivation and performance in STEM (Nakamura et al., 2023). The test, in which over 500 students were polled, revealed that problem-solving efficiency was boosted by 20% when instruction was supplemented with chatbots. Nevertheless, there were increased ethical concerns regarding relying too heavily on AI and the potential for AI-based tutors to inadvertently enhance biases present in the data.

The use of chatbots in metaverse classrooms presents a revolutionary learning method, enhancing interaction and personalization. However, addressing AI fairness, ethical concerns, and privacy risks must be addressed to ensure inclusive and safe learning environments. Future research needs to focus on developing unbiased AI models, well-defined ethical guidelines, and robust data protection protocols to establish an inclusive and trustworthy learning experience in the metaverse.

9. CONCLUSION

This integration of chatbots in the Metaverse-based classroom forms a new era in the education landscape, bringing much potential for enhancing both teaching and learning. The use of this immersive and interactive Metaverse platform will enable chatbots to provide personalized on-demand support to students, further stir the engagement of students in the task, and facilitate collaborative learning that was deemed impossible in the traditional setups of education. These AI-driven tools can act as virtual teaching assistants that guide the students through complex content, respond to questions in real time, and offer customized feedback based on individual learning needs. Additionally, chatbots scale learning experiences, catering the attention and resources needed by students of different backgrounds and abilities to participate in virtual classes to foster inclusivity and equity.

Yet, with the integration, some challenges and limitations have to be addressed. Technological infrastructure, interaction quality between the chatbot, concerns over data privacy, and ease of access for learning are some of the issues to consider to ensure that chatbots actually improve learning experience rather than impede it. Additionally, the ethical issues concerning AI biases, data security, and over-reliance on automated systems need to be addressed to ensure fairness, transparency, and trust in these educational tools. Despite all these challenges, the future of chatbots in the Metaverse classroom is incredibly promising. More evolutions of the AI technology and the resultant complexities will further deepen the level of personalization, empathy, and engagement from a chatbot; it would, therefore, eventually integrate seamlessly into other new developments, like virtual and augmented realities.

It depends on thoughtful designs and implementation which will enable this to succeed without replacing the educator but supplement them in bringing a meaningful learning experience. With the right balance between innovation and responsibility, chatbots have the capacity to revolutionize education by making learning environments more dynamic, more inclusive, and personalized for each one of the students. As Metaverse expands and redefines the boundaries of education, there's no doubt that chatbots will play a role that will determine the future virtual classrooms to the benefit of learners and educators alike, in ways that have been unimaginable so far.

REFERENCES

Bailenson, J. N. (2018). *Experience on demand: What virtual reality is, how it works, and what it can do*. W. W. Norton & Company.

Baker, R., & Hawn, A. (2021). Bias in AI-driven education: Addressing fairness and transparency. *Educational Technology Research and Development, 69*(4), 567–589.

Baker, R. S., Baker, R., & Copeland, R. (2020). *Educational chatbots: Enhancing learning through AI-driven communication*. Springer.

Bower, M., Cavanagh, M., & Moloney, R. (2020). *Designing for a digital world: The role of artificial intelligence in education*. Springer.

Chaudhary, A., Gupta, P., & Rao, S. (2023). Privacy challenges in the metaverse: Implications for education. *Journal of Digital Learning and Ethics, 15*(2), 112–128.

Cummings, J. J., & Bailenson, J. N. (2016). How immersive is enough? A psychological comparison of traditional and virtual reality mediated environments. *Computers in Human Behavior, 55*, 28–37. DOI: 10.1016/j.chb.2015.09.056

Dede, C. (2020). The Metaverse as an educational environment. *Journal of Virtual Learning, 23*(2), 56–72. DOI: 10.1080/10890045.2020.1780910

Fryer, L. (2017). The role of chatbots in education: A survey of the use of conversational agents in education. *Journal of Educational Technology & Society, 20*(4), 40–50.

Huang, T. C., Chiang, M. H., & Li, H. C. (2020). AI-based education: The role of chatbots in enhancing student engagement and learning outcomes. *Computers & Education, 149*, 103795. DOI: 10.1016/j.compedu.2020.103795

Lee, J., & Kim, H. (2022). EduVerse: Leveraging AI for immersive K-12 learning. *International Journal of Virtual Learning, 9*(3), 289–305.

Mikropoulos, T. A., & Natsis, A. (2011). Educational virtual environments: A ten-year review of empirical research (1999-2009). *Computers & Education, 56*(3), 769–780. DOI: 10.1016/j.compedu.2010.10.020

Nakamura, Y., Takahashi, R., & Ito, M. (2023). Impact of AI tutors in metaverse classrooms: A case study from Japan. *Journal of Educational AI, 18*(1), 45–63.

Patel, R., Singh, M., & Zhao, L. (2023). Assessing chatbot effectiveness in metaverse learning environments. *Educational Research Journal, 20*(1), 78–95.

Shawar, B. A., & Atwell, E. (2007). Chatbots: Are they really useful? *LNAI, 4762*, 392–397. DOI: 10.1007/978-3-540-76314-9_48

Smith, J., & Johnson, L. (2023). AI tutors in virtual reality classrooms: An empirical analysis. *Journal of Emerging Educational Technologies, 14*(2), 321–340.

Steed, A., Waller, D., & Stott, L. (2021). Immersive environments and the Metaverse: Current research and emerging opportunities. *International Journal of Human-Computer Studies, 144*, 102502. DOI: 10.1016/j.ijhcs.2020.102502

Vasalou, A., Joinson, A. N., Bänziger, T., & Kappas, A. (2020). Building and assessing virtual learning environments. *Computers & Education, 156*, 103939. DOI: 10.1016/j.compedu.2020.103939

Zawacki-Richter, O., Marín, V. I., & Bond, M. (2022). Ethical dilemmas in AI-driven education. *Journal of Educational Ethics, 11*(1), 88–104.

Chapter 2

Gamification Elements in Language-Learning Chatbots

Rohit Yadav
https://orcid.org/0000-0002-7573-8005
IILM University, Greater Noida, India

Xuan-Hoa Nghiem
https://orcid.org/0000-0003-2292-0257
International School, Vietnam National University, Hanoi, Vietnam

Mohit Yadav
https://orcid.org/0000-0002-9341-2527
O.P. Jindal Global University, India

ABSTRACT

This chapter explores the role of gamification in language-learning chatbots, examining its core elements, advanced features, benefits, and challenges. Gamification, which integrates game mechanics such as points, badges, and leaderboards, enhances learner motivation, engagement, and retention. By analyzing key theoretical foundations, including Self-Determination Theory, the chapter discusses how gamification fosters intrinsic and extrinsic motivation in language learners. Case studies of successful applications

DOI: 10.4018/979-8-3693-9974-3.ch002

such as Duolingo, Babbel, and Mondly demonstrate the effectiveness of these gamified systems in real-world settings. Additionally, the chapter highlights challenges such as learner diversity, content overload, and the balance between intrinsic and extrinsic motivation. Finally, future trends, including the integration of AI, NLP, augmented reality, and social learning, promise to revolutionize the gamified language-learning experience. This comprehensive analysis underscores the transformative potential of gamification in language education.

1. INTRODUCTION

Language-learning chatbots have been one of the most dominant tools for supporting language acquisition in recent years. Built on the principle of simulation, these systems create conversational interactions where users engage their language skill practice in any corner of the world (Vázquez-Cano, 2020). Chatbots have mainly been used for customer service and technical support but are now rapidly transforming into being used in educational fields. Language learning chatbots use NLP and machine learning algorithms to personalize educational content for individual users, making learning experiences highly personalized (Fogg, 2003). In this regard, gamification, the use of game-like elements such as rewards, levels, and challenges in non-game contexts, has been a powerful way to increase the engagement and motivation of language learners (Deterding et al., 2011).

Gamification has been an effective application in educational environments, using the psychological mechanisms of rewards and progress to motivate learners (Anderson & Rainie, 2020). It corresponds with intrinsic and extrinsic motivation theories where learners are motivated both to achieve mastery of new skills through the eagerness to learn and the rewards associated with achievement (Ryan & Deci, 2000). The gamified aspects and language learning chatbots should make highly engaging and effective learning experiences since the learners are highly motivated to continue their studies by the interactive and rewarding nature of the platform (Sailer et al., 2017). This chapter deals with the incorporation of gamification elements in language learning chatbots, with a lot of attention to their theoretical underpinnings, core features, and how they improve language acquisition. By analyzing the state of gamified language learning chatbots, this chapter focuses on how such tools help in enhancing learner engagement, skill development, and general effectiveness in a particular activity of the language learning process.

2. THE THEORETICAL UNDERPINNINGS OF GAMIFICATION IN EDUCATION

The use of gamification in education draws from different psychological and educational theories in the attempt to understand human motivation and behavior. Two theories of motivation are prominent in this regard, Self-Determination Theory (SDT) and Flow Theory, because they are pivotal in understanding why gamification might be effective or not in a learning environment. According to SDT, Ryan and Deci (2000) suggested that people are motivated to the extent that their basic psychological needs of autonomy, competence, and relatedness are met. Gamification makes such needs feasible because it provides learners with opportunities to make choices in their learning processes, information about their performance, and social interaction that boost intrinsic motivation and maintained interest. Therefore, for example, offering learners the chance to choose between tasks or challenges while navigating a gamified chatbot can go a long way in helping learners feel autonomous while clear goals and rewards will add up in real competence.

Other significant theoretical frameworks are those of Flow Theory, which was first identified by Csikszentmihalyi (1990). According to this theory, flow refers to the state wherein the individual is fully centred or immersed in an activity. The balance between challenge and skill is one of the most important characteristics of flow. This means that the individual perceives the task as neither too easy nor too difficult. In gamification, levels, challenges, and feedback systems are used to help learners enter and maintain this state of flow. Since the difficulty of tasks is continuously adjusted to match a learner's ability, the ideal conditions for flow are created by gamified language-learning chatbots, known to improve focus and learning outcomes (Csikszentmihalyi, 1990). The balance ensures that learners feel challenged but capable, thus promoting deep learning and enjoyment.

Gamification also draws from operant conditioning (Skinner, 1953), a behavioral theory that explains how behaviors can be shaped through rewards and punishments. The positive reinforcement of gamified language learning through chatbots could be represented through points, badges, or other progress markers; these reinforce learning efforts by creating a continued impetus toward a specific goal of learning. Language learning specifically requires constant practice in terms of vocabulary, grammar, and pronunciation. Moreover, the achievement motivation theory by McClelland (1961) is a common foundation for the gamification techniques since learners receive motivation in achieving the completion of a challenge or simply leveling up. The game-like characteristics invoke the feeling of accomplishment, which further propels them to be more participative.

The grounds are the same, but the terms should not be used synonymously. Game-based learning involves using fully fledged games for content, while gamification involves bringing game design elements into a non-game space, like a language-learning chatbot, with scoring, badges, and leaderboards. This is different from game-based learning, because gamification is more about how one can best exploit these elements for the improvement of user engagement and motivation without turning the whole experience into a game (Deterding et al., 2011). The game elements can be inculcated in the chatbots so that the educators could make use of the motivational power of games in the educational format to enable the learners to garner benefits from the both intrinsic as well as extrinsic motivation.

To sum it up, the theoretical base of gamification in education comes from established psychological theories with regard to motivation, feedback, and challenge. Building on these theories, a gamified language-learning chatbot can create environments that encourage motivation, mastery, and engagement, thereby facilitating better educational outcomes.

3. CORE ELEMENTS OF GAMIFICATION IN CHATBOTS

Language learning chatbots typically implement a few core elements of gamification, as widely used in game design, to increase learner engagement, motivation, and retention. Most simple gamification elements consist of the PBL. PBL is the awarding of points to learners based on task completion, be it answering questions correctly or other criteria set by the process of learning. These are forms of immediate reinforcement, rewarding the effort and inviting users to continue participation (Deterding et al., 2011). Badges are symbolic rewards for the achievement or mastery of particular skills. These serve as visual recognition of learner's progress and achievements, thus motivating learners with clear, tangible markers of their success. This incorporates the competition while learning, so there is also a leaderboard of users that compete with one another in their advancement. But that can sometimes become a compulsion for the performance of users, as it boosts them to increase their rank, and this type of situation calls for the combination of factors which should not exceed the threshold, making the condition unbearable for them (Sailer et al., 2017).

The second prominent gamification feature is quests and challenges, which provide a structured learning experience in a way that seems to be like mission-based gameplay. The quests might involve a number of tasks or problems to be solved by a learner in steps of increasing difficulty that align with the growth in the learner's competence (Fogg, 2003). For example, a language learning chatbot might present the user with a challenge that will make them use the new vocabulary in different contexts, or even a quest which requires them to complete certain exercises within a set time. Such an approach will keep the learners' minds occupied and also the content fresh for their level and areas of improvement. In doing so, this way of inculcating challenges, the chatbot lets excitement and the sense of urgency prevail over the user, making engagement better.

Levels and achievements further motivate the learners. When there are levels, it allows for a well-defined sense of progression, thereby letting learners feel that they see their journey on a game-like structure. Since they are bettering their skills, they perceive that they “level up” each time that they complete the tasks and attain new milestones. Incremental progression towards mastery, since it makes the learners keep on moving through the material, offers them a definite path to it. Achievements, for example, can be regarded as accomplishments of significant events in the learning process, like mastering a certain language skill or completing a chain of challenging tasks (Deterding et al., 2011). Usually, achievements are celebrated in the chatbot itself, giving the learner a feeling of accomplishment and reinforcing the value of his/her effort.

Feedback and rewards in gamified systems are directly affecting learners' motivation and self-efficacy. Immediate and formative feedback can be given to language learners in chatbots, allowing them to recognize errors and correct them in real time. Positive reinforcement, such as earning extra points or receiving a congratulatory message, encourages learners to continue their efforts, while corrective feedback helps them identify areas for improvement (Ryan & Deci, 2000). Besides direct feedback, many gamified chatbots include virtual rewards, such as unlocking new content or access to special features upon achieving certain goals. These incentives raise the value perceived by one upon completing tasks and maintaining their engagement with the learning material.

The core elements of gamification in language learning chatbots would include points, badges, leaderboards, quests, challenges, levels, achievements, feedback, and rewards; these are aspects that enhance learners' motivation through an engaging learning experience. Utilizing these mechanics of games with language-learning chatbots enhances an educational experience over time, enabling learners to retain interest in this process of gaining a new language.

4. ADVANCED GAMIFICATION IN LANGUAGE LEARNING CHATBOTS

More advanced gamification attributes are likely to be integrated in the continued evolutions of chatbots for learning languages, further enhancing learner engagement, successful learning outcomes, and overall learning experience. In this regard, storytelling and narrativity can represent an added sense of immersion, emotional investment into the learning, and a meaning of purpose into the learning flow. In this way, by establishing a narrative flow, chatbots can transform what otherwise might be just routine executions of language tasks into parts of a larger story, while learners feel part of something greater. For instance, students may be challenged to complete 'language exercises' to unlock new chapters of a story, solve mysteries, or help the characters overcome challenges. This narrative approach takes a bonus, exploiting the fact that individuals love stories and, therefore, increases motivation by adding an element of adventure and personal involvement (Ryan & Deci, 2000). Besides making learning more enjoyable, stories also tend to deepen interaction with the content, and the memory involved in learning new information is made easier for learners.

Customization and personalization is another advanced feature by which a learner can learn anything according to his or her preference. Most of the gamified chatbots offer to personalize avatars, select a preferred topic, or even choose learning paths based on their interests or goals. This is not only motivational but also increases the sense of autonomy, a crucial element in intrinsic motivation (Ryan & Deci, 2000). The responses by the chatbot can be further personalized based on the learner's progress, strengths, and weaknesses. For example, the difficulty of tasks undertaken by the chatbot may be changed in real time; this means that more challenging exercises would be given to a learner if he or she is moving at a rapid pace, and conversely, support would be added if the learner is struggling with certain concepts. This flexibility sustains a flow state, where learners are constantly challenged but not overwhelmed (Csikszentmihalyi, 1990).

Social interaction and collaboration is another powerful gamification feature, which engages learners through peer involvement and community-driven goals. Social elements can be as simple as leaderboards that compare the progress of the learners or even more complex interactions, such as multiplayer, in which learners interact to achieve a common goal. Learners might interact through the challenges, co-operative tasks or direct communication of them with the interface of the chatbot. The social feature relates to relatedness, where there is the need for having a sense of belonging and reciprocated support (Ryan & Deci, 2000). For one, social gamification features make the learner more responsible and motivated since they will continue engaging due to pressure or encouragement from peers, hence a better continuation of engaging with the language.

Lastly, some learning chatbots have adopted adaptive learning algorithms, which take it a step further by tailoring experience further through learner behavior observation and anticipation of learner needs. Learners' strengths, weaknesses, and speed of learning are taken into account in order to dynamically alter the subject matter and difficulty of the challenges a user is exposed to. For example, if a learner keeps getting the same vocabulary or grammatical structures wrong, the chatbot might start throwing those elements up more often until the learner gets it right. The reason is that motivation of learners together with the correct kind of support at the appropriate time maximizes both learning efficiency and learner satisfaction (Molenaar et al., 2013).

Lastly, integrating augmented reality and virtual reality can be considered to be an emergent trend and takes gamified language learning one step further ahead. Here, learners live interactive scenarios in real life as they practice their language skills in context in an amalgamation of immersive AR/VR technologies that come with gamified elements. For instance, in a VR game, learners could immerse themselves in the virtual marketplace or restaurant where, using the target language, they have to accomplish certain tasks and communicate with virtual characters. This fusion of gamification and immersion technologies creates a very engaging, highly realistic context for language learning that allows learners to practice in circumstances that simulate real life (Huang et al., 2016).

These sophisticated gamification techniques, such as storytelling, personalization, social interaction, adaptive learning, and AR/VR integration, would revolutionize learner engagement with language education. Benefits not only derive from motivation enhancement but also deeper and more efficient learning, transforming the environment through which learners find their success-creating dynamism, personalization, and immersiveness.

Language-learning chatbots have become more advanced, incorporating gamification aspects to boost engagement and allow more efficient language learning. Some chatbots excel at combining artificial intelligence (AI) and game mechanics to develop rich learning experiences.

Duolingo's AI-driven chat system is one such chatbot that embeds role-playing situations, adaptive difficulty levels, and real-time feedback to mimic real-life conversations. By combining streak rewards, experience points (XP), and achievement badges, Duolingo promotes regular practice, reinforcing vocabulary and grammar patterns in a manner that is more game-like than study. The chatbot's capacity to offer contextual hints and corrective suggestions in real time keeps learners interested while making consistent progress in their target language.

Another significant example is ChatGPT-based language tutors, which leverage AI's conversational capabilities to create dynamic, open-ended dialogues. Unlike rule-based chatbots that rely on scripted responses, these models generate natural, contextually relevant interactions, making them highly effective for practicing fluency. By incorporating elements such as quiz challenges, interactive storytelling, and gamified role-play scenarios, these chatbots allow learners to explore language in creative and personalized ways. The ability to select topics of conversation and difficulty levels adds to their utility, appealing to both beginners and advanced learners.

Likewise, Mondly's chatbot features speech recognition and real-life simulation capabilities, enabling learners to practice comprehension and pronunciation using gamified conversation exercises. The chatbot involves users in interactive lessons in which they earn points, progress to new levels, and get instant pronunciation feedback. This game-like yet systematic process maintains motivation while reinforcing key linguistic skills.

A more niche example is Lingvist's AI-based chatbot, which uses spaced repetition algorithms and gamification mechanics to maximize vocabulary retention. By combining flashcards, rewards for correct responses, and adaptive learning pathways, Lingvist guarantees that users concentrate on the most pertinent words and phrases, speeding up their language learning process.

These chatbots illustrate the revolutionizing power of gamification in language learning. By integrating game features like challenges, rewards, competition, and progress tracking, they provide an interactive and stimulating environment that maximizes motivation and retention. The application of AI-powered natural language processing (NLP) enables personalized feedback and realistic conversational practice, making language learning more accessible, enjoyable, and effective. As technology advances, these gamified chatbots will increasingly be at the center of assisting learners in acquiring new languages more efficiently and confidently.

5. ADVANTAGES OF GAMIFICATION IN LEARNING LANGUAGES

This gives numerous benefits to the language learning process, including motivating learners, enhancing engagement and retention, and eventually leading to greater learning outcomes. This is, arguably, what boosts motivation and engagement. Conventional language learning methods often lack the interest in learning among the learners, as the learning is carried out over a very long period and loses interest with exercises that seem to be repetitive and complicated grammar rules. Gamification, through integrating features like points, badges, and challenges into game-like learning processes, has proved to make learning very lively and interesting. The interesting aspects with fun as well as competition will engage the minds of learners to visit lessons more frequently. This will encourage them to keep moving forward to unlock new levels or achievements, since their main motivators are rewards and recognition and achievement of satisfactory levels upon completion of their goals (Deterding et al., 2011). Gamification, on the other hand relates to intrinsic motivation, since learners work for both external rewards and the enjoyment and personal growth at the completion of new skills mastered (Ryan & Deci, 2000).

With gamification, there is further support for better retention and learning outcome. Traditional learning of language usually breaks away from context, which contributes to shallow knowledge hard to retain over long periods. Yet, when linked with gamification elements such as spaced repetition, real-time feedback, and diversified learning challenges, language learners become better at holding information over long periods. For example, a great majority of chatbots aimed at multiplying languages use a spaced repetition algorithm, which displays formerly learned words or concepts at increasingly longer intervals, in order to be retained or reinforced (Anderson & Rainie, 2020). Gamification helps learners connect more meaningfully with the content through interactive and engaging ways that support long-term retention as opposed to passive absorption of information. The gamified environment, in terms of levels, challenges, and achievements, provides a sense of progression that instills learners into reviewing and practicing material more than usual, boosting retention.

Another significant contribution of gamification is immediacy. In any traditional classroom teaching, feedback can be delayed because of the waiting time for submitting language tasks in class. Actually, actual feedback is given to students through gamified learning chatbots for languages when they try to interact in the system. Immediately correcting learners upon errors or complicating them on some issues by a chatbot would be one of the helpful hints to be able to point them towards correction. Such an immediate reinforcement assists learners in comprehending their errors, learning from them, and changing their behavior (Fogg, 2003). Moreover, gamified chatbots may modify the difficulty level of tasks according to learner performance, always challenging the learner but never overwhelming them. By adapting the learning experience to the individual's needs, these systems optimize the efficiency of learning and maintain the learner's motivation and engagement.

Gamification also fosters a sense of accomplishment and progress, which is critical in sustaining long-term engagement. When learners earn badges, unlock new levels, or complete challenges, they develop a sense of accomplishment that strengthens their efforts. This is particularly the case in language learning, which is a notoriously slow or even invisible process at times. This kind of quick success in vocabulary sets or successful completion of hard challenges will definitely motivate learners in pursuing their learning journey. With this goes a well-designed progression system that motivates learners to continue achieving learning objectives (Sailer et al., 2017).

Lastly, gamification brings social interaction and sense of community with the integration of social features from chatbots like leaderboards, challenges, or collaborative tasks. Learners acquire a feeling of belongingness by competing or cooperating with others to enhance the social aspects of learning a language. This social interaction might produce increased accountability as learners have more urges to produce better when their progression is visible to others. Moreover, many learners feel highly motivated by friendly competition or cooperation with each other to achieve common goals (Ryan & Deci, 2000). The social aspect of gamification in language learning supports engagement through enjoyment and lack of isolation.

The advantages of gamification in language learning are too many to list. To begin with, gamification motivates the learner as it turns the learning process into more engaging, enjoyable, and rewarding. It also enhances retention as content is presented in ways that reinforce memory and the aspect of active learning. Providing immediate feedback, personalized learning paths, and a sense of accomplishment greatly enhances the learning process. It also involves gamified features, which allow the learner to interact socially, creating a supportive community that encourages him to go on with his language-learning plans. Ultimately, gamification strengthens not only the effectiveness of language learning but enjoyment and the spirit of learners as well.

6. CHALLENGES AND CONSIDERATIONS

Although gamification has many benefits in language learning, it also comes with several challenges and considerations that need to be taken into account and addressed to make it effective. One of the main concerns is that extrinsic motivation is overemphasized, especially through rewards and competition. While points, badges, and leaderboards work well to motivate learners in the short term, there is also a risk of learners becoming focused on external rewards rather than internal enjoyment of the learning process itself. This could threaten the sustainability of motivation into the longer term and impede the development of a deeper personal connection to the language being learned (Deci, Vallerand, Pelletier & Ryan, 1991). To combat this, there is a need to balance intrinsic and extrinsic motivation and ensure that the programmatic and game elements support learners in autonomy, competence, and relatedness, as it is proposed in Self Determination Theory (Ryan & Deci, 2000).

Another challenge is that learning may not be equitable in terms of outcomes because learners' populations are diverse, and learners may have different levels of prior knowledge, learning styles, and abilities. Even though gamified elements, including algorithms that perceive and adapt content according to the needs of the learners, always take into consideration that some tasks might always prove either too easy or too difficult for some learners and frustrate these learners to even disengage. Other learners, particularly those who are more uncomfortable with the use of technology, may be confused by technical nature of gamified chatbots and have their learning experience negatively affected (Vogel et al., 2006). To address this, gamified systems should therefore be designed with flexible levels of difficulty, user-friendly interfaces, and support for diverse learning styles so that all learners have the equal opportunity to win.

Content overload is another critical aspect to be considered in designing gamified language learning systems. While gamification may engage learners in levelling up, completing challenges, and getting rewards, an excessive amount of content or too many tasks leads to burnout or fatigue. New language learners, for example, or learners not yet fluent with the target language may be discouraged by too many challenges or complex tasks rather than motivated. Chatbots need to carefully design the pacing and sequencing of tasks so that learners are not exposed to too much information at one time and are given sufficient time to absorb and master each concept before being presented with more challenging material. Pacing mechanisms, such as breaks or rest periods, can be integrated to help manage cognitive load and avoid learner overload (Sweller, 1988).

Another aspect would be the danger of dependency on the chatbot. Although gamified chatbots may provide impressive support in language learning, overdependency on the technology may act to hinder other essential skills that the language learner has to master-such as conversational fluency, listening comprehension, and culture awareness. Authentic interaction with native speakers and authentic situations are indispensable parts of successful language learning. Hence, language learning chatbots would be used as complements to other methods and experience in real-life usage by the learners during which learners master all the competencies needed. Furthermore, using chatbots, it is possible to supplement the learning experience with the social and emotional aspects of language learning, which cannot be easily replicated through chatbots, to prevent complete isolation of learners from the social aspects of learning the language (Tharp, 1993).

Finally, there are ethical considerations regarding the use of gamification in education. For instance, collecting user data is often necessary for personalized learning experiences, which raises concerns about privacy and data security. Furthermore, the design of gamified systems must ensure inclusivity, avoiding stereotypes and biases that could alienate certain groups of learners. For instance, culturally biased content and exclusion of learners with disabilities undermine the effectiveness of gamified learning systems and reduce their reach. Therefore, accessibility and equity have to be top priorities in designing gamified chatbots so that the experience is enjoyable and effective for all learners, regardless of background or ability (Anderson et al., 2016).

While gamification entails many advantages, the problems introduced by gamifying must also be taken into deep consideration. Successful gamified design of language learning chatbots incorporates the delicate extrinsic/intrinsic motivation balance of learners, cultural and personal variability of the latter, a hazard of information explosion, a fear of excessive technological dependency, as well as critical ethical questions, which require balanced consideration of one another for implementing effective, appealing, and learner-friendly gamification.

7. CASE STUDIES AND REAL APPLICATIONS

Several real-world applications have been constructed as an outcome of gamification from language learning-based chatbots, and those show the efficiency of this approach. A very prominent example of such an application is the extremely popular language-learning application Duolingo, which uses a variety of gamification elements to encourage learners. Duolingo uses a combination of points, levels, badges, and streaks to encourage its users to continually practice their target language. The progression in the app is designed such that learners open up to new levels and challenges as soon as lessons are completed. There is also real-time feedback on mistakes made. This competitive factor, applied by Duolingo through the use of leaderboards, extends user engagement because learners can see how they fare in comparison to other users. Duolingo's gamified design, as shown through studies, helps increase learner motivation and persistence considerably, with chances of returning users and maintaining the practice schedule considerably higher (Vesselinov & Grego, 2012).

Thus, this result proves that the power of gamification is maintained by keeping interest in the language practice.

Another case study which shows the power of gamification in language learning is Babbel, a learning other languages platform based on game mechanics for lessons. Babbel differs slightly from Duolingo. It takes a structured lesson method with motivational elements of game mechanics, including tracking progress and achievement badges as well as review of one's performance. The system continuously adjusts the levels of difficulty during lessons to depend on how they are performing-never challenging someone too much to be unable to handle the materials. The popularity of Babbel can be tied to its convergence of gamification with more linear, organized methodology for teaching one a new language, increasing involvement and sticking through. A company-led study found that Babbel learners significantly improved their language skills, demonstrating the effectiveness of gamification with high-quality educational content (Babbel, 2019). Babbel's user-centered gamification, such as customized lesson paths and rewards for completing lessons, is a testament to the growing trend in personalized, gamified education.

Another example of gamification in language education is the Mondly language-learning chatbot. Mondly offers some gamification features advanced, such as a VR experience and interactive chatbots powered by AI. The interface is specifically designed to put learners in a scenario like they were speaking to locals face to face for real-time conversations in a target language, simulating real-life interactions as it's been designed to allow users for vocabulary, pronunciation, and grammar practice, in a dynamic, gamified environment. Mondly creates virtual environments in which learners interact with objects and characters in the target language by using augmented reality. This provides an immersive experience, game-like in nature, that simulates real-life conversations, which is very important to language learners struggling with conversational fluency. Studies on Mondly have shown gamified features can significantly enhance engagement and retention for the learner, especially for the younger target audiences who have become more accustomed to interactive technologies as part of their daily life (Bai & Furlong, 2019). Success with Mondly brings attention to opportunities for using augmented reality in combination with gamification to more effectively create immersive language learning experiences.

One more example is Busuu, which brings a gamified language learning application with social capabilities to interact directly with native speakers by using community-based approaches. Gamified elements of Busuu are represented by levels, points, achievements, and daily challenges that usually keep students involved. While Busuu's strength is on the social aspect where users will have the chance to submit exercises for review in a native-speaker context. This peer-to-peer learning aspect improves the skills of learners through authentic interaction but also produces a sense of community that enhances motivation and engagement. Social features applied by Busuu within a gamified framework trigger an attractive learning environment where language skills can be exercised in support and interactive settings (Bai & Furlong, 2019). The success of the platform in the fluency of language shows the importance of the integration of social components with gamified features for a more holistic learning experience.

Case studies on real-world applications, such as Duolingo, Babbel, Mondly, and Busuu, indicate that gamified language-learning systems are highly successful. These platforms rely on game mechanics, such as points, badges, levels, and social interaction, to sustain learner motivation, increase engagement, and enhance learning outcomes. Combining personalized learning, adaptive difficulty, and immersive experiences with gamification results in more effective language acquisition and a deeper connection to the learning process. These case studies are excellent examples for further development and refinement of gamified language-learning chatbots, providing insight into how systems can be designed that are both engaging and pedagogically sound.

8. FUTURE DIRECTIONS AND TRENDS

With the evolution of gamification, several promising directions and trends emerge in the development of language-learning chatbots. One of the significant future trends would be to include artificial intelligence (AI) and machine learning into the learning platform to provide learners with even more personalized and adaptive learning experiences. Using the power of AI, a learner's behavior, learning preferences, and progress can be tracked in real-time so that the type of tasks, learning materials, and feedback can be appropriately changed on the fly by the chatbot. Machine learning algorithms can continuously improve the system's understanding of a learner's needs so that, at any point, the content presented is relevant and engaging. For example, an AI-based chatbot may notice patterns in the errors made by a learner and will offer lessons that are targeted to specific weak areas. This dynamics personalization will most likely increase learner retention and overall language acquisition because it is more tailored and responsive in nature towards learning the language (Woolf, 2010).

The other significant development is the use of natural language processing and speech recognition technology; hence, chatbots will be more interactive and realistic in the context of any language learning experience. With NLP, the chatbots would better understand the input of users in a way more human-like so that their conversation with others becomes more fluent and natural in the target language. Together with speech recognition that evaluates the pronunciation and fluency of learners, the ability of the chatbot to give the most accurate and effective feedback possible will be more pronounced, almost like a native speaker speaking. These will allow learners not only to get enough practice speaking and listening but also produce more authentic communication in virtual environments (Budzianowski et al., 2021). The integration of these advanced technologies may lead to immersive experiences that closely mimic real-life interactions, thus raising learners' confidence in their use of language in authentic contexts.

Gamified language learning will also have augmented and virtual reality play increasingly big roles. Both AR and VR would be fully immersive in order to allow learners to experience realistic, context-based situations in their target language. For example, AR would superimpose language learning over actual settings in their lives-for example, by identifying objects in the learner's home or neighborhood-while VR would place learners in totally virtual scenarios that could include navigating a foreign marketplace or restaurant. Such immersive settings allow learners to practice their language skills in more meaningful and richer context, providing opportunities for interactivity and hands-on learning. There is an enormous scope for gamified language-learning experiences that are powered by AR and VR. Learners would be able to engage with the language not only through tasks but in real-life simulations, boosting their conversational fluency and cultural understanding (Zhao, 2020).

Social and collaborative elements of learning features are also poised to dominate in the future trend of gamifying language learning. Current gamified chatbots, for example already have some mode of sociality, such as leaderboards as well as through peer feedback for the students using them. These future trends of gamification into language learning include far more integrative collaborative and multiplayer mode aspects or colearning tasks. These features would allow for learners to work with each other on language challenges, friendly competition, or jointly complete missions and thereby provide the element of community and mutual support for learners. This social feature can work to create even greater motivation since learners have the ability to be in a community with peers who could help in the achievement of those same objectives and challenges within an engaging and social form of learning. Furthermore, learner interactions with others, particularly native speakers, add to a learner's engagement with the target language as well as cultural awareness (Godwin-Jones, 2017).

The gamified language-learning platforms that easily blur with daily life will gain more popularity as mobile and flexible learning demands grow. Future language-learning chatbots will leverage the increased use of smartphones, wearables, and other mobile devices. It will be a platform that will enable learners to practice their target language anywhere, anytime, converting mundane tasks, such as commuting or exercising, into opportunities for language practice. If the gamification aspects are involved within the normal, daily operations like sending of reminders or day-by-day tiny challenges, students would be pushed toward constant practicing without getting annoyed or burdened. The practice can then very easily become ingrained in day-to-day lives to increase comfort and convenience levels and accessibility toward more sustainable language learning, benefiting various lifestyles and time schedules for its users (Kukulska-Hulme, 2020).

Future trends in gamification-related language-learning chatbots focus on further advances in AI, NLP, speech recognition, AR/VR technologies, and social learning features, which appear to produce more adaptive, contextual, and collaborative learning experience. In the overall, these emerging trends will probably enhance motivation, retention, and fluency among learners in these enhanced environment conditions. The integration of gamification in language-learning chatbots will continually be pushing education boundaries, bringing innovative ways in which learners interact with languages and cultures on their own terms.

9. CONCLUSION

Ultimately, the gamification of elements in language-learning chatbots holds a lot of promise to improve the level of engagement and motivation as well as general effectiveness for the learners. Integrating game-like elements such as points, levels, badges, and real-time feedback with instruction creates an engaging, dynamic learning environment that will attract intrinsic as well as extrinsic motivators. This implies that in fact, applications like Duolingo, Babbel, Mondly, and Busuu have the proof of effectiveness towards raising the retention of a learner as well as enhancing acquisition when it involves increased joy and accessibility in acquiring those languages.

However, gamification of language learning is not free from its problems as well. For instance, there could be over-reliance on extrinsic rewards, content overload, learner diversity, and technical accessibility to name others that might make the experience unbalanced, exclusive, or even pedagogically unsound. With these challenges, as technology continues to advance, including such features as artificial intelligence, natural language processing, augmented reality, and social aspects, the obstacles will be easily overcome, making the learning process more efficient and effective.

The future prospects of gamified language-learning chatbots seem truly promising in this regard, moving even more intensely personal, more immersive, and socially engaging than ever. Thus, using some of the state-of-the-art AI advancements integrated with speech recognition and AR/VR technologies will probably continue with the improvement for language-learning experiences that are significantly richer and, in nature more interactive, promoting conversational fluency and rich cultural understanding from learners. Additionally, as language learning becomes more integrated with daily routines through mobile apps and wearable devices, learners will have more opportunities to practice their target language anytime, anywhere, ensuring consistent engagement and progress.

Ultimately, gamification can revolutionize language learning. The innovative technologies adopted and the design of systems to focus on learner autonomy, motivation, and social interaction can all be supported by gamified chatbots, enhancing a variety of learners' experience in a far more enjoyable, effective, and sustainable way. With further development, this field has the potential to make language learning truly accessible, engaging, and rewarding.

REFERENCES

Anderson, C. A., Shibuya, A., Ihori, N., Swing, E. L., & Bushman, B. J. (2016). Video game play, aggression, and prosocial behavior. *Psychological Science*, *27*(6), 777–790. DOI: 10.1177/0956797616634463

Anderson, J. Q., & Rainie, L. (2020). *The future of education: How technology is reshaping learning*. Pew Research Center. https://www.pewresearch.org

Babbel. (2019). *Babbel language learning: Impact on language proficiency*. Retrieved from https://www.babbel.com

Bai, X., & Furlong, C. (2019). Mondly: The use of augmented reality in language learning. *Journal of Educational Technology Development and Exchange*, *12*(3), 31–44.

Budzianowski, P., Sima, J., & Rudzicz, F. (2021). Towards conversational artificial intelligence for language learning. *Journal of Language and Education Technology*, *7*(2), 42–55. DOI: 10.1057/jlet.2021.39

Csikszentmihalyi, M. (1990). *Flow: The psychology of optimal experience*. Harper & Row.

Deci, E. L., Vallerand, R. J., Pelletier, L. G., & Ryan, R. M. (1991). Motivation and education: The self-determination perspective. *Educational Psychologist*, *26*(3–4), 325–346. DOI: 10.1080/00461520.1991.9653137

Deterding, S., Dixon, D., Khaled, R., & Nacke, L. (2011). From game design elements to gamefulness: defining" gamification". In *Proceedings of the 2011 annual conference on Human factors in computing systems* (pp. 9-15). DOI: 10.1145/2181037.2181040

Fogg, B. J. (2003). *Persuasive technology: Using computers to change what we think and do*. Morgan Kaufmann. DOI: 10.1016/B978-155860643-2/50011-1

Godwin-Jones, R. (2017). Emerging technologies: Language learning and social media. *Language Learning & Technology*, *21*(1), 6–19.

Huang, T., Su, C., & Lin, Y. (2016). Application of augmented reality in language learning: A case study on Chinese language learning. *Computers & Education*, *102*, 38–50. DOI: 10.1016/j.compedu.2016.06.001

Kukulska-Hulme, A. (2020). Mobile language learning. In *The Cambridge Handbook of Technology and Language* (pp. 391–409). Cambridge University Press., DOI: 10.1017/9781108330307.024

McClelland, D. C. (1961). *The achieving society*. Free Press. DOI: 10.1037/14359-000

Molenaar, I., Chiu, M. M., & van der Maas, H. L. (2013). The role of adaptive learning in the design of interactive educational technologies: An evaluation of two types of interventions. *Journal of Educational Psychology*, *105*(4), 1043–1057. DOI: 10.1037/a0032412

Ryan, R. M., & Deci, E. L. (2000). Self-determination theory and the facilitation of intrinsic motivation, social development, and well-being. *The American Psychologist*, *55*(1), 68–78. DOI: 10.1037/0003-066X.55.1.68 PMID: 11392867

Sailer, M., Hense, J. U., Mayr, S. K., & Mærkedahl, J. (2017). How gamification motivates: An experimental study of the effects of specific game design elements on psychological need satisfaction. *Computers in Human Behavior*, *69*, 10–17. DOI: 10.1016/j.chb.2016.12.033

Skinner, B. F. (1953). *Science and human behavior*. Macmillan.

Sweller, J. (1988). Cognitive load during problem solving: Effects on learning. *Cognitive Science*, *12*(2), 257–285. DOI: 10.1207/s15516709cog1202_4

Tharp, R. G. (1993). *Teaching transformed: Achieving excellence, fairness, inclusion, and harmony*. Pergamon Press.

Vázquez-Cano, E. (2020). *Language learning with technology: A practical guide for language educators*. Springer.

Vesselinov, R., & Grego, J. (2012). *Duolingo effectiveness study*. City University of New York. Retrieved from https://www.duolingo.com

Vogel, J. J., Vogel, D. L., Cannon-Bowers, J. A., Bowers, C. A., Muse, K., & Wright, M. (2006). Computer gaming and interactive simulations for learning: A meta-analysis. *Journal of Educational Computing Research, 34*(3), 229–243. DOI: 10.2190/FLHV-K4WA-WPVQ-H0YM

Woolf, B. P. (2010). *Building intelligent interactive tutors: Student-centered strategies for learning*. Morgan Kaufmann.

Zhao, Y. (2020). Emerging trends in virtual and augmented reality for language learning. *Journal of Educational Technology & Society, 23*(4), 101–115. DOI: 10.2307/26834692

Chapter 3
Adaptive AI in Metaverse Language Education

Rohit Yadav
https://orcid.org/0000-0002-7573-8005
IILM University, Greater Noida, India

Xuan-Hoa Nghiem
https://orcid.org/0000-0003-2292-0257
International School, Vietnam National University, Hanoi, Vietnam

Mohit Yadav
https://orcid.org/0000-0002-9341-2527
O.P. Jindal Global University, India

ABSTRACT

This chapter explores the integration of Adaptive AI in Metaverse language education, examining how AI-driven platforms and immersive virtual environments are revolutionizing language learning. By combining artificial intelligence, augmented reality (AR), and virtual reality (VR), the Metaverse offers personalized and interactive experiences tailored to individual learning needs. This chapter covers the evolution of language learning technologies, the potential benefits and features of Adaptive AI,

DOI: 10.4018/979-8-3693-9974-3.ch003

and how it enhances language acquisition within the Metaverse. It also addresses key ethical concerns, challenges such as data privacy, accessibility, and AI biases, and the future trajectory of this educational approach. The future promises even more sophisticated learning environments, with emotionally intelligent AI tutors, real-time translation, and multilingual communication tools. This emerging paradigm reshapes how languages are learned globally, fostering accessibility and cross-cultural understanding.

1. INTRODUCTION

Adaptive AI based on metaverse technology in language learning is one of the paradigm shifts in teaching and learning approaches. Current language teaching methodologies, like traditional curricula, do not have room for the natural learner's difference, making it a formidable task to accommodate diverse needs in learning (Pérez & Murray, 2021). However, adaptive AI engages machine learning, NLP, and real-time data analysis to adapt every learner's learning experience according to his skill level, activity level, and progress in the learning processes (Chen et al., 2022).

On the other hand, the metaverse is a dynamic and engaging learning environment for language learners. This immersive virtual world created with AR, VR, and blockchain technologies differs from the traditional classroom as it provides real-time communication, AI-created avatars, and gamified experiences that condition language acquisition through social interaction and contextual immersion (Li, 2023). This aligns with constructivist learning theories, where learning is explained to result from active participation and engagement in meaningful contexts (Vygotsky, 1978).

Adaptive AI brings together with metaverse technologies the all-inclusive, engaging, and efficient possibilities of language education. AI-based language tutors can evaluate pronunciation, grammar, and fluency in real-time and provide instant feedback and customized learning pathways (Yang & Sun, 2023). Furthermore, AI-based conversational agents and virtual peers can enhance social learning by simulating authentic language interactions in immersive digital environments (Huang et al., 2021). These developments are most useful to those learning the second language since most of these people face issues related to in situ exposure and opportunity to interact within low-stakes, building confidence scenarios (Smith & Jones, 2020).

There is much that promises from including adaptive AI into language education that happens within metaverse, and data privacy and accessibility issues become part of its drawbacks, coupled with the biased decision-making abilities of AI (Kumar & Singh, 2022). However, the synergy of such technologies has remained unprecedented in the sense that they have made learning language highly engaging, personal, and accessible throughout the world due to its revolution through continued improvement in AI and sophisticated development in metaverse platforms (Zhou et al., 2023).

2. HISTORICAL DEVELOPMENT OF LANGUAGE LEARNING TECHNOLOGIES

Language learning witnessed drastic change throughout the past hundred years. The changes went from traditional classroom-based methodologies towards technology-supportive, AI-driven approaches for learning language. Early approaches were based on behaviorist theories that relied heavily on rote memorization and repetition, like the audio-lingual method that was so prevalent in the middle of the 20th century (Skinner, 1957). Effective for grammatical structures and pronunciation, it didn't leave space for meaningful interaction, thereby failing to give the learner opportunities to develop communicative competence (Richards & Rodgers, 2001). The 1970s gave rise to CLT, focusing on communication in the real world. It encouraged interaction and contextual learning (Hymes, 1972). However, traditional CLT was still confined to classroom-based instruction and teacher-centered approach.

The advent of CALL in the 1980s and 1990s brought more active roles of technology in language education (Levy, 1997). The early CALL programs used text-based exercises and language drills, giving learners automated feedback and structured practice. But, such systems did not accommodate individual learner needs, so they just settled for one size fits all (Hubbard, 2009). Early in the 2000s, internet-based learning platforms appeared: Duolingo and Rosetta Stone have popularized a shift toward self-paced and interactive learning (Godwin-Jones, 2011). These used multimedia, gamification, and speech recognition to attract learners but still remained mostly on a set learning track instead of adapting to the progress of the learner.

Language learning was dramatically shifted with adaptive learning technologies from the 2010s through incorporating AI and NLP into adaptive learning processes to tailor instruction to the performance of the learner (Wang & Vasquez, 2021). These real-time speech analyses, conversational AI tutors, and data-driven learning recommendations through AI-powered platforms are made into personalized experiences (Colpaert, 2018). Other applications for creating human-like simulations include virtual assistants and language chatbots that may simulate actual conversation practice (Hwang et al., 2022).

The most recent evolution is the application of AI in metaverse environments, which provide virtual reality and augmented reality, creating immersive and interactive spaces for language acquisition (Dede, 2022). Metaverse-based learning, unlike digital platforms, encourages embodied cognition, through which learners can experience language in contextualized virtual environments, such as simulated marketplaces, restaurants, or social events (Schwienhorst, 2002). These experiences fall in with sociocultural learning theories that focus on the social process and embracing cultural practice in the development of language (Vygotsky, 1978). In addition, metaverse AI adaptive learning systems will evaluate learner behavior, speech patterns, and their engagement level to derive appropriate customized learning paths and give immediate feedback (Zhang et al., 2023).

As adaptive AI and metaverse technology evolve, so does language learning move from being linear and structured to interactive and dynamic, from teacher-centeredness to learner-centricity. Second language acquisition should become more accessible, engaging, and efficient using these innovations to shift the paradigms through which languages can be taught in the digital world (Lu et al., 2022).

3. THE CONCEPT OF ADAPTIVE AI IN LANGUAGE LEARNING

This paradigm shift in how learners acquire new languages is brought about by the integration of adaptive AI in language education. In contrast to traditional learning methods, which are rigid and have a set curriculum that proceeds at the same pace for everyone, adaptive AI-driven language education tailors instruction to individual progress, learning styles, and performance (Chen et al., 2022). Adaptive AI relies on ML, NLP, and real-time data analytics to generate adaptive and interactive learning environments that continuously respond to each learner's needs to maximize engagement and retention (Wang & Vasquez, 2021).

3.1 What is Adaptive AI?

Adaptive AI refers to adaptive smart learning systems that can adjust content, learning difficulty, and teaching approach based on real-time interactions of learners with the system (Pérez & Murray, 2021). These AI-based educational platforms analyze learner input, responses, and engagement patterns to provide personalized recommendations, feedback, and lesson modifications. Adaptive AI ensures that learners obtain content at the right level of difficulty, neither too challenging nor too easy to maintain motivation and maximize learning progress (Colpaert, 2018).

3.2 Key Technologies Driving Adaptive AI in Language Learning

Some of the newest technologies that facilitate adaptive AI systems to personalize experiences in language learning are:

- Natural Language Processing (NLP): NLP allows an AI to process, decipher, and create human language. To analyze speech in real time, for conversational AI tutors and interactive chatbot-based learning, Hwang et al., 2022. AI-powered speech recognition systems will track pronunciation, fluency, and grammatical correctness and provide immediate feedback to enable the conversation on the same (Yang & Sun, 2023).

- Machine Learning (ML): ML algorithms analyze learner behavior, track progress, and predict areas of difficulty, enabling AI to adjust lesson plans dynamically (Zhang et al., 2023). These systems continuously refine their models based on new data, making learning increasingly personalized over time (Godwin-Jones, 2021).
- Artificial Intelligence-Powered Speech Synthesis: AI-generated voices help learners practice pronunciation by simulating native-like speech patterns, adjusting tones, and offering real-time corrections (Lu et al., 2022).
- Data-Driven Learning Analytics: AI aggregates and analyzes big chunks of learner performance data to detect trends and predict the learner's needs for future learning (Wang et al., 2020). Data-driven methods can more efficiently provide learners with personalized paths, customized learning plans according to the individual strengths and weaknesses.

3.3 Personalization and Real-Time Feedback in Language Learning

Another critical advantage of adaptive AI in language learning is its provision of prompt, personalized feedback, allowing the learner to make adjustments on the spot rather than waiting for an instructor's review (Chen et al., 2022). AI-driven systems can break down pronunciation, grammatical errors, and issues of fluency while providing context-based explanations that help improve the learning process (Hubbard, 2018). Adaptive AI also takes into account the speed of learning, attention span, and levels of engagement to adjust lessons to maintain learner interest (Kumar & Singh, 2022).

For instance, Duolingo and Babbel are language learning applications powered by AI that use adaptive algorithms to provide exercises based on a learner's ability. If a student fails to grasp verb conjugations, the AI will instantly produce more focused practice exercises and descriptions to make the concept more concrete before allowing them to move on (Wang & Vasquez, 2021). In metaverse-based AI learning environments, learners can engage in interactive role-playing dialogues in which AI-constructed avatars respond in real-time to their speech, thereby mimicking actual conversations without judgment or stress (Zhou et al., 2023).

3.4 Advantages of Adaptive AI for Language Learning

Adaptive AI in language teaching offers the following benefits:

- Personalized learning paths: AI will update the lesson instantly based on the learner's performance, and they are allowed to have a tailored process of learning (Yang & Sun, 2023).
- High interaction and motivation: Adaptive AI gamifies learning, incorporating rewards and challenges and providing real-time feedback to keep learners motivated (Pérez & Murray, 2021).
- Efficient Skill Development: AI-based pronunciation analysis and speech recognition tools assist learners in developing speaking skills through an engaging and confidence-building platform (Lu et al., 2022).
- Scalability and Accessibility: AI-based learning platforms are accessible 24/7, ensuring that quality language education is provided to learners anywhere in the world, including in remote locations (Wang et al., 2020).

3.5 Challenges and Limitations

There are many challenges that adaptive AI in language education has to deal with:

- Bias and Fairness: The AI system is likely to inherit biases from its training data, making the feedback offered and lesson recommendations possess linguistic and cultural bias (Kumar & Singh, 2022).
- Data Privacy Issues: AI systems collect and analyze huge amounts of data regarding the users, bringing up ethical questions about security of the data, consent of the users, and confidentiality (Huang et al., 2021).

- dependency on technology: The overdependence on AI-powered learning decreases human interaction and analysis, both of which play a crucial role in real-world language learning (Zhou et al., 2023).
- Lack of contextual insight: AI systems cannot grasp the subtlety in the usage of expressions or idiomatic expression and cultural context, all these aspects are crucial for fluency and real-life communication (Colpaert, 2018).

3.6 Future Direction of Adaptive AI in Language Learning

Future advances will be made through deep learning, AI-human interaction, and multimodal language processing. The further development of AI will mean the better contextual understanding, emotional involvement, and culture-specific language for future models, making interactions sound more authentic, human-like (Lu et al., 2022). The integration of metaverse-based learning will further enhance immersion, providing learners with opportunities to engage in simulated real-world conversations with AI-powered avatars and multilingual virtual environments (Zhang et al., 2023).

By combining the adaptability of AI with the immersive potential of the metaverse, the future of language education will be more engaging, personalized, and effective than ever before.

4. THE METAVERSE AS A LANGUAGE LEARNING ENVIRONMENT

The metaverse is the collective virtual shared space created by the convergence of virtually enhanced physical reality and physically persistent virtual spaces, which are transforming the learning landscape of languages. This digital universe is fully immersive, and highly interactive environments in which learners acquire language within the fabric of their everyday virtual experiences. The metaverse situates learners in context-rich, virtual worlds, allowing for a form of experiential learning that is deeply aligned with constructivist educational theories, which emphasize learning through active participation and social interaction (Dede, 2022).

4.1 Virtual Classrooms and Immersive Learning Spaces

Virtual classrooms in the metaverse transcend the constraints of physical spaces, providing customizable and interactive settings that suit different learning preferences (Lu et al., 2022). For example, virtual field trips to historical sites or cultural landmarks allow learners to engage in contextualized language practice that would be almost impossible to replicate in a physical classroom. It is not rare for such settings to include AI-based content enrichments, like virtual teaching assistants and real-time language translation tools, that modify their content based on the learner's needs (Zhang et al., 2023). Such adaptability can create powerful, fully personalized, immersive experiences, thus boosting engagement and retention by leaps and bounds.

4.2 Social Interaction and AI-driven Conversational Agents

Among the most promising aspects of a metaverse for language learning is the opportunities it provides for authentic social interaction. This can be through AI-driven, conversational agents, or virtual characters, as these can effectively simulate real-world conversations in which learners find low-pressure outlets for practicing the speaking and listening skills (Huang et al., 2021). These AI agents are designed to engage with learners in natural language, allowing them to use these agents in different kinds of conversational contexts-such as ordering food in a virtual café, to negotiating within a business setting. These interactions promote pragmatic competence, as they prepare learners to better and more appropriately use language in social environments (Schwienhorst, 2002).

Additionally, the social feature of the metaverse allows learners to interact and communicate with their peers anywhere in the world as well as collaborative language learning. In the virtual communities, the learners can participate in group activities that include projects, cultural collaborations, and linguistic games but are aimed at developing communication skills in an interesting yet interactive manner (Yang & Sun, 2023). The social connection that the metaverse provides also supports peer feedback and cooperative learning, vital elements in the development of communicative competence (Vygotsky, 1978).

4.3 Gamification and AI-based Motivation Strategies

The metaverse lends itself to gamified learning where language acquisition is embedded within game-like experiences that motivate and challenge learners (Pérez & Murray, 2021). AI algorithms track learners' progress and adjust game difficulty levels, ensuring an optimal balance between challenge and skill, a key principle of flow theory (Csikszentmihalyi, 1990). As an example, learners may engage in quests that require the completion of a puzzle or mission based on a set of tasks that the target language must efficiently accommodate. This contextual and goal-oriented approach tends to heighten intrinsic motivation and ensures that more consistent practice is maintained (Wang & Vasquez, 2021).

Besides motivation, AI-based adaptive feedback systems in the metaverse provide instant corrections and encouragement tailored to individual performance. Such personalized feedback loops have been proven to enhance language acquisition outcomes because they help learners recognize and correct errors promptly, reinforcing accurate language use (Chen et al., 2022).

4.4 Cultural Immersion and Empathy Building

The immersive nature of the metaverse also offers unprecedented opportunities for cultural immersion, which is an essential part of language learning that is often overlooked in traditional settings (Li, 2023). Participating in virtual cultural festivals, markets, or day-to-day activities exposes learners to the nuances and norms that frame the use of language in real-world contexts. This level of immersion creates cultural empathy and sensibility, both of which are essential ingredients in truly effective communication (Smith & Jones, 2020).

Moreover, VR and AR in the metaverse can be utilized to create scenarios that make cross-cultural communication-related decisions more practical, thus helping students develop strategies for effective intercultural dialogue. This makes learners understand the language and the cultural contexts that influence meaning and interpretation (Zhou et al., 2023).

4.5 Challenges and Future Directions

The metaverse is exciting but poses a challenge. The access to participate in the metaverse requires an equal distribution of technology, thereby worsening the divide (Kumar & Singh, 2022). In addition, the accumulation of vast data regarding personal behavior and personal identifiable information increases vulnerability to data breaches and loss in security due to AI-driven platform use (Hwang et al., 2022). That requires a robust policy and ethical framework that can provide the safety net to learning rights while creating an open and friendly digital environment.

Haptic technologies and AI-driven emotional recognition could be the ultimate upgrades for the metaverse as a language learning space. Learners may be able to receive real-time emotional feedback that would lead to more empathetic, responsive interactions (Lu et al., 2022). Future development in these areas could transform the metaverse from being a mere language learning tool into a holistic educational ecosystem that fosters global citizenship and cultural literacy.

5. ADAPTIVE AI FEATURES FOR LANGUAGE LEARNING IN THE METAVERSE

The metaverse unlocks transformational opportunities for language education through adaptive AI features. Advanced AI technologies integrated into the metaverse will provide learners with a highly personalized, dynamic environment that differentiates according to one's individual needs, preferences, and learning pace. These features go way beyond basic tools and enable meaningful interaction with language content in the context. This chapter expands on some of the most important features around adaptive AI used in language learning and which can apply to language learning within the metaverse.

5.1 Dynamic Content Personalization and Customization

One of the most powerful features of adaptive AI in the metaverse is that it can personalise content to meet the specific needs of the learners based on their progress. It keeps track of the learner's strengths and weaknesses in real-time by adjusting the complexity and scope of the language material (Pérez & Murray, 2021). For example, if a learner continuously finds himself in difficulties when using verb conjugations in the target language, then the AI system will show more exercises or immersed scenarios with regard to that skill. With that being said, in making sure learners only experience the most relevant content to their individual progress, the personalized learning journey in the metaverse can dramatically increase motivation and retention (Chen et al., 2022).

This will allow giving learners personalized virtual learning environments where they can train the language under real-life experience in various conditions and contexts. The adaptive learning environments range from virtual shops, restaurants, or marketplaces, even city streets, to serve particular cultural and linguistic contexts where learners can deeply engage in goal-oriented authentic practice (Huang et al., 2021). Such experiences ensure that learners can practice not only textbook language but also social nuances and cultural cues necessary for real-world communication.

5.2 Real-time Language Feedback and Correction

The second significant feature of adaptive AI is real-time feedback and correction. In the metaverse, AI-driven speech recognition and NLP systems can assess learners' spoken and written language in real time to provide immediate, personalized feedback on pronunciation, grammar, and vocabulary use (Yang & Sun, 2023). For instance, AI can analyze pronunciation errors during virtual role-playing exercises and then give personal suggestions for improvement, such as by adjusting a voice model to indicate how native speakers might pronounce certain words or phrases. The feedback loop is very immediate, hence helping the learner adjust his language use immediately for rapid improvement.

The AI system in the metaverse can provide learners with corrective techniques through the use of an interactive correction by giving hints to the learner or alternative phrases. Unlike the typical classroom where feedback may only come after assignments have been graded, real-time correction through adaptive AI ensures that errors are corrected before learners reinforce bad habits (Godwin-Jones, 2021). This leads to effective use of the language in the long run and more confident application by the learner.

5.3 Immersive Conversational AI Agents

The metaverse offers an excellent opportunity to make learners interact with AI-driven conversational agents or virtual tutors who bring it as close as possible to real communication exchange. Such agents, based on NLUs and machine learning algorithms, can automatically create spontaneous conversations, change responses based on the input from learners, and provide real-time feedback (Schwienhorst, 2002). Such versatile AI agents make them ideal practice tools for actual conversations, especially if learners wish to improve their fluency, vocabulary, or pronunciation.

Another adaptability feature highlights the virtual tutor's ability to be sensitive to the learner's conversational speed. For instance, if a learner cannot keep up with a conversation, the AI agent could slow its speech, use simpler words, or even break down complex sentences into simpler words for easy comprehension (Zhou et al., 2023). This is the core reason learners are not given tasks that overwhelm them to the point that they cannot create the foundation for error-making and slow improvement on a topic of learning.

Furthermore, there is contextual intelligence provided with the conversational agents that it can sense the social and cultural context in which a conversation takes place. For example, if a student is chatting with a local shopkeeper or tour guide in a virtual city, the AI will add culturally suitable responses, accents, and idiomatic expressions so that students feel the language as it should be in their living lives (Lu et al., 2022).

5.4 Gamification and Motivation Strategies

Gamification is another crucial element in the metaverse adaptive AI toolset for language learning-an exciting and motivational approach. Such AI-driven gamified learning conditions as language learning challenges, missions, or quests are far more engaging and rewarding for learners to experience. Among such tasks would be solving a dialogue puzzle or role-playing in a given situation or linguistic challenges, aiming at creating the required level of learner's language proficiency while maintaining at higher levels the engagement and motivation (Wang & Vasquez, 2021).

As in the metaverse, learners earn rewards and move on to increasingly challenging tasks after completing language learning tasks, developing a sense of accomplishment that perpetuates continued engagement. AI algorithms monitor individual students' progress in order to incrementally increase difficulty to match increased competence. For intrinsic motivation, adaptive difficulty progression is critical-it encourages learners to push themselves and not be forced to do anything that is significantly too difficult to accomplish (Pérez & Murray, 2021).

This is not only this but also AI-fed loops of feedback that have learners feel motivated by getting them engaged towards achievements, thus keeping them feeling better and where they should improve. Indeed, these factors of gamified elements are enhanced with the interactive presence of learning with 3D spaces where learners can enhance their emotional immersion as well when using a metaverse-based learning environment (Lu et al., 2022).

5.5 Contextual and Cultural Adaptation

The most advanced functionality of adaptive AI in the metaverse is the ability to offer contextual as well as cultural adaptation in the learning of the language. Through this, by allowing learners to interact virtually through AI-driven avatars, this system adjusts content for language studies on a given cultural scenario for interaction. For example, a learner learning Spanish in a virtual Spanish market may be exposed to region-specific vocabulary and cultural practices, such as local greetings or customs, which reflect the varied linguistic and cultural landscapes within the target language (Zhou et al., 2023). Such contextualization of language learning makes it far more relevant and effective than isolated grammar drills or vocabulary exercises.

Adaptive AI systems can also be used to measure the emotions of a learner and adjust the feedback tone and presentation. When a learner appears frustrated, the AI will adjust the tone to encourage and empathize with the learner in order to avoid burnout and keep him motivated. This emotive aspect of emotional intelligence will further add a holistic nature to the learning experience so that learners are supported all the way through their learning journey (Yang & Sun, 2023).

5.6 Continuous Learning and Adaptive Assessment

In the metaverse, AI-driven adaptive assessments ensure that learners are not only constantly engaged but also evaluated correctly based on their individual progress. AI systems can continuously assess learners' language skills in real-time, adjusting the frequency and complexity of assessments to match their development (Zhang et al., 2023). For example, learners can take micro-assessments after each learning task or immersive experience, enabling AI to recalculate their next learning steps.

Moreover, adaptive assessments within the metaverse focus on various language competencies, such as reading comprehension, listening skills, vocabulary, and fluency in speaking. AI-based systems can integrate conventional assessments into immersive, scenario-based assessments in virtual environments, for example, testing the fluency of a conversation by holding real-life conversations (Lu et al., 2022). This is a continuous adaptation learning cycle, which supports learners' short-term needs while keeping their learning path aligned with long-term goals and competency milestones.

6. CHALLENGES AND ETHICAL CONSIDERATIONS

Although the inclusion of adaptive AI and the metaverse in language education opens up tremendous opportunities for change, there are several challenges and ethical issues that must be addressed to create equitable and effective learning environments. These include technological limitations, privacy concerns, bias in AI systems, accessibility differences, and the psychological effects of virtual learning. This section will discuss these challenges and the necessary ethical frameworks for responsible implementation.

6.1 Technological Limitations and Infrastructure Challenges

The future of AI and the metaverse for language learning seems promising. However, the implementation of such technology may face significant challenges from technological limitations. High-quality hardware such as VR headsets, motion sensors, and high-speed internet may not be available to all learners (Chen et al., 2022). For example, virtual reality environments require high computing power to ensure smooth, immersive experiences. These opportunities will leave learners in regions with low technological infrastructure or inadequate access to powerful computing devices. Such a development would be seen as creating a digital divide (Pérez & Murray, 2021).

In addition, AI algorithms, particularly real-time language feedback systems, rely on high-quality data and are large in training. Bad quality in the training datasets or underpowered AI models will yield wrong feedback, including the misidentification of accents or failure to recognize local language variations (Zhang et al., 2023). Over-reliance on technology for AI-driven systems may actually lead to knowledge gaps or wrong usage of language because the technology has not been fine-tuned to handle the diversity of learners and languages.

6.2 Data Privacy and Security Issues

Adaptive AI and the metaverse have major privacy and security issues with regard to language learning. The data collected by AI systems is used to tailor the learning experience; this includes speech patterns, progress metrics, and user behavior. Such data is usually stored on cloud-based servers, thereby opening up data breach, unauthorized access, and sensitive information misuse issues (Hwang et al., 2022). For instance, during learner's voice recordings or in the personal process of learning if mishandled, the metaverse immersion environment may result in invasion of privacy and exploitation of private data.

Biometric collection, for instance, heart rate and facial expressions, while one is immersed within a metaverse environment poses the ethical concerns over consent and data usage. A data protection policy between institutions and companies offering language learning services and their clients should be quite strict to ensure that privacy prevails among learners and the data of all participants is only for educational purposes. Data policies need to be crystal-clear to the users and not difficult to read or understand while protecting individual rights, according to Lu et al. (2022).

6.3 Bias and Inclusivity in AI Systems

AI systems are inherently biased by the data they are trained on, which can introduce biases that affect the effectiveness of language learning. If the training datasets are not diverse enough, AI-powered language models may not be as effective in recognizing accents, dialects, or regional variations of a language (Zhang et al., 2023). For instance, speech recognition algorithms may fail for speakers with non-native accents or for languages with diverse phonetic structures.

Moreover, the design of AI avatars and virtual environments can inadvertently perpetuate negative stereotypes. The use of generic, ethnocentric representations of characters may create a lack of diversity and cultural sensitivity in metaverse-based language lessons, which could alienate learners from diverse backgrounds (Pérez & Murray, 2021). It is important for developers to ensure cultural inclusivity in the AI systems, ensuring that learners see themselves represented in the avatars, accents, and scenarios that they encounter.

Ensuring that AI systems are fair and unbiased requires constant testing, diversification of training data, and the inclusion of underrepresented languages and accents in AI models. Moreover, virtual environments must be designed with cultural sensitivity and tailored to meet the needs of a diverse global audience.

6.4 Psychological Impact and Social Interaction Concerns

The immersive nature of the metaverse, along with AI-driven learning experiences, brings new psychological concerns related to learners. Long periods of immersion in virtual environments can lead to an overdependence on AI tutors and avatars, which can curtail face-to-face social interaction and affect pragmatic language skills development in the face-to-face setting. They might have become more comfortable with AI-driven conversations, hence ill-prepared when it matters most-that is, when meeting more authentic social environments where facial expressions, body language, and cultural context constitute important cues in interaction (Wang et al., 2020).

Immergence in these metaverse environments also could solidify a feeling of disconnection or isolation from life in reality. Although the platforms enable students to interact with each other in virtual learning settings, social presence could be characterized by lack of physical co-presence, hence thwarting critical heights of interpersonal relation (Lu et al., 2022). For others, the higher level of social exposure in virtual worlds can even prompt social anxiety and disembodiment, as the design options for the user interface or the interaction avatar.

To counteract these effects, balance needs to be incorporated into the learning experience, ensuring that learners have access to real-world interaction opportunities and human-centered guidance. Regular breaks from virtual learning environments and fostering social connections outside of the metaverse should be emphasized to reduce any potential psychological impact (Hwang et al., 2022).

6.5 Equity and Access Issues

Just like everything technological, applying adaptive AI and metaverse in teaching language is likely to exacerbate current inequalities in access to education. High-end equipment like the VR headsets expensive, while stable internet connectivity that it requires may deny the tools to some low-income or rural students (Chen et al., 2022). Further, the proper implementation of these systems requires technological literacy, in which some learners cannot even navigate AI-based interfaces or interact with complex virtual environments.

The global digital divide might hinder access to the tools and infrastructure that learners from developing countries or remote areas need to reach their potential in AI-driven language education from the metaverse. The onus rests with schools and developers to develop accessible learning platforms at affordable prices that work across multiple devices with varying technical requirements (Zhang et al., 2023).

Further, as the AI and metaverse applications are developed according to different kinds of learning abilities, cultural influences, it is sure to consider all learners devoid of any favoritism when it comes to socioeconomic classes, geographical locality, and a level of computer literacy (Lu et al., 2022).

6.6 Ethical Guidelines and Regulation

Therefore, the need to erect proper ethical standards and law-based guidelines over the development and deployment of adaptive AI and metaverse learning technologies is critical. These policies must guarantee the protection of the rights of learners to privacy, ensure there is minimal bias in the AI systems, and, in a way, utilize these technologies to enhance social good (Wang & Vasquez, 2021).

In addition, regulations on data protection and access and responsible use of AI in the learning model should be implemented by regulatory bodies. These would ensure that all AI algorithms are constantly checked for bias and discrimination; the immersive environments are safe and a tool that is effective for learning (Pérez & Murray, 2021).

7. CONCLUSION: THE FUTURE OF ADAPTIVE AI IN METAVERSE LANGUAGE LEARNING

Adaptive AI in the metaverse will dramatically change the future of language education, as applied to metaverse technologies, which are making tremendous strides in AI capabilities, immersion technologies, and next-generation personalized learning. The integration of AI with the metaverse will further take language education into a future that has been widely anticipated-accessible, intuitive, and immersive in a way that reaches a large audience of learners from all walks of life: beginner, advanced speaker, cultures, regions, and linguistic backgrounds.

Increasingly advanced AI algorithms are likely to be developed. With advancing machine learning models, AI will be able to better understand the nuances of human language, including regional dialects, even slang, and emotional tones. Thus, students can enjoy very high personalization in language experiences- for example, real-time conversations with AI-generated avatars or other learners in natural-sounding dialogue. These interactions will feel more like human communication, as they will include adaptive responses and feedback tailored to the learner's needs, pace, and proficiency level. AI can generate learning paths based on real-time performance; this means language learning will be more efficient and ensure learners not only correct mistakes but progress toward mastery at their own pace.

There would be more vivid and immersive surroundings in the metaverse, taking interaction beyond a mere text-to-voice context in the far-off future. We will notice, for instance, more prevalence of haptic feedback, tracking body movement due to AI powers, and experiences related to multiversity learning forming the core framework of language instruction in the metaverse. These innovations promise learners a much more holistic, feel-based experience in practicing their speaking, writing, listening, and reading within virtual realities impossible to distinguish from the real one. For example, learners would be able to practice conversational Spanish while talking with AI chefs, native speakers, and even real-world situations in a virtual cooking class located somewhere in Spain. Such environments will enhance engagement and retention by putting learners in real-world contexts.

Another significant change on the horizon is the extension of language learning from individual experience to a more social and collaborative model. The metaverse will bring together global learners in virtual spaces where they can practice their language skills in dynamic, real-world social situations. From a virtual conference to a language exchange event or even a simulated marketplace, students will apply their skills in culturally rich contexts and engage with native speakers across the globe. This turn toward social interaction bridges the gap between theoretical knowledge and practical communication—the backbone of fluency in any language.

The future will continue to demand an adaptive AI in the metaverse to make language learning more inclusive. With better AI that comes more powerful, accessible, and neurodiverse-sensible, there will be more appreciation of diverse learning styles. For instance, AI will sense every type of learning, such as visual, auditory, or kinesthetic, and supplement the content to fill in the gaps appropriately. Henceforth, this is going to enable language training for the metaverse to be in greater reachability to people carrying cognitive impairments, physical troubles, or perhaps neurodiverse individuals who often require highly unique and varied communication modes.

During its maturity, technology advances will also render AI-led language learning services even cheaper and hence available to a far wider range of users in the long run. Improvements in cloud computing, among other aspects, as well as affordable hardware in forms such as AR glasses and VR headsets, will result in lower entry barriers for both learners and institutions offering language education. This ensures language education offers easier access in regions where education was underutilized or the economically deprived parts of the globe and can use such innovation.

Building the future of adaptive AI in language education is where AI ethics comes into play. As AI continues to integrate itself into our learning environments, such systems need to be designed with fairness, transparency, and respect for data privacy. Better regulations and more ethical standards would make the risk of algorithmic bias, data exploitation, and breach of privacy things of the past. With such a safeguard in place, learners would be able to engage in the metaverse confidently, knowing their personal information was safe and AI systems operated on an ethical scale.

Adaptive AI in the metaverse's future language learning promises a profound change in how we learn and interact with languages. It is going to become more immersive, engaging, and inclusive with the combination of the very latest AI technology, immersive metaverse environments, and personalized experiences in language education. With these technologies at their advancement, learning any language will not only be effective but reduce cultural barriers, linguistic barriers, and geographic barriers, fostering a global community of learners who will be able to engage, collaborate, and communicate as never before in their first language or second language. This vision for the future of language education has nothing to do with teaching a new language; it is bringing together, cross-cultural understanding, and a world where the language is no longer a barrier but a bridge.

8. CONCLUSION

The merge of Adaptive AI in the Metaverse marks a revolution in the language education sector that had never been seen before, an unprecedented opportunity to change the status quo of the process of learning and teaching and even practicing languages. This technology will continue to evolve, allowing learners to interact with new languages in ways that were previously unimaginable. Adaptive AI in the Metaverse promises not only to cater to individual learning needs by adjusting to a learner's cognitive style, proficiency level, and emotional state but also to provide highly contextual and culturally rich learning experiences. These accomplishments will allow language learners to exercise in real contexts, engage with AI-driven avatars, and receive real-time, person-centered feedback, thus making learning a language more productive and enjoyable.

At the same time, challenges need to be overcome as this technology is deployed more and more. Equity, privacy, bias, and accessibility issues will need to be ensured so that there is fair access to these benefits for all learners. The possibility of data breaches, AI biases, and unequal access to the needed hardware demands strong ethical guidelines, robust regulatory frameworks, and innovative solutions for ensuring fair and equal access in AI-infused learning environments. Besides that, while highly supportive AI can be a windfall of benefits, the human educator plays the most important role since that embodies all aspects of human needs such as emotional intelligence and critical thinking as well as cultural context through which AI would not be able to deliver.

Looking forward, the future of Adaptive AI in Metaverse language education looks very promising, cutting-edge technology, personalized learning experiences, and global connectivity. With technological, ethical, and societal challenges to be overcome, AI and the Metaverse can make language learning an accessible, dynamic, and enriching journey for all people on Earth, leading to a new era of global communication, cultural exchange, and linguistic diversity. It's going to be shaped before us as the future of language education, and this complexity is possibly going to open the gateway toward breaking linguistic barriers and making people from different cultures unite toward a more cohesive and inclusive society.

REFERENCES

Chen, L., Zhang, W., & Lin, T. (2022). AI-driven personalization in language education: Adaptive learning models and their impact. *Educational Technology Research and Development*, *70*(4), 523–541.

Colpaert, J. (2018). Artificial intelligence in language learning: The quest for meaning. *Computer Assisted Language Learning*, *31*(5-6), 409–420.

Csikszentmihalyi, M. (1990). *Flow: The psychology of optimal experience*. Harper & Row.

Dede, C. (2022). Immersive learning in the metaverse: Educational opportunities and challenges. *Educational Technology Research and Development*, *70*(2), 341–357.

Dwivedi, Y. K., Hughes, D. L., Baabdullah, A. M., Ribeiro-Navarrete, S., Giannakis, M., Al-Debei, M. M., Dennehy, D., Metri, B., Buhalis, D., Cheung, C. M. K., Conboy, K., Doyle, R., Dubey, R., Dutot, V., Felix, R., Goyal, D. P., Gustafsson, A., Hinsch, C., Jebabli, I., & Wamba, S. F. (2022). Metaverse beyond the hype: Multidisciplinary perspectives on emerging challenges, opportunities, and agenda for research, practice, and policy. *International Journal of Information Management*, *66*, 102542. DOI: 10.1016/j.ijinfomgt.2022.102542

Godwin-Jones, R. (2011). Emerging technologies: Mobile apps for language learning. *Language Learning & Technology*, *15*(2), 2–11.

Godwin-Jones, R. (2021). Emerging AI applications for language learning: From chatbots to virtual tutors. *Language Learning & Technology*, *25*(2), 3–15.

Huang, R., Liu, D., & Wang, Y. (2021). AI-enhanced virtual tutors: Redefining language education in immersive learning environments. *Computers & Education*, *167*, 104187.

Hubbard, P. (2009). *Computer-assisted language learning: Critical concepts in linguistics*. Routledge.

Hubbard, P. (2018). Computer-assisted language learning and artificial intelligence. *ReCALL, 30*(1), 1–10.

Hwang, W. Y., Shadiev, R., & Lin, Y. T. (2022). Conversational AI for language learning: Trends, challenges, and future directions. *Computers & Education, 174*, 104335.

Hymes, D. (1972). On communicative competence. In Pride, J. B., & Holmes, J. (Eds.), *Sociolinguistics* (pp. 269–293). Penguin.

Kumar, N., & Singh, P. (2022). Ethical implications of AI in education: Data privacy and bias considerations. *AI & Society, 37*(1), 123–140.

Levy, M. (1997). *Computer-assisted language learning: Context and conceptualization*. Oxford University Press. DOI: 10.1093/oso/9780198236320.001.0001

Li, X. (2023). Metaverse and foreign language learning: A review of emerging trends and pedagogical strategies. *Language Learning & Technology, 27*(1), 1–15.

Lu, X., Fang, Y., & He, J. (2022). AI-enhanced metaverse learning: Bridging virtual reality and language acquisition. *Interactive Learning Environments, 30*(4), 621–639.

Pérez, M., & Murray, J. (2021). Personalized learning with AI: A framework for adaptive language instruction. *Journal of Educational Computing Research, 59*(3), 487–505.

Richards, J. C., & Rodgers, T. S. (2001). *Approaches and methods in language teaching*. Cambridge University Press. DOI: 10.1017/CBO9780511667305

Schwienhorst, K. (2002). The state of VR-based language learning. *ReCALL, 14*(2), 253–267.

Skinner, B. F. (1957). *Verbal behavior*. Appleton-Century-Crofts. DOI: 10.1037/11256-000

Smith, R., & Jones, T. (2020). Virtual environments and second language acquisition: Insights from AI-driven learning models. *Language Teaching Research, 24*(5), 678–693.

Vygotsky, L. S. (1978). *Mind in society: The development of higher psychological processes.* Harvard University Press.

Wang, Y., & Vasquez, C. (2021). AI-driven adaptive learning: A game changer for second language acquisition? *Language Teaching Research, 25*(6), 891–916.

Yang, F., & Sun, Y. (2023). Artificial intelligence in immersive language learning: Real-time feedback and adaptive assessment. *Educational Review, 75*(2), 311–330.

Zhang, W., Chen, L., & Xu, T. (2023). Metaverse-assisted language education: AI-driven personalization and adaptive learning models. *Computers in Human Behavior, 140*, 107583.

Zhou, K., Wang, L., & Chen, J. (2023). The future of AI and metaverse in education: Opportunities, challenges, and pedagogical shifts. *Computers in Human Behavior, 139*, 107564.

Chapter 4
The Future of Education in the Metaverse:
Immersive, Interactive, and Collaborative Learning

Andi Asrifan
https://orcid.org/0000-0002-9934-6129
Universitas Negeri Makassar, Indonesia

Nurul Aini
Nahdlatul Ulama University, Indonesia

Khristianto
https://orcid.org/0000-0002-6565-2670
Universitas Muhammadiyah Purwokerto, Indonesia

ABSTRACT

This chapter examines the metaverse's transformational potential in education, highlighting its ability to improve immersive learning experiences via sophisticated technologies like virtual reality (VR) and augmented reality (AR). It examines how these technologies may provide realistic simulations, enabling students to participate in interactive learning settings that enhance their comprehension and retention of knowledge. The chapter emphasizes the significance of personalized learning paths

DOI: 10.4018/979-8-3693-9974-3.ch004

supported by data analytics and artificial intelligence, which provide customized educational experiences that address specific student requirements. Furthermore, it analyzes novel evaluation techniques that enhance critical thinking and problem-solving abilities, as well as the function of collaborative tools in facilitating peer feedback and teamwork. The chapter ultimately articulates a vision for a future in which education is more interesting, accessible, and successful, propelled by the incorporation of immersive technology inside the metaverse.

INTRODUCTION TO THE METAVERSE AND EDUCATION

1.1 Defining the Metaverse

The metaverse is a shared virtual realm that integrates physical and digital realities, allowing users to engage with a computer-generated environment and connect with other users in real-time (Alpala et al., 2022; Alam, 2024). This concept originates from science fiction, particularly in Neal Stephenson's 1992 novel "Snow Crash," which depicts a virtual reality-based replacement to the internet (Johri et al., 2024). Throughout the years, the phrase has developed to include many technologies like as virtual reality (VR), augmented reality (AR), and mixed reality (MR), all of which facilitate immersive experiences.

The metaverse's origins can be traced to early online communities and virtual worlds, including MUDs (Multi-User Dungeons) and subsequent platforms like Second Life, which enabled users to create avatars and engage in a shared digital environment (Mourtzis et al., 2022). The initial versions established the foundation for the advanced metaverse we observe today, distinguished by improved graphics, real-time interactions, and the use of blockchain technology, facilitating the ownership of digital assets.

With technological advancements, the potential of the metaverse has similarly evolved. The expansion of high-speed internet, robust computing devices, and cost-effective VR/AR technology has rendered it progressively accessible (Xiong et al., 2021; Bibri & Jagatheesaperumal, 2023). Prominent technology firms, such as Meta (previously Facebook), Google, and Microsoft, are significantly investing in metaverse development, perceiving it as the forthcoming progression of the internet—a completely immersive, interconnected digital realm where individuals may interact, work, and learn.

The metaverse offers a transformative opportunity within the realm of education. Conventional educational frameworks frequently fail to engage students effectively, resulting in a disconnection between learners and the content (Divanji et al., 2023). The metaverse provides immersive, interactive, and collaborative learning experiences that accommodate various learning styles. Students can investigate intricate subjects via simulations, engage in virtual excursions, and connect with classmates worldwide in real-time.

Furthermore, the metaverse cultivates a sense of presence and community frequently absent in traditional online learning settings. Utilizing the metaverse, educators may develop dynamic and engaging curriculum that improve information retention and equip students for a future when digital literacy and flexibility are essential (Li & Yu, 2022; Huang et al., 2023).

1.2 The Intersection of Education and Technology

The convergence of education and technology has undergone substantial transformation over the centuries (Rahm, 2023; Alam & Mohanty, 2023). From the development of the printing press to the emergence of the internet, each technological advancement has transformed the educational environment, improving access to knowledge and modifying the methods of information dissemination and consumption.

The printing press, invented in the 15th century, transformed education by enhancing the accessibility and affordability of books (Strielkowski et al., 2024; Musarat et al., 2023). The democratization of knowledge facilitated the dissemination of ideas and literacy, establishing the foundation for the contemporary education system. With the proliferation of literature, educational institutions thrived, resulting in the formation of universities and structured curriculum.

The 20th century witnessed the emergence of audiovisual aids, including film and radio, which enhanced the educational experience by offering varied methods of content engagement (Nicolaou et al., 2021).

These technologies enabled educators to deliver material in more dynamic formats, accommodating diverse learning styles. The emergence of television significantly broadened educational prospects, with shows tailored for instructing various subjects, including science and history.

The digital revolution of the late 20th and early 21st centuries signified a crucial turning point in education. The advent of personal computers and the internet revolutionized the interaction between students and educators with knowledge (Rizvi & Nabi, 2021). Digital platforms, like educational websites and online libraries, offered unparalleled access to extensive information. This transition not only promoted self-directed learning but also permitted distant education, enabling students to study from any location globally.

With the progression of technology, its incorporation into the classroom also evolved. Learning management systems (LMS) developed, offering venues for educators to disseminate content, monitor student progress, and facilitate communication (Veluvali & Surisetti, 2022; Simelane-Mnisi, 2023). The proliferation of mobile devices has augmented learning opportunities, allowing students to access educational resources remotely and interact with programs that foster active learning.

We are on the cusp of a new age in education with the advent of the metaverse. This immersive digital environment integrates components of virtual reality, augmented reality, and mixed reality, establishing a venue for unprecedented learning experiences. The metaverse facilitates experiential learning, enabling students to interact with intricate topics via simulations and collaborative projects inside a communal virtual environment (Jovanović & Milosavljević, 2022; Chen & Huang, 2024).

1.3 The Need for Innovative Learning Environments

Conventional education systems, although essential in developing knowledge and skills, frequently encounter considerable constraints that impede their efficacy in the swiftly evolving contemporary landscape (Haleem et al., 2022; Yu, 2023). These constraints underscore the pressing necessity for creative educational settings that can accommodate the varied requirements of learners and the expectations of the contemporary labor market.

A fundamental problem of conventional education is its uniform approach (Tran, 2021). Traditional classrooms generally utilize uniform curricula and pedagogical approaches that may not accommodate the diverse learning styles and rates of individual pupils. This inflexibility can result in disengagement, since students who do not connect with the subject or pedagogical approach may find it difficult to comprehend fundamental concepts. As a result, numerous learners lag, leading to decreased motivation and a reduced sense of agency in their education.

Furthermore, conventional schooling frequently prioritizes rote memorization and standardized assessments, thus inhibiting creativity and critical thinking (Jabali et al., 2024; Javed, 2025). In a time when problem-solving and innovation are crucial, the capacity for critical thinking and the application of knowledge in practical situations is vital. The emphasis on examinations and grades may foster an environment in which students emphasize performance over authentic comprehension, so constraining their capacity for profound engagement with the topic.

The worldwide landscape is continually transforming due to technological breakthroughs and changing economic demands. The competencies demanded in the labor market are evolving, with a growing focus on digital literacy, teamwork, and adaptability (Nikou et al., 2022; Bennett & McWhorter, 2021). Conventional education methods, frequently deficient in incorporating technology and practical applications, may inadequately equip students for emerging difficulties. Consequently, there is an increasing demand for educational frameworks that cultivate abilities pertinent to the 21st century.

The metaverse provides an effective resolution to these issues by delivering immersive, interactive, and collaborative educational experiences (Jovanović & Milosavljević, 2022; Damaševičius & Sidekerskienė, 2024). In the metaverse, students can interact with content dynamically, investigating intricate concepts through simulations and virtual environments that facilitate experiential learning. This method not only improves comprehension but also fosters creativity and critical thinking, as students can engage in experimentation and collaboration in ways that conventional classrooms cannot support.

Additionally, the metaverse facilitates customized learning experiences, enabling students to advance at their own speed and access resources specifically designed to meet their unique requirements (Roa et al., 2025). This flexibility cultivates a sense of ownership in their education, enabling learners to assume control of their learning experiences.

IMMERSIVE LEARNING EXPERIENCES

2.1 Virtual Reality (VR) in Education

Virtual Reality (VR) technology has emerged as a revolutionary instrument in education, providing immersive learning experiences that surpass the constraints of conventional classroom environments (Kayyali; 2024; AlGerafi et al., 2023). Virtual reality facilitates student engagement with instructional information through a simulated environment that allows interaction with three-dimensional locations and objects in a profoundly experiential way. This chapter examines the utilization of virtual reality in education and its capacity to revolutionize learning.

Fundamentally, VR technology immerses people in a computer-generated environment, enabling exploration and manipulation of virtual worlds (Alpala et al., 2022; Zhao & Guo, 2022). This immersive quality is especially advantageous in educational settings, where intricate concepts can be visualized and experienced directly. For example, in disciplines such as science and history, students can undertake virtual excursions to historical civilizations or examine the complexities of the human anatomy. Such interactions not only augment comprehension but also cultivate a sense of presence that conventional learning approaches frequently lack.

A notable advantage of VR in education is its capacity to accommodate various learning styles (Marougkas et al., 2023). Visual learners can gain from the extensive pictorial depictions of subjects, and kinesthetic learners can participate in tactile activities within the virtual environment. This versatility renders VR an inclusive instrument capable of addressing diverse educational requirements, hence enhancing student engagement and retention.

Furthermore, virtual reality enhances experiential learning, essential for cultivating critical thinking and problem-solving abilities (Huang et al., 2023). Medical students can perform surgical procedures in a risk-free virtual environment, enabling them to refine their skills without the burden of real-life repercussions. Engineering students can replicate intricate systems and evaluate their designs in a virtual laboratory, promoting innovation and creativity.

Collaboration becomes a pivotal element of virtual reality in education (Alpala et al., 2022). Numerous VR technologies provide simultaneous user interaction inside a shared virtual environment, promoting joint endeavors and dialogues. Students can collaboratively engage in problem-solving exercises, exchange insights, and learn from each other in real-time, irrespective of their physical location. This collaborative element reflects the social character of learning, augmenting communication abilities and teamwork.

Notwithstanding its myriad advantages, the incorporation of VR in education presents certain problems. The expense of VR equipment and the requirement for technical proficiency may hinder general adoption (Maqsoom et al., 2023; Matsika & Zhou, 2021). As technology progresses and becomes more economical, the prospect of virtual reality transforming education becomes increasingly feasible.

2.2 Augmented Reality (AR) and Mixed Reality (MR)

Augmented Reality (AR) and Mixed Reality (MR) are innovative technologies that improve real-world educational experiences by superimposing digital information onto the actual environment (Constantinescu et al., 2024). These immersive technologies offer interactive components that engage students in ways unattainable by conventional teaching techniques, promoting enhanced comprehension and retention of content.

Augmented Reality (AR) technology overlays digital content—including photos, videos, and 3D models—onto the physical environment via devices such as smartphones, tablets, or AR glasses (Syed et al.; 2022; Mendoza-

Ramírez et al., 2023). This ability enables children to conceptualize intricate ideas in a concrete framework. In a biology class, students can utilize AR applications to examine 3D models of human anatomy, facilitating interactive exploration of organs and systems. This practical method enhances engagement and aids students in comprehending complex subtleties that may be challenging to discern from textbooks alone.

MR advances this concept by integrating the physical and digital realms, enabling users to engage with both concurrently. In mixed reality environments, digital objects can react to real-world conditions, facilitating a seamless integration of virtual and physical aspects (Hatami et al., 2024). For example, in an engineering course, students can utilize MR tools to construct a bridge, enabling them to envision their project in real-time within the context of its actual environment. This interactive experience promotes experimentation and critical analysis, enabling students to evaluate the practicality of their designs within a realistic framework.

Both augmented reality (AR) and mixed reality (MR) facilitate active learning, which is crucial for cultivating fundamental abilities such as problem-solving, teamwork, and creativity (Lombardi et al., 2021; Chang et al., 2023). These tools promote discovery and inquiry by involving students in interactive tasks. In a history lesson, students might utilize augmented reality to discover historical items within their local area, thereby fostering a connection with their community's legacy and enhancing their research abilities.

Moreover, augmented reality (AR) and mixed reality (MR) can enhance individualized learning experiences (Halkiopoulos & Gkintoni, 2024). Students may advance at their own speed, reviewing intricate subjects via interactive simulations tailored to their specific learning requirements. This versatility is especially advantageous in heterogeneous settings, as students exhibit variable levels of comprehension and distinct learning modalities.

Notwithstanding the significant promise of augmented reality (AR) and mixed reality (MR) in education, obstacles persist. Addressing the necessity for dependable technology, access to devices, and the creation of superior instructional content is essential for effective deployment (Timotheou et al., 2023). As these technologies advance and become increasingly available, their incorporation into educational environments is expected to grow.

2.3 Case Studies of Immersive Learning

The adoption of immersive learning technologies, including Virtual Reality (VR), Augmented Reality (AR), and Mixed Reality (MR), has increased in many educational environments, showcasing its ability to improve engagement and comprehension (Muzata et al., 2024; Tan, 2023). This section presents various successful case studies that demonstrate the transforming effects of immersive learning experiences.

1. Stanford University's Virtual Reality Lab

The Virtual Reality Lab at Stanford University has innovated the application of virtual reality in education, especially within psychology (Li et al., 2025; Soliman et al., 2021). A significant initiative entailed developing a VR simulation that enables students to experience social interactions from various perspectives, including those of individuals with social anxiety. This immersive program promotes empathy and equips students with practical tools for handling challenging social situations. By empathizing with others, students acquire insights unattainable through conventional lectures, so enhancing their comprehension of psychological subjects.

2. The University of Illinois' AR in Anatomy

The University of Illinois has effectively used augmented reality technology into its medical curriculum (Niu, 2023). Medical students can utilize AR applications to visualize three-dimensional representations of human anatomy overlaid on their physical environment. This participatory method enables students to examine anatomical structures thoroughly, improving their understanding of intricate systems. The capacity to manipulate and analyze these models in real-time has demonstrated significant value for students, resulting in enhanced material retention and increased confidence in their practical abilities.

3. Case Western Reserve University's HoloAnatomy

Case Western Reserve University has created an advanced MR application named HoloAnatomy, which employs Microsoft HoloLens for anatomical education (Dolega-Dolegowski et al., 2022). This program enables students to engage with life-sized holograms of human bodies, facilitating dissection and exploration of anatomical features in a virtual setting. This practical experience not only augments learning but also equips students for actual medical operations. Student feedback has been predominantly favorable, with numerous individuals indicating that HoloAnatomy markedly enhanced their comprehension of anatomy relative to conventional techniques.

4. The National Museum of Natural History's AR Experiences

The Smithsonian Institution's National Museum of Natural History has adopted augmented reality to improve visitor interaction (Smith, 2024; Bell, 2024). Visitors can utilize an AR application to direct their devices at exhibitions, thereby accessing supplementary content, including 3D models, films, and interactive quizzes. This immersive experience converts a conventional museum visit into an engaging educational journey, enabling people to investigate scientific subjects in an enjoyable and participatory manner. The success of this effort has resulted in heightened visitor satisfaction and a greater respect for the museum's treasures.

5. Google Expeditions

Google Expeditions is a platform enabling educators to conduct virtual field trips globally (Parmaxi et al., 2021). Educators can facilitate immersive experiences for pupils, such as exploring the Great Barrier Reef or traversing ancient Rome, all within the classroom setting. This platform has been particularly helpful in engaging pupils who lack the opportunity to travel, so extending their perspectives and igniting interest about the world.

INTERACTIVE LEARNING IN THE METAVERSE

3.1 Gamification of Education

Gamification, the incorporation of game design aspects into non-game contexts, has become a potent tool in education, especially inside the immersive realms of the metaverse (Sharma et al., 2024). By utilizing game elements, educators can improve student engagement, motivation, and learning results, converting conventional educational encounters into dynamic and participatory endeavors.

Gamification fundamentally leverages the intrinsic human yearning for accomplishment, rivalry, and social engagement. Educators can enhance the learning environment by integrating components like points, badges, leaderboards, and challenges (Hellín et al., 2023; Sousa-Vieira et al., 2021). Students can accumulate points by completing projects, engaging in conversations, or cooperating with others, so cultivating a sense of achievement and promoting active involvement. This incentive system not only incentivizes students to interact with the subject but also fosters a growth attitude in which effort and progress are acknowledged and applauded.

A notable benefit of gamification in education is its capacity to establish a secure environment for experimentation and failure (López-Jiménez et al., 2021; Rodrigues et al., 2022). In conventional educational environments, the apprehension of committing errors might obstruct learning. In a gamified atmosphere, students are motivated to take risks and learn from their errors without the burden of real-world repercussions. This method cultivates resilience and adaptation, crucial competencies in the contemporary, swiftly evolving environment.

Furthermore, gamification fosters teamwork among pupils. Numerous educational games and platforms within the metaverse are structured for cooperative play, fostering communication and collaboration (Damaševičius & Sidekerskienė, 2024). Students may collaborate to resolve intricate problems or accomplish tasks, learning to utilize one other's abilities and viewpoints. This collaborative element enhances the educational experience and reflects the social dynamics of contemporary workplaces, equipping students for future jobs.

The immersive characteristics of the metaverse enhance the efficacy of gamification (Flavián et al., 2024). In virtual environments, students can investigate imaginative realms, engage in role-playing activities, and partake in simulations that enhance the learning experience. A history lecture could evolve into an interactive quest in which students embody historical individuals, confronting difficulties and making decisions that influence the trajectory of their experience. This degree of participation cultivates profound connections to the content, rendering learning more remembered and significant.

Moreover, gamification facilitates individualized learning experiences. Educators can customize challenges and quests to address unique student requirements, guaranteeing that each learner advances at their own rate (Adera, 2025). This versatility is especially advantageous in heterogeneous settings, as students exhibit variable levels of comprehension and distinct learning modalities.

3.2 Collaborative Tools and Platforms

The metaverse provides numerous collaborative tools and platforms that enhance interaction between students and instructors, reshaping the educational landscape into a dynamic, interconnected environment (Damaševičius & Sidekerskienė, 2024; Onu et al., 2024). These tools increase communication and collaboration while fostering a sense of community and shared learning experiences, which are vital for effective education in the 21st century.

Mozilla Hubs is a leading platform in the metaverse, providing a virtual reality area for people to create and share immersive surroundings. Educators can create tailored environments for conversations, presentations, or collaborative projects, facilitating real-time interaction among students irrespective of their geographical location. The platform accommodates diverse media formats, such as 3D models, movies, and photos, facilitating comprehensive multimedia presentations that augment comprehension and engagement. The capacity to personalize environments promotes creativity and a sense of ownership, motivating students to engage actively in their educational setting (Zamiri & Esmaeili, 2024; mSidhu et al., 2024).

Another important instrument is Spatial, which integrates augmented reality and virtual reality to establish collaborative work environments (Orel, 2022). Spatial enables people to engage with three-dimensional content and collaborate on projects in real-time. Students can generate ideas, interact with virtual objects, and participate in debates as if they were in a physical classroom. This immersive experience fosters active engagement and improves communication skills, enabling students to express their ideas and work efficiently in a virtual environment.

Microsoft Teams and Google Workspace have adapted to the demands of the metaverse by incorporating collaborative capabilities that facilitate remote learning (Orel, 2022; Pathak & Malpani, 2025). These systems provide instruments for video conferencing, document sharing, and project management, allowing educators to conduct group work and conversations effortlessly. By integrating conventional collaborative tools with immersive experiences, educators can establish hybrid learning environments that address varied student requirements.

Gather is a unique platform that integrates gaming features with collaborative learning (Perry, 2021). In Gather, users construct avatars and traverse a virtual environment to engage with peers, attend lectures, and partake in collaborative activities. The platform's design facilitates social interaction, enabling students to connect and engage in a more informal, engaging setting. The social dimension is essential for cultivating relationships and promoting a sense of belonging among students, especially in online learning environments.

Moreover, ClassroomVR offers educators a comprehensive array of tools for the creation and management of collaborative VR experiences (Álvarez et al., 2024). Educators can create classes that necessitate collaborative efforts among students in virtual settings, addressing challenges or accomplishing objectives that foster collaboration and critical analysis. This platform prioritizes experiential learning, enabling students to implement their knowledge in practical situations while engaging with their peers.

3.3 Real-Time Feedback and Assessment

The integration of interactive technology inside the metaverse has transformed the delivery of feedback and assessment in education. Real-time feedback mechanisms improve the learning experience and establish adaptive learning paths that address specific student needs, promoting a more personalized educational journey (Gligorea et al., 2023; Strielkowski et al., 2024).

A primary benefit of interactive technology in the metaverse is their capacity to deliver instantaneous feedback. Conventional assessment techniques sometimes entail deferred feedback, requiring students to await graded papers or examinations to gauge their performance (Fynn & Mashile, 2022). Conversely, metaverse platforms can provide immediate feedback via diverse interactive components. Educational games and simulations can evaluate student activities in real-time, offering insights into their comprehension and performance while interacting with the material. This immediacy enables students to recognize areas for enhancement and modify their learning tactics in real-time, fostering a more proactive educational approach.

Adaptive learning systems augment this feedback loop by customizing educational experiences for individual learners (Gligorea et al., 2023; Strielkowski et al., 2024). By examining student interactions and performance metrics, these systems can calibrate task complexity, recommend supplementary resources, or alter learning trajectories to better accommodate individual student requirements. For example, if a learner encounters difficulty with a specific idea in a virtual arithmetic simulation, the system can offer additional exercises or alternative explanations to enhance comprehension. This tailored method not only enables students to comprehend difficult content but also cultivates a sense of autonomy in their educational journey.

Furthermore, the immersive characteristics of the metaverse provide novel assessment techniques that surpass conventional testing procedures (Damaševičius & Sidekerskienė, 2024). Educators might create interactive examinations that necessitate pupils to utilize their knowledge in practical situations. In a scientific lesson, students may perform virtual experiments requiring them to hypothesis, test, and interpret outcomes. The system offers immediate feedback on techniques and findings, fostering critical thinking and problem-solving abilities. This experiential learning method not only measures knowledge but also tests students' capacity to apply concepts in real-world scenarios.

Moreover, collaborative tools in the metaverse enhance peer input, so augmenting the assessment process. Students may participate in group projects that facilitate constructive criticism among peers, promoting a collaborative learning atmosphere (Herrera-Pavo & Chen, 2021). This peer-to-peer engagement not only improves comprehension but also cultivates communication and collaboration skills, vital for success in the contemporary industry.

COLLABORATIVE LEARNING ENVIRONMENTS

4.1 Building Virtual Learning Communities

As education progressively shifts into the metaverse, the establishment of virtual learning communities is vital for promoting cooperation, participation, and a sense of belonging among students (Herrera-Pavo, 2024; Archambault et al., 2022). These communities not only enrich the educational experience but also equip students for a future in which collaboration and communication are essential. This chapter examines effective ways for cultivating dynamic virtual learning communities inside immersive settings.

Establishing Clear Communication Channels

Effective communication is fundamental to the success of any learning community. Educators in virtual environments should utilize diverse communication technologies, including chat features, discussion boards, and video conferencing, to enhance student participation (Zamiri & Esmaeili, 2024; Zamiri & Esmaeili, 2024). Platforms such as Discord and Microsoft Teams can be incorporated into the educational setting, facilitating student connectivity, idea exchange, and project collaboration. Establishing communication norms, such as promoting respectful discourse and active listening, fosters a good environment where all perspectives are esteemed.

Creating Collaborative Projects

Involving kids in collaborative projects is an effective method for fostering community. Educators can promote collaboration among students by assigning group assignments that necessitate teamwork, enabling them to share responsibility and utilize each other's skills (Benner et al., 2023). In a virtual science class, students may cooperate on a research project, employing shared digital tools to collect data and deliver their conclusions. This collaborative method not only improves educational results but also cultivates relationships among classmates, as students learn to address obstacles and enjoy achievements collectively.

Utilizing Gamification Elements

Integrating gamification components into the virtual learning environment can markedly improve community development (Mystakidis, 2021; Vetrivel et al., 2024). By implementing challenges, leaderboards, and incentives, educators may stimulate students to participate actively and interact with their peers. Establishing a pleasant competition in which groups accumulate points for collaboration and participation can cultivate camaraderie and motivate students to assist one another. This engaging method of learning dismantles obstacles and fosters a sense of collaboration.

Encouraging Peer Mentorship

Implementing a peer mentorship program within the virtual community can augment collaboration (Carvalho & Santos, 2022; Aquino et al., 2022). Pairing seasoned students with novices cultivates a friendly atmosphere conducive to the exchange of knowledge and skills. Mentors can assist their colleagues in overcoming problems, offer constructive comments, and promote engagement in discussions. This relationship enriches mentees and empowers mentors, boosting their comprehension of the content and enhancing their leadership abilities.

Hosting Virtual Social Events

Fostering a sense of community extends beyond academic collaboration; it also include social contact. Facilitating virtual social events, including game evenings, study groups, or casual meet-and-greets, enables students to establish personal connections (Aravena-Bravo et al., 2024). These events facilitate student bonding, experience sharing, and relationship development, which are essential for cultivating a supportive learning environment.

Providing Continuous Feedback and Support

Educators must prioritize ongoing feedback and support to cultivate the virtual learning community. Consistent evaluations, questionnaires, and open discussion platforms enable educators to assess student happiness and resolve any issues. By exhibiting a dedication to student welfare and achievement, educators can foster a constructive community environment in which students feel esteemed and inspired to participate (Tripon et al., 2023).

4.2 Cross-Cultural and Global Learning Opportunities

The metaverse offers unparalleled prospects for cross-cultural and global education, dismantling geographical barriers and linking learners from varied origins (Alfaisal et al., 2024). This connection enhances the educational experience and promotes a profound comprehension of global viewpoints, cultural diversity, and collaborative problem-solving. As education advances in the metaverse, the opportunity to provide inclusive, multicultural learning settings grows in importance.

Bridging Geographical Divides

A notable feature of the metaverse is its capacity to connect students globally in real-time (Hatami et al., 2024; Sidhu et al., 2024). Virtual classrooms facilitate the participation of learners from diverse nations, enabling them to engage in debates, exchange experiences, and work on projects irrespective of geographical limitations. A cohort of students from various continents might collaborate on a global environmental initiative, exchanging knowledge regarding their local ecosystems and formulating solutions to shared concerns. This cooperative method not only improves education but also cultivates a sense of global citizenship.

Cultural Exchange and Understanding

The metaverse functions as a medium for cultural exchange, allowing pupils to acquire knowledge of and value other cultures (Lai et al., 2024; Buragohain et al., 2024). Virtual field tours enable students to investigate historical locations, museums, and cultural icons globally, acquiring direct understanding of various traditions and customs. Moreover, immersive experiences may incorporate guest speakers from many cultural backgrounds, who can convey their narratives and viewpoints, so enhancing the educational atmosphere. This exposure to varied perspectives fosters empathy and comprehension, vital attributes in an ever more linked society.

Collaborative Problem-Solving

Collaboration across cultures in the metaverse can yield novel answers to global challenges (Vaz, 2024; Mahindru et al., 2024). By uniting students from diverse backgrounds and experiences, instructors may foster discussions that question assumptions and stimulate innovative thinking. Students from many nations may collaborate on a project focused on climate change, combining their distinct perspectives and methodologies to formulate comprehensive strategies. This collaborative problem-solving promotes critical thinking abilities and enables students to address real-world difficulties in diverse teams.

Language Learning and Communication Skills

The metaverse offers a distinctive possibility for language acquisition and the enhancement of communication abilities. Students may participate in language exchange programs to practice speaking with peers from diverse linguistic backgrounds (O'Dowd, 2021; Itoi & Mizukura, 2024). This immersive experience enables learners to enhance their language proficiency in genuine circumstances, so boosting their confidence and fluency. Moreover, the imperative of good communication in collaborative endeavors cultivates vital talents that are progressively sought after in the global employment market.

Building Global Networks

Ultimately, the metaverse facilitates the establishment of worldwide networks for students that transcend the confines of the classroom. Students can forge enduring friendships and professional connections by engaging with peers from diverse cultures (Tan et al., 2023; Gradiski et al., 2022). These linkages enhance their educational experience and offer significant insights into various career choices and opportunities within a globalized economy.

CHALLENGES AND FUTURE DIRECTIONS

5.1 Addressing Equity and Access

With the emergence of the metaverse as a revolutionary educational environment, prioritizing fairness and access is essential (Nahi et al., 2023; Singh, 2024). The digital divide—the disparity between individuals with access to digital technologies and those without—presents considerable obstacles to the fair execution of metaverse schooling. Facilitating immersive, interactive, and collaborative learning experiences for all learners is crucial for promoting inclusion and optimizing the potential of this novel educational model.

Understanding the Digital Divide

The digital gap includes multiple aspects, such as access to gadgets, dependable internet connectivity, and digital literacy (Lythreatis et al., 2022; Jamil, 2021). In numerous countries, especially in low-income and rural communities, children may be deprived of the requisite technology to engage in metaverse education. This mismatch can result in considerable educational disparities, wherein just a fraction of students can participate in immersive learning experiences while others are excluded. Understanding the complex nature of the digital divide is essential for formulating successful ways to close these disparities.

Infrastructure Development

Investment in infrastructure is crucial to tackle these difficulties. Governments, educational institutions, and corporate entities must cooperate to enhance internet connectivity in underserved communities (Faturoti, 2024). Expanding broadband networks, offering subsidized gadgets, and creating community technology centers can ensure that all students possess the necessary tools for participation in metaverse education. By emphasizing infrastructure development, stakeholders may establish a more egalitarian basis for digital education.

Promoting Digital Literacy

Equitable access to the metaverse necessitates an emphasis on digital literacy. Students must possess the abilities to navigate virtual environments, employ collaboration tools, and interact with immersive information proficiently. Educational programs that prioritize digital literacy can equip students to become proficient technology users, allowing them to engage fully in metaverse learning experiences (Lee & Hwang, 2022). Moreover, professional development for educators is crucial, guaranteeing that teachers are equipped to assist pupils in cultivating these fundamental abilities.

Inclusive Content and Design

Developing inclusive material and educational experiences is a vital component of promoting fairness in the metaverse (Othman et al., 2024; Radanliev et al., 2024). Educational resources must embody various viewpoints and be accessible to all students, including individuals with impairments. By integrating universal design principles, educators may guarantee that virtual environments are accessible and stimulating for all individuals. This dedication to inclusivity not only improves the educational experience but also cultivates a sense of belonging among all pupils.

Policy and Advocacy

Ultimately, tackling fairness and access in metaverse schooling necessitates robust policy frameworks and advocacy initiatives. Policymakers must prioritize equal access to technology and digital resources within their educational agendas (Imran, 2023; Gallegos-Rejas et al., 2023). This encompasses sponsoring projects designed to bridge the digital gap and foster inclusive practices in educational institutions. Advocacy organizations can significantly contribute to enhancing awareness regarding the significance of equity in education and galvanizing support for efforts that tackle these issues.

5.2 Privacy and Security Concerns

As education progressively transitions into the metaverse, the ethical ramifications concerning data privacy and security emerge as essential issues that require attention. Immersive environments, although providing novel educational opportunities, also present considerable issues related to the acquisition, storage, and utilization of personal data (Pellas et al., 2021). Comprehending these problems is crucial for establishing safe and secure educational experiences in the metaverse.

Data Collection and Usage

Educational platforms in the metaverse frequently gather extensive data from users, encompassing personal information, learning practices, and activities inside virtual settings (Zhang et al., 2022). This data can be important in augmenting individualized learning experiences and enhancing educational outcomes. The acquisition of such sensitive information prompts ethical inquiries regarding consent and the possibility of misuse. Students, especially adolescents, may lack a comprehensive understanding of the ramifications of data sharing, raising issues about informed consent and privacy protection.

Security Risks

The immersive characteristics of the metaverse present distinct security vulnerabilities. Cybersecurity concerns, such data breaches and hacking, can jeopardize sensitive information, putting students and instructors at risk of potential harm (Aslan et al., 2023). Educational institutions must establish stringent security protocols to safeguard user data from illegal access and guarantee the safety of virtual environments for all users. This entails utilizing encryption, robust authentication techniques, and periodic security assessments to detect and address problems.

Ethical Use of Data

The ethical utilization of data in educational environments is a significant issue (Akgun & Greenhow, 2022). Although data analytics can yield insights into student performance and engagement, there exists a potential that such information may be utilized to profile students or influence decisions affecting their educational opportunities. Algorithms that examine student data may unintentionally perpetuate biases or result in discriminatory practices. Educators and administrators must remain diligent in assuring the responsible and ethical use of data, prioritizing kids' best interests.

Transparency and Accountability

To foster confidence in the metaverse, educational institutions must emphasize transparency and accountability in their data operations. Transparent communication on the data obtained, its utilization, and the individuals with access is crucial for cultivating a culture of trust (Van et al., 2021; Tyagi et al., 2022). Institutions must have rules that delineate data privacy practices and guarantee that students and parents are apprised of their rights concerning personal information. Furthermore, establishing avenues for feedback and reporting issues might enable consumers to express their concerns regarding data protection.

Regulatory Compliance

Ultimately, traversing the intricate terrain of data privacy legislation is essential for educational institutions functioning within the metaverse (Fadhel et al., 2024). Legislation such as the Family Educational Rights and Privacy Act (FERPA) in the United States and the General Data Protection Regulation (GDPR) in Europe establishes stringent protocols for the management of student data. Institutions must adhere to these standards to safeguard student privacy and prevent legal consequences. This may necessitate ongoing training for educators and staff on data privacy best practices and the execution of policies that conform to regulatory standards.

5.3 The Future of Education in the Metaverse

The future of education in the metaverse is poised to be revolutionary, propelled by technological developments and creative pedagogical methods. The incorporation of immersive, interactive, and collaborative learning experiences is poised to transform educational delivery, enhancing engagement, personalization, and accessibility (Bizami et al., 2023). This chapter examines significant forecasts and trends poised to influence the future of education within the metaverse.

Enhanced Immersive Learning Experiences

Progress in virtual reality (VR) and augmented reality (AR) technology will persist in improving immersive learning experiences (Al-Ansi et al., 2023). As hardware becomes more economical and accessible, educational institutions will progressively integrate VR and AR technologies to develop realistic simulations and interactive experiences. Students will have the opportunity to investigate historical locations, do virtual scientific experiments, and participate in intricate problem-solving scenarios, all inside a secure and regulated environment. This practical method will enhance comprehension and retention of information, rendering learning more significant.

Personalized Learning Pathways

The metaverse will enable the creation of customized learning trajectories designed to meet the specific needs of each student. Utilizing data analytics and artificial intelligence (AI), educational platforms can evaluate student performance in real-time and modify learning experiences accordingly (Kaur et al., 2024). This indicates that students may advance at their individual speed, with tailored help and resources aligned with their distinct learning styles and preferences. This customisation will enable learners to assume responsibility for their education, enhancing motivation and engagement.

Global Collaboration and Cultural Exchange

The metaverse will dismantle geographical barriers, allowing students from many backgrounds to collaborate on projects and participate in cultural exchanges. Virtual classrooms will accommodate students globally, enabling the exchange of opinions, ideas, and experiences (Vahed & Rodriguez, 2021). This international collaboration will enhance the educational experience and equip students for a multicultural workforce, improving their communication and teamwork abilities in a progressively interconnected world.

Integration of Gamification and Game-Based Learning

Gamification will significantly influence the future of education in the metaverse (Damaševičius & Sidekerskienė, 2024; Yang et al., 2024). Integrating game design aspects into educational encounters can augment student engagement and motivation. Game-based learning environments will promote exploration, experimentation, and collaboration, enhancing the enjoyment and efficacy of education. As students navigate hurdles and attain rewards, they will cultivate critical thinking and problem-solving abilities vital for success in the contemporary world.

Lifelong Learning and Professional Development

The metaverse will facilitate continuous education and career advancement. As sectors progress and new competencies arise, individuals will pursue possibilities for upskilling and reskilling in immersive settings. Online courses, workshops, and training programs will increase in prevalence, enabling learners to obtain high-quality education from any location globally (Pregowska et al., 2021; Cui et al., 2023). This transition will foster a culture of perpetual learning, allowing individuals to adjust to evolving employment markets and technology progressions.

Ethical Considerations and Data Privacy

With the expansion of schooling in the metaverse, ethical considerations and data privacy will continue to be paramount (Li et al., 2022). Institutions must prioritize transparency, security, and appropriate data practices to foster trust among students and instructors. Formulating comprehensive policies and procedures is crucial to guarantee that the advantages of immersive education are attained without jeopardizing personal privacy or security.

CONCLUSION

The future of education in the metaverse signifies a transformative transformation that aims to reshape the learning environment via immersive, interactive, and collaborative experiences. This transition is propelled by technological developments in Virtual Reality (VR), Augmented Reality (AR), and Mixed Reality (MR), which provide distinctive options for student engagement that conventional educational models frequently do not accomplish. The metaverse enables learners to investigate intricate concepts via simulations, engage in virtual excursions, and connect with peers worldwide, generating a feeling of community frequently absent in traditional online education.

A principal advantage of metaverse-based learning is its capacity to accommodate various learning styles. Conventional education often employs a uniform methodology, resulting in disengagement among pupils who do not connect with standardized curricula. The metaverse enables customized learning experiences, allowing students to advance at their own speed and access resources suited to their own needs. This adaptability not only improves comprehension but also enables learners to assume responsibility for their educational paths.

Furthermore, the incorporation of gamification within the metaverse enhances the educational experience by incentivizing students with game-like components such as points, badges, and leaderboards. This method promotes active engagement and cultivates a growth attitude, wherein effort and progress are acknowledged and applauded. The immersive characteristics of the metaverse provide real-time feedback and evaluation, permitting instructors to track student progress and modify learning trajectories as needed.

Nonetheless, as we adopt these advancements, it is imperative to confront concerns pertaining to fairness and access, data privacy, and the ethical application of technology. Providing all students with the requisite resources for participation in metaverse education is essential for fostering an inclusive learning environment. By emphasizing these factors, the future of education in the metaverse can serve as a transformational catalyst that not only improves learning results but also equips students for a swiftly changing digital landscape.

REFERENCES

Adera, N. (2025). Innovative learning spaces and blended learning: Quest for 21st century competency teaching and learning approaches. Creating Dynamic Space in Higher Education: Modern Shifts in Policy, Competencies, and Governance, 139-174.

Akgun, S. & Greenhow, C. (2022). Artificial intelligence in education: Addressing ethical challenges in K-12 settings. AI and Ethics. springer.com

Al-Ansi, A. M., Jaboob, M., Garad, A., & Al-Ansi, A. (2023). Analyzing augmented reality (AR) and virtual reality (VR) recent development in education. [sciencedirect.com]. *Social Sciences & Humanities Open*, *8*(1), 100532. DOI: 10.1016/j.ssaho.2023.100532

Alam, A., & Mohanty, A. (2023). Educational technology: Exploring the convergence of technology and pedagogy through mobility, interactivity, AI, and learning tools. Cogent Engineering. tandfonline.com

Alam, T. (2024). Metaverse of Things (MoT) applications for revolutionizing urban living in smart cities. Smart Cities. mdpi.com

Alfaisal, R., Hashim, H., & Azizan, U. H. (2024). Empowering the Metaverse in Education: ChatGPT's Role in Transforming Learning. In Breaking Barriers with Generative Intelligence. Using GI to Improve Human Education and Well-Being: First International Workshop, BBGI 2024, Thessaloniki, Greece, June 10, 2024 [Springer Nature.]. *Proceedings*, *2162*, 13.

AlGerafi, M. A. M., Zhou, Y., Oubibi, M., & Wijaya, T. T. (2023). Unlocking the potential: A comprehensive evaluation of augmented reality and virtual reality in education. Electronics. mdpi.com

Alpala, L. O., Quiroga-Parra, D. J., Torres, J. C., & Peluffo-Ordóñez, D. H. (2022). Smart factory using virtual reality and online multi-user: Towards a metaverse for experimental frameworks. [mdpi.com]. *Applied Sciences (Basel, Switzerland)*, *12*(12), 6258. DOI: 10.3390/app12126258

Álvarez, I. M., Manero, B., Romero-Hernández, A., Cárdenas, M., & Masó, I. (2024). Virtual reality platform for teacher training on classroom climate management: Evaluating user acceptance. [springer.com]. *Virtual Reality (Waltham Cross)*, *28*(2), 78. DOI: 10.1007/s10055-024-00973-6

Aquino, J. F., Riss, R. R., Multerer, S. M., Mogilner, L. N., & Turner, T. L. (2022). A step-by-step guide for mentors to facilitate team building and communication in virtual teams. [tandfonline.com]. *Medical Education Online*, *27*(1), 2094529. DOI: 10.1080/10872981.2022.2094529 PMID: 35762578

Aravena-Bravo, P., Cristia, A., Garcia, R., Kotera, H., Nicolas, R. K., Laranjo, R., & Woon, F. T. (2024). Towards Diversifying Early Language Development Research: The First Truly Global International Summer/ Winter School on Language Acquisition (/L+/) 2021. [mpg.de]. *Journal of Cognition and Development*, *25*(2), 242–260.

Archambault, L., Leary, H., & Rice, K. (2022). Pillars of online pedagogy: A framework for teaching in online learning environments. *Educational Psychologist*.

Aslan, Ö, Aktuğ, S. S., Ozkan-Okay, M., Yilmaz, A. A., & Akin, E. (2023). A comprehensive review of cyber security vulnerabilities, threats, attacks, and solutions. Electronics. mdpi.com

Bell, J. (2024). *Unseen connections: Exhibiting the global stories of cellular telephony at the Smithsonian's National Museum of Natural History*. Museums and the History of Computing. DOI: 10.4324/9781003424703-3

Benner, G. J., Rock, M. L., Strycker, L. A., Lee, E. O., Bailey, P., & Virgin, A. S. (2023). Working together: Leveraging teacher study groups to improve social and emotional learning in the classroom. [sagepub.com]. *Beyond Behavior*, *32*(1), 24–35. DOI: 10.1177/10742956221143497

Bennett, E. E., & McWhorter, R. R. (2021). Virtual HRD's role in crisis and the post Covid-19 professional lifeworld: Accelerating skills for digital transformation. [sagepub.com]. *Advances in Developing Human Resources*, *23*(1), 5–25. DOI: 10.1177/1523422320973288

Bibri, S. E. & Jagatheesaperumal, S. K. (2023). Harnessing the potential of the metaverse and artificial intelligence for the internet of city things: Cost-effective XReality and synergistic AIoT technologies. Smart Cities. mdpi.com

Bizami, N. A., Tasir, Z., & Kew, S. N. (2023). Innovative pedagogical principles and technological tools capabilities for immersive blended learning: a systematic literature review. Education and Information Technologies. springer.com

Buragohain, D., Meng, Y., Deng, C., Li, Q., & Chaudhary, S. (2024). Digitalizing cultural heritage through metaverse applications: challenges, opportunities, and strategies. Heritage Science. springer.com

Carvalho, A. R. & Santos, C. (2022). Developing peer mentors' collaborative and metacognitive skills with a technology-enhanced peer learning program. Computers and Education Open. sciencedirect.com

Chang, C. Y., Kuo, H. C., & Du, Z. (2023). The role of digital literacy in augmented, virtual, and mixed reality in popular science education: a review study and an educational framework development. Virtual Reality. springer.com

Chen, C. M. & Huang, M. Y. (2024). Enhancing programming learning performance through a Jigsaw collaborative learning method in a metaverse virtual space. International Journal of STEM Education. springer.com

Chen, R. H. (2021). Fostering students' workplace communicative competence and collaborative mindset through an inquiry-based learning design. Education sciences. mdpi.com

Constantinescu, G. G., Silion, D., & Iftene, A. (2024). Using Artificial Intelligence and Mixed Realities to Create Educational Applications of the Future. Procedia Computer Science. sciencedirect.com

Cui, Y., Ma, Z., Wang, L., Yang, A., Liu, Q., Kong, S., & Wang, H. (2023). A survey on big data-enabled innovative online education systems during the COVID-19 pandemic. [sciencedirect.com]. *Journal of Innovation & Knowledge*, *8*(1), 100295. DOI: 10.1016/j.jik.2022.100295

Damaševičius, R. & Sidekerskienė, T. (2024). Virtual worlds for learning in metaverse: a narrative review. Sustainability. mdpi.com

Divanji, R. A., Bindman, S., Tung, A., Chen, K., Castaneda, L., & Scanlon, M. (2023). A one stop shop? Perspectives on the value of adaptive learning technologies in K-12 education. [sciencedirect.com]. *Computers and Education Open*, *5*, 100157. DOI: 10.1016/j.caeo.2023.100157

Dolega-Dolegowski, D., Proniewska, K., Dolega-Dolegowska, M., Pregowska, A., Hajto-Bryk, J., Trojak, M., Chmiel, J., Walecki, P., & Fudalej, P. S. (2022). Application of holography and augmented reality based technology to visualize the internal structure of the dental root–a proof of concept. [springer.com]. *Head & Face Medicine*, *18*(1), 12. DOI: 10.1186/s13005-022-00307-4 PMID: 35382839

Fadhel, M. A., Duhaim, A. M., Albahri, A. S., Al-Qaysi, Z. T., Aktham, M. A., Chyad, M. A., Abd-Alaziz, W., Albahri, O. S., Alamoodi, A. H., Alzubaidi, L., Gupta, A., & Gu, Y. (2024). Navigating the metaverse: Unraveling the impact of artificial intelligence—a comprehensive review and gap analysis. [springer.com]. *Artificial Intelligence Review*, *57*(10), 264. DOI: 10.1007/s10462-024-10881-5

Faturoti, B. (2022). Online learning during COVID19 and beyond: A human right based approach to internet access in Africa. *International Review of Law Computers & Technology*, *36*(1), 68–90.

Flavián, C., Ibáñez-Sánchez, S., Orús, C., & Barta, S. (2024). The dark side of the metaverse: The role of gamification in event virtualization. [sciencedirect.com]. *International Journal of Information Management*, *75*, 102726. DOI: 10.1016/j.ijinfomgt.2023.102726

Fynn, A. & Mashile, E. O. (2022). Continuous online assessment at a South African open distance and e-learning institution. Frontiers in Education. frontiersin.org

Gallegos-Rejas, V. M., Thomas, E. E., Kelly, J. T., & Smith, A. C. (2023). A multi-stakeholder approach is needed to reduce the digital divide and encourage equitable access to telehealth. [sagepub.com]. *Journal of Telemedicine and Telecare*, *29*(1), 73–78. DOI: 10.1177/1357633X221107995 PMID: 35733379

Gligorea, I., Cioca, M., Oancea, R., Gorski, A. T., Gorski, H., & Tudorache, P. (2023). Adaptive learning using artificial intelligence in e-learning: A literature review. [mdpi.com]. *Education Sciences, 13*(12), 1216. DOI: 10.3390/educsci13121216

Gradiski, I. P., Borovecki, A., Ćurković, M., San-Martín, M., Delgado Bolton, R. C., & Vivanco, L. (2022). Burnout in international medical students: Characterization of professionalism and loneliness as predictive factors of burnout. [mdpi.com]. *International Journal of Environmental Research and Public Health, 19*(3), 1385. DOI: 10.3390/ijerph19031385 PMID: 35162399

Haleem, A., Javaid, M., Qadri, M. A., & Suman, R. (2022). Understanding the role of digital technologies in education: A review. Sustainable operations and computers, 3, 275-285. sciencedirect.com

Halkiopoulos, C. & Gkintoni, E. (2024). Leveraging AI in e-learning: Personalized learning and adaptive assessment through cognitive neuropsychology—A systematic analysis. Electronics. mdpi.com

Hatami, M., Qu, Q., Chen, Y., Kholidy, H., Blasch, E., & Ardiles-Cruz, E. (2024). A Survey of the Real-Time Metaverse: Challenges and Opportunities. [mdpi.com]. *Future Internet, 16*(10), 379. DOI: 10.3390/fi16100379

Heinrich, W. F., Louson, E., Blommel, C., & Green, A. R. (2021). Who coaches the coaches? The development of a coaching model for experiential learning. [springer.com]. *Innovative Higher Education, 46*(3), 357–375. DOI: 10.1007/s10755-020-09537-3

Hellín, C. J., Calles-Esteban, F., Valledor, A., Gómez, J., Otón-Tortosa, S., & Tayebi, A. (2023). Enhancing student motivation and engagement through a gamified learning environment. [mdpi.com]. *Sustainability (Basel), 15*(19), 14119. DOI: 10.3390/su151914119

Herrera-Pavo, M. Á. (2021). Collaborative learning for virtual higher education. *Learning, Culture and Social Interaction, 28*, 100437.

Huang, H., Hwang, G. J., & Chang, S. C. (2023). Facilitating decision making in authentic contexts: An SVVR-based experiential flipped learning approach for professional training. *Interactive Learning Environments, 31*(8), 5219–5235. DOI: 10.1080/10494820.2021.2000435

Huang, X., Li, H., Huang, L., & Jiang, T. (2023). Research on the development and innovation of online education based on digital knowledge sharing community. BMC psychology. springer.com

Imran, A. (2023). Why addressing digital inequality should be a priority. [wiley.com]. *The Electronic Journal on Information Systems in Developing Countries, 89*(3), e12255. DOI: 10.1002/isd2.12255

Itoi, K., & Mizukura, R. (2024). Experience of Japanese exchange students in EMI programmes: Benefits and issues of translanguaging. *International Journal of Multilingualism, 21*(3), 1434–1453. DOI: 10.1080/14790718.2023.2177652

Jabali, O., Hamamra, B., & Ayyoub, A. (2024). Critical thinking, assessment, and educational policy in Palestinian universities. [springer.com]. *International Journal for Educational Integrity, 20*(1), 12. DOI: 10.1007/s40979-024-00160-9

Jamil, S. (2021). From digital divide to digital inclusion: Challenges for wide-ranging digitalization in Pakistan. *Telecommunications Policy, 45*(8), 102206. DOI: 10.1016/j.telpol.2021.102206

Javed, F. (2025). Preparing for Tomorrow: Evaluating and Innovating Educational Systems for Future Competence. In Fostering Teacher Skills and Critical Thinking in Modern Education (pp. 43-78). IGI Global Scientific Publishing.

Johri, A., Sayal, A., Chaithra, N., Jha, J., Aggarwal, N., Pawar, D., & Gupta, A. (2024). Crafting the techno-functional blocks for Metaverse-A review and research agenda. [sciencedirect.com]. *International Journal of Information Management Data Insights, 4*(1), 100213. DOI: 10.1016/j.jjimei.2024.100213

Jovanović, A. & Milosavljević, A. (2022). VoRtex Metaverse platform for gamified collaborative learning. Electronics. mdpi.com

Kaur, S., Budhraja, K., Pahuja, A., Nayyar, V., & Saluja, S. (2024). Leveraging Artificial Intelligence in Education: Enhancing Learning Experience. In Ethical AI and Data Management Strategies in Marketing (pp. 125-140). IGI Global.

Kayyali, M. (2024). Immersive Technologies: Virtual and Augmented Reality in Higher Education. In Reshaping Learning with Next Generation Educational Technologies (pp. 99-114). IGI Global.

Lai, Y. H., Lin, Y. S., Chang, Y. C., & Chen, S. Y. (2024). Cyber-physical metaverse learning in cultural sustainable education. *Library Hi Tech*. Advance online publication. DOI: 10.1108/LHT-12-2023-0585

Lee, H. J. & Hwang, Y. (2022). Technology-enhanced education through VR-making and metaverse-linking to foster teacher readiness and sustainable learning. Sustainability. mdpi.com

Li, J., Zhang, X., & Liu, X. C. (2025). Exploring the motivational factors and learning outcomes of Virtual Reality educational games for middle school students: A unity 3D case study. *Interactive Learning Environments*, 1–21. DOI: 10.1080/10494820.2024.2446536

Li, M. & Yu, Z. (2022). Teachers' satisfaction, role, and digital literacy during the COVID-19 pandemic. Sustainability. mdpi.com

Li, Y., Wei, W., & Xu, J. (2022). The exploration on ethical problems of educational metaverse. *International Conference on Metaverse*. DOI: 10.1007/978-3-031-23518-4_3

Lombardi, D., & Shipley, T. F., & Astronomy Team, Biology Team, Chemistry Team, Engineering Team, Geography Team, Geoscience Team, and Physics Team. (2021). The curious construct of active learning. *Psychological Science in the Public Interest*, *22*(1), 8–43.

López-Jiménez, J. J., Fernández-Alemán, J. L., García-Berná, J. A., López González, L., González Sequeros, O., Nicolás Ros, J., Carrillo de Gea, J. M., Idri, A., & Toval, A. (2021). Effects of gamification on the benefits of student response systems in learning of human anatomy: Three experimental studies. [mdpi.com]. *International Journal of Environmental Research and Public Health, 18*(24), 13210. DOI: 10.3390/ijerph182413210 PMID: 34948818

Lythreatis, S., Singh, S. K., & El-Kassar, A. N. (2022). The digital divide: A review and future research agenda. [HTML]. *Technological Forecasting and Social Change, 175*, 121359. DOI: 10.1016/j.techfore.2021.121359

Mahindru, R., Kumar, A., Bapat, G., & Rroy, A. D., Kavita, & Sharma, N. (2024). Metaverse unleashed: Augmenting creativity and innovation in business education. *Engineering Proceedings, 59*(1), 207.

Maqsoom, A., Zulqarnain, M., Irfan, M., Ullah, F., Alqahtani, F. K., & Khan, K. I. A. (2023). Drivers of, and barriers to, the adoption of mixed reality in the construction industry of developing countries. [mdpi.com]. *Buildings (Basel, Switzerland), 13*(4), 872. DOI: 10.3390/buildings13040872

Marougkas, A., Troussas, C., Krouska, A., & Sgouropoulou, C. (2023). Virtual reality in education: a review of learning theories, approaches and methodologies for the last decade. Electronics. mdpi.com

Matsika, C., & Zhou, M. (2021). Factors affecting the adoption and use of AVR technology in higher and tertiary education. *Technology in Society, 67*, 101694. DOI: 10.1016/j.techsoc.2021.101694

Mendoza-Ramírez, C. E., Tudon-Martinez, J. C., Félix-Herrán, L. C., Lozoya-Santos, J. D. J., & Vargas-Martínez, A. (2023). Augmented reality: Survey. [mdpi.com]. *Applied Sciences (Basel, Switzerland), 13*(18), 10491. DOI: 10.3390/app131810491

Mourtzis, D., Panopoulos, N., Angelopoulos, J., Wang, B., & Wang, L. (2022). Human centric platforms for personalized value creation in metaverse. *Journal of Manufacturing Systems, 65*, 653–659. DOI: 10.1016/j.jmsy.2022.11.004

Musarat, M. A., Irfan, M., Alaloul, W. S., Maqsoom, A., & Ghufran, M. (2023). A review on the way forward in construction through industrial revolution 5.0. [mdpi.com]. *Sustainability (Basel), 15*(18), 13862. DOI: 10.3390/su151813862

Muzata, A. R., Singh, G., Stepanov, M. S., & Musonda, I. (2024). Immersive Learning: A Systematic Literature Review on Transforming Engineering Education Through Virtual Reality. Virtual Worlds. mdpi.com

Mystakidis, S. (2021). *Motivation enhancement methods for community building in extended reality*. Augmented and Mixed Reality for Communities. DOI: 10.1201/9781003052838-17

Nahi, A. A., Ghaib, A. A., & Ali, A. A. A. A. (2023, December). Metaverse Applications and Its Use in Education. In International Multi-Disciplinary Conference-Integrated Sciences and Technologies (pp. 61-80). Cham: Springer Nature Switzerland. DOI: 10.1007/978-3-031-51716-7_5

Nelson, W. & Luetz, J. M. (2021). The impact of short-term cross-cultural experience on the intercultural competence of participating students: A case study of Australian high school students. Social Sciences. mdpi.com

Nicolaou, C., Matsiola, M., Karypidou, C., Podara, A., Kotsakis, R., & Kalliris, G. (2021). Media studies, audiovisual media communications, and generations: The case of budding journalists in radio courses in Greece. [mdpi.com]. *Journalism and Media*, *2*(2), 155–192. DOI: 10.3390/journalmedia2020010

Nikou, S., De Reuver, M., & Mahboob Kanafi, M. (2022). Workplace literacy skills—How information and digital literacy affect adoption of digital technology. [emerald.com]. *The Journal of Documentation*, *78*(7), 371–391. DOI: 10.1108/JD-12-2021-0241

Niu, Y. (2023). Integrated physical education and medicine in general physical education at universities in the age of educational technologies. BMC Medical Education. springer.com

O'Dowd, R. (2021). What do students learn in virtual exchange? A qualitative content analysis of learning outcomes across multiple exchanges. International Journal of Educational Research. sciencedirect.com

Onu, P., Pradhan, A., & Mbohwa, C. (2024). Potential to use metaverse for future teaching and learning. Education and Information Technologies. springer.com

Orel, M. (2022). Collaboration Potential in Virtual Reality (VR) Office Space: Transforming the Workplace of Tomorrow.

Othman, A., Chemnad, K., Hassanien, A. E., Tlili, A., Zhang, C. Y., Al-Thani, D., & Altınay, Z. (2024). Accessible Metaverse: A Theoretical Framework for Accessibility and Inclusion in the Metaverse. [mdpi.com]. *Multimodal Technologies and Interaction*, *8*(3), 21. DOI: 10.3390/mti8030021

Parmaxi, A., Athanasiou, A., & Demetriou, A. (2021). Introducing a student-led application of Google Expeditions: An exploratory study. *Educational Media International*, *58*(1), 37–59. DOI: 10.1080/09523987.2021.1908497

Pathak, S., & Malpani, D. (2025). Leveraging Virtual Reality to Improve Communication and Collaboration in Remote Work: Enhancing Team Dynamics and Engagement Through Immersive Technologies. In Optimizing Virtual Reality and Metaverse for Remote Work and Virtual Team Collaboration (pp. 191-224). IGI Global.

Pellas, N., Mystakidis, S., & Kazanidis, I. (2021). Immersive Virtual Reality in K-12 and Higher Education: A systematic review of the last decade scientific literature. *Virtual Reality (Waltham Cross)*, *25*(3), 835–861. DOI: 10.1007/s10055-020-00489-9

Perry, B. (2021). Gamified mobile collaborative location-based language learning. Frontiers in Education. frontiersin.org

Pregowska, A., Masztalerz, K., Garlińska, M., & Osial, M. (2021). A worldwide journey through distance education—from the post office to virtual, augmented and mixed realities, and education during the COVID-19 pandemic. Education Sciences. mdpi.com

Radanliev, P., De Roure, D., Novitzky, P., & Sluganovic, I. (2024). Accessibility and inclusiveness of new information and communication technologies for disabled users and content creators in the Metaverse. [tandfonline.com]. *Disability and Rehabilitation. Assistive Technology*, *19*(5), 1849–1863. DOI: 10.1080/17483107.2023.2241882 PMID: 37585705

Rahm, L. (2023). Educational imaginaries: Governance at the intersection of technology and education. Journal of Education Policy. tandfonline.com

Ramírez-Montoya, M. S., Andrade-Vargas, L., Rivera-Rogel, D., & Portuguez-Castro, M. (2021). Trends for the future of education programs for professional development. [mdpi.com]. *Sustainability (Basel)*, *13*(13), 7244. DOI: 10.3390/su13137244

Rizvi, Y. S., & Nabi, A. (2021). Transformation of learning from real to virtual: An exploratory-descriptive analysis of issues and challenges. [emerald.com]. *Journal of Research in Innovative Teaching & Learning*, *14*(1), 5–17. DOI: 10.1108/JRIT-10-2020-0052

Roa González, J., Sánchez Sánchez, N., Seoane Pujol, I., & Díaz Palencia, J. L. (2025). Challenges and perspectives in the evolution of distance and online education towards higher technological environments. [tandfonline.com]. *Cogent Education*, *12*(1), 2447168. DOI: 10.1080/2331186X.2024.2447168

Rodrigues, L., Pereira, F. D., Toda, A. M., Palomino, P. T., Pessoa, M., Carvalho, L. S. G., Fernandes, D., Oliveira, E. H. T., Cristea, A. I., & Isotani, S. (2022). Gamification suffers from the novelty effect but benefits from the familiarization effect: Findings from a longitudinal study. [springer.com]. *International Journal of Educational Technology in Higher Education*, *19*(1), 13. DOI: 10.1186/s41239-021-00314-6

Sharma, W., Lim, W. M., Kumar, S., Verma, A., & Kumra, R. (2024). Game on! A state-of-the-art overview of doing business with gamification. [sciencedirect.com]. *Technological Forecasting and Social Change*, *198*, 122988. DOI: 10.1016/j.techfore.2023.122988

Sidhu, M. S., Mousakhani, S., Lee, C. K., & Sidhu, K. K. (2024). Educational impact of Metaverse learning environment for engineering mechanics dynamics. *Computer Applications in Engineering Education, 32*(5), e22772. DOI: 10.1002/cae.22772

Simelane-Mnisi, S. (2023). Effectiveness of LMS Digital Tools used by the academics to Foster Students' Engagement. Education Sciences. mdpi.com

Singh, M. (2024). Exploring the possibilities to implement metaverse in higher education institutions of India. Education and Information Technologies. springer.com

Smith, S. L. (2024). The American Museum of Natural History. In Connecting with Our Ancestors: Human Evolution Museum Experiences (pp. 93-135). Cham: Springer Nature Switzerland. DOI: 10.1007/978-3-031-69429-5_4

Soliman, M., Pesyridis, A., Dalaymani-Zad, D., Gronfula, M., & Kourmpetis, M. (2021). The application of virtual reality in engineering education. [mdpi.com]. *Applied Sciences (Basel, Switzerland), 11*(6), 2879. DOI: 10.3390/app11062879

Sousa-Vieira, M. E., Ferrero-Castro, D., & López-Ardao, J. C. (2021). Design, development and use of a digital badges system in higher education. Applied Sciences. mdpi.com

Strielkowski, W., Grebennikova, V., Lisovskiy, A., Rakhimova, G., & Vasileva, T. (2024). AI-driven adaptive learning for sustainable educational transformation. Sustainable Development. wiley.com

Syed, T. A., Siddiqui, M. S., Abdullah, H. B., Jan, S., Namoun, A., Alzahrani, A., Nadeem, A., & Alkhodre, A. B. (2022). In-depth review of augmented reality: Tracking technologies, development tools, AR displays, collaborative AR, and security concerns. [mdpi.com]. *Sensors (Basel), 23*(1), 146. DOI: 10.3390/s23010146 PMID: 36616745

Tan, S. (2023). Harnessing immersive technologies for innovation in teaching and learnings. In *Learning intelligence: Innovative and digital transformative learning strategies: Cultural and social engineering perspectives* (pp. 305–334). Springer Nature Singapore. DOI: 10.1007/978-981-19-9201-8_7

Tan, Y., Lo, L., Li, W., & Pang, G. (2023). Intellectual capital and student mobility. *Journal of Ethnic and Migration Studies, 49*(18), 4641–4661. DOI: 10.1080/1369183X.2023.2270332

Timotheou, S., Miliou, O., Dimitriadis, Y., Sobrino, S. V., Giannoutsou, N., Cachia, R., Monés, A. M., & Ioannou, A. (2023). Impacts of digital technologies on education and factors influencing schools' digital capacity and transformation: A literature review. [springer.com]. *Education and Information Technologies, 28*(6), 6695–6726. DOI: 10.1007/s10639-022-11431-8 PMID: 36465416

Tran, C. D. T. T. (2021). Cost efficiency–one size fits all? A university-level analysis of economies of scale and scope in Vietnamese higher education. *Asia Pacific Journal of Education, 41*(2), 336–355. DOI: 10.1080/02188791.2020.1735996

Tripon, C., Gon a, I., & Bulgac, A. (2023). Nurturing minds and sustainability: an exploration of educational interactions and their impact on student well-being and assessment in a sustainable university. Sustainability. mdpi.com

Tyagi, S., Sibal, R., & Suri, B. (2022). Empirically developed framework for building trust in distributed agile teams. *Information and Software Technology, 145*, 106828. DOI: 10.1016/j.infsof.2022.106828

Vahed, A., & Rodriguez, K. (2021). Enriching students' engaged learning experiences through the collaborative online international learning project. *Innovations in Education and Teaching International, 58*(5), 596–605. DOI: 10.1080/14703297.2020.1792331

Van der Burg, S., Wiseman, L., & Krkeljas, J. (2021). Trust in farm data sharing: Reflections on the EU code of conduct for agricultural data sharing. [springer.com]. *Ethics and Information Technology, 23*(3), 185–198. DOI: 10.1007/s10676-020-09543-1

Vaz, E. (2024). The Role of the Metaverse and the Geographical Dimension of Knowledge Management. In Regional Knowledge Economies: Exploring the Intersection of Technology, Geography, and Innovation in the Digital Era (pp. 23-40). Cham: Springer Nature Switzerland. DOI: 10.1007/978-3-031-76906-1_3

Veluvali, P. & Surisetti, J. (2022). Learning management system for greater learner engagement in higher education—A review. Higher Education for the Future. sagepub.com

Vetrivel, S. C., Arun, V. P., Maheswari, R., & Saravanan, T. P. (2024). Technology integration in online learning platforms: Blended learning gamification. In Transdisciplinary Teaching and Technological Integration for Improved Learning: Case Studies and Practical Approaches (pp. 219-247). IGI Global.

Xiong, J., Hsiang, E. L., He, Z., Zhan, T., & Wu, S. T. (2021). Augmented reality and virtual reality displays: Emerging technologies and future perspectives. [nature.com]. *Light, Science & Applications*, *10*(1), 1–30. DOI: 10.1038/s41377-021-00658-8 PMID: 34697292

Yang, W., Fang, M., Xu, J., Zhang, X., & Pan, Y. (2024). Exploring the Mediating Role of Different Aspects of Learning Motivation between Metaverse Learning Experiences and Gamification. Electronics. mdpi.com

Yu, H. (2023). Reflection on whether Chat GPT should be banned by academia from the perspective of education and teaching. Frontiers in Psychology. frontiersin.org

Zamiri, M. & Esmaeili, A. (2024). Methods and technologies for supporting knowledge sharing within learning communities: A systematic literature review. Administrative Sciences. mdpi.com

Zamiri, M. & Esmaeili, A. (2024). Strategies, methods, and supports for developing skills within learning communities: A systematic review of the literature. Administrative Sciences. mdpi.com

Zhang, X., Chen, Y., Hu, L., & Wang, Y. (2022). The metaverse in education: Definition, framework, features, potential applications, challenges, and future research topics. Frontiers in Psychology. frontiersin.org

Zhao, K. & Guo, X. (2022). Analysis of the application of virtual reality technology in football training. Journal of Sensors. wiley.com

Chapter 5

Integrating AI Into Task-Based Language Teaching: Large Language Models in the Designing of Web Quests

Pinelopi Krystalli
https://orcid.org/0000-0001-5262-7495
Aristotle University of Thessaloniki, Greece

Panagiotis Arvanitis
https://orcid.org/0000-0003-1863-4135
Aristotle University of Thessaloniki, Greece

ABSTRACT

Communication in a foreign language requires more than linguistic proficiency, incorporating communicative, general, and digital skills. The chapter emphasizes the importance of equipping students to become active producers of digital discourse rather than passive consumers of unfiltered information. Leveraging the new technological advancements, it advocates integrating tools like webquests into language education. Webquests, research-oriented tasks, enhance motivation, critical thinking, and digital literacy within a social-constructivist framework. The chapter

DOI: 10.4018/979-8-3693-9974-3.ch005

explores the potential of LLMs chatbots (e.g., ChatGPT, Gemini, Claude, Grok2) in tailoring webquests to proficiency levels, thereby fostering linguistic and digital competencies. A theoretical framework addresses task-based learning, webquests, and LLMs integration, while a practical section provides guides for language educators to optimize AI tools and extending learning beyond the classroom.

INTRODUCTION

The recent advent of chatbots such as OpenAI's ChatGPT, Google's Gemini, Anthropic's Claude, and X-AI's Grok2—powered by Large Language Models (LLMs)—marks a significant milestone in the advancement of Artificial Intelligence (AI). Built upon sophisticated deep neural network architectures, these chatbots are trained on vast textual datasets, enabling them to process and generate human-like language with remarkable nuance and complexity (Brown et al., 2020).

The capabilities of these models have opened new horizons across various research and professional domains (Naveed et al., 2020), so consequently, they cannot be overlooked in the field of education, particularly in language teaching and learning.

Today, it is widely acknowledged that language teaching requires a coordinated and multifaceted approach that integrates human interaction, an understanding of contextual communication, the dynamic development of instructional materials, diverse written and oral learning activities, and the continuous creation of engaging language-learning scenarios.

In the above context, LLMs serve as valuable assistants, offering multiple ways to support both language educators and students. Current Large Language Models (LLMs) have the potential to serve as advanced digital tools in addressing the complex challenges of language didactics. They offer unprecedented support to both educators and learners by facilitating the creation of diverse and adaptive didactic materials, generating comprehensive lesson plans, developing assessment resources, and providing detailed, analytical, and personalized feedback on linguistic errors (Caines et al., 2023). Furthermore, they can serve as virtual conversation partners by facilitating real-time autonomous language practice, or by simulating authentic communication scenarios (Huang et al, 2023).

In the context of language learning, students also develop critical digital skills as they learn to interact effectively with AI tools, enhancing their ability to navigate the complex digital landscape of contemporary communication. This dual focus on linguistic competence and digital literacy positions chatbots as significant transformative agents in modern language didactics.

1. DIGITAL LITERACY IN LANGUAGE LEARNING: ADVANCING 21ST-CENTURY COMPETENCIES

Digital literacy refers to an individual's ability to perform tasks effectively in a digital environment, where "digital" encompasses information in numeric form primarily utilized by computers. This concept includes the ability to read and interpret various media forms (e.g., text, sound, images), manipulate data, and critically evaluate and apply new knowledge obtained from digital sources (Jones-Kavalier & Flannigan, 2006, p. 9).

A crucial component of digital literacy involves developing skills to locate, synthesize, and apply information. Students need to learn how to critically assess digital content, understanding that online information is often shaped by individual perspectives, introducing potential bias or incompleteness. Consequently, consulting multiple sources is essential to gain a well-rounded and comprehensive understanding of any given topic (Gibson, 2010; Hafner, Chik, & Jones, 2015; Pegrum et al., 2018).

Digital literacy also fosters creative engagement with information, encouraging students to transform it into new insights rather than merely consuming existing content. This transformative approach promotes a critical attitude toward technology, prompting learners to consider its societal impact both now and in the future. Ultimately, digital literacy seeks to develop responsible, skilled users of technology who can navigate and contribute meaningfully to the digital world (Gibson, 2010).

These skills are closely linked to essential 21st-century competencies, including collaboration, critical thinking, problem-solving, creativity, and lifelong learning (Mishra & Kereluik, 2011; Gee, 2013). In today's digital age, a digitally literate individual can effectively leverage technology to identify and evaluate information, collaborate with others, produce and share original content, and use digital tools to achieve academic, professional, and personal objectives (eLearning Department, 2015).

Importantly, digital literacy extends beyond basic reading and writing in digital formats. It encompasses a broader skill set, enabling individuals to interpret, produce, manage, and share meaning across diverse digital communication channels (Hafner, Chik, & Jones, 2015). This comprehensive understanding necessitates the adoption of innovative pedagogical approaches, particularly in foreign language teaching, to ensure the parallel development of linguistic and digital competencies (Jones & Hafner, 2012; Dudeney, Hockly, & Pegrum, 2013).

One such pedagogical approach is the WebQuest, a task-based methodology aligned with the constructivist theory and principles, as highlighted in the Common European Framework of Reference for Languages (CEFR). A well-designed WebQuest provides structured, inquiry-based activities that foster critical thinking, collaboration, and digital literacy, aligning seamlessly with language learning objectives

2. TASK-BASED LEARNING

Task-based learning, as introduced by David Nunan (1989) and Rod Ellis (2003), has become a cornerstone of the action-oriented approach outlined in the Common European Framework of Reference for Languages (CEFR, 2001). This approach emphasizes meaning making over linguistic form, encouraging learners to engage their receptive, productive, and mediated language skills, as well as abilities crucial for both written and oral interaction. Ellis (2003: 16) defines a pedagogical task as a workplan that requires learners to process language pragmatically to achieve an outcome, which is evaluated based on whether the appropriate propositional content has been conveyed. This necessitates students' focus on meaning and the use of their linguistic resources, although task design may also prompt attention to specific forms. Thus, tasks should involve language use that mirrors real-world communication, either directly or indirectly, and may engage productive or receptive, oral or written skills, along with various cognitive processes.

According to Nunan (1989), a task should be structured with a clear beginning, middle, and end, allowing it to function independently as a meaningful communicative act. To qualify as a task, it must engage students in authentic language use, involve cognitive processes, and lead to a specific outcome that enables students to assess whether they have met the task's objective (Ellis, 2003). Moreover, tasks should promote interaction and collaboration among participants, often culminating in written or oral production.

As Mangenot (2017) emphasizes, tasks should mirror established social practices and aim to achieve social objectives (Soubrié, 2008; Puren, 2009). This illustrates that task-based language learning is learner-centered, fosters collaborative learning, and incorporates authentic texts. Unlike the communicative approach, which centers on authentic texts as the basis for activities, task-based learning uses these texts primarily as informational sources, focusing on their morphological characteristics (Mangenot, 2017).

Many linguists, didacticians, and language specialists recognize the benefits of integrating tasks into foreign language classrooms. Ellis (2003: 27) distinguishes between two approaches to incorporating tasks into language teaching:

1. Task-supported language teaching, where tasks complement traditional teaching methods,
2. Task-based language teaching, where tasks are central to the curriculum.

In both approaches, tasks enhance the communicative and interactive aspects of language learning, allowing learners to develop the ability to use the language authentically in real-world contexts. Tasks thus serve two main functions: fostering interaction and facilitating the exchange of information (Alrabadi, 2012). The interactional function of tasks helps initiate and sustain communication. Mangenot and Louveau (2006: 38) assert that tasks "are not only plausible in terms of similarity with real life but also interactionally justified in the community where they take place (the class, in general)." Consequently, tasks should encourage genuine communication between learners, supporting the natural process of language acquisition.

In addition, tasks serve a transactional function, facilitating the exchange of information among interlocutors. By engaging in real communication situations, tasks allow learners to develop both interactional and transactional skills. From the actional perspective, language acquisition occurs through communication, where learners discover the target language system by participating in communicative processes, rather than through isolated language structure learning (Alrabadi, 2012).

Bourguignon (2001) underscores the importance of the actional perspective, connecting tasks to real-life scenarios and problem-solving. These tasks may be completed individually or in groups, requiring students to strategically apply their knowledge and skills to achieve specific outcomes (Council of Europe, 2001, p. 15). The CEFR Companion Volume (Council of Europe, 2018, p. 26) stresses the importance of designing educational programs that address real-world communication needs, based on tasks aligned with language proficiency descriptors.

These tasks, which reflect everyday life across personal, public, educational, and professional domains, are diverse and complex, requiring not only linguistic but also other competencies. The complexity of a task is influenced by factors such as the learners' abilities, educational objectives, learning methods, and task conditions (Council of Europe, 2001, pp. 121-123). One example of task implementation in a foreign language lesson is web exploration, which integrates the internet as a learning tool.

3. OPTIMIZING ONLINE INFORMATION RETRIEVAL: THE ROLE OF WEBQUESTS IN LANGUAGE LEARNING

The Internet serves as a vast and diverse repository of information, offering numerous opportunities for academic exploration (Leu et al., 2004). However, its unstructured and expansive nature can make it difficult for school learners to locate reliable and relevant resources. The potential for time loss due to irrelevant, outdated, or erroneous content is considerable. To overcome these challenges, WebQuest stands out as an effective instructional tool, as will be discussed in the following section.

3.1 Definition of the WebQuest

The WebQuest model, introduced by Dodge and March in 1995 at the Educational Technology Department of San Diego State University, is a structured, inquiry-based learning approach designed to optimize internet use for educational purposes. Unlike traditional online searches, it relies on a curated selection of resources pre-determined by the teacher, ensuring a focused and secure learning experience. This approach is particularly effective in fostering higher-order thinking skills, such as analysis, synthesis, and evaluation, by shifting the focus from simply searching for information to utilizing it in meaningful ways (Dodge, 2001). Since its inception, the WebQuest model has been widely embraced by educators (Wang & Hannafin, 2008) for its ability to engage students with authentic, contextually rich materials. This engagement facilitates meaningful interactions (Dodge, 2001; Strickland, 2005), promotes deeper connections with the target language, and exposes learners to diverse cultural contexts.

WebQuests emphasize the development of higher-order cognitive skills, such as analysis, synthesis, and evaluation, which aligns with Bloom's Taxonomy (Lacina, 2007). By reducing the cognitive load and time spent searching for information, WebQuests allow learners to focus more on complex tasks like problem-solving, research, and writing. As defined by Dodge (1997), a WebQuest is a research-oriented task conducted partially or entirely on the Internet, where students work in small groups to solve problems using teacher-guided online resources. In this process, learners evaluate, select, and synthesize information, justifying their choices—distinguishing it from simple web browsing (Starr, 2012). This methodology is grounded in constructivist principles, emphasizing that knowledge is actively constructed through the integration of prior knowledge and new information (Catroux, 2004). Furthermore, WebQuest promotes the idea that knowledge is not just a collection of facts but is shaped by the student's active engagement and experiences (Von Glaserfeld, 1996).

Additionally, utilizing the Web as a source of real-world information supports modern language teaching by incorporating authentic language materials, an approach emphasized by Godwin-Jones (2004). A WebQuest often provides students with a topic-focused "hotlist" of websites to begin their research, thus ensuring relevance and quality in the information gathered. Furthermore, it exposes learners to authentic electronic documents—professional materials not initially intended for educational use—offering a richer, more realistic context for learning (Catroux, 2005).

3.2 Key WebQuest Elements

WebQuest offers a structured approach to inquiry-based learning, combining online resources with elements that promote knowledge acquisition, critical thinking, and problem-solving. The following table highlights the key components of an effective WebQuest.

Table 1. Key WebQuest Elements

Key WebQuest Elements	Purpose
Introduction	The introduction sets the context for the task, providing relevant background information and presenting the problem that students are expected to solve.
Task	This section defines the objective of the task and specifies the expected format for the final deliverable.
Process	This section outlines the steps students must follow to complete the task, providing guidance on organizing their work
Resources:	A curated list of pre-selected online sources is provided to ensure relevance, reliability, and appropriateness for the task.
Evaluation	Clear criteria are established to assess students' work, often incorporating self-reflection, peer assessment, or instructor evaluation.
Conclusion	The conclusion allows students to reflect on their learning experience, summarize their findings, and consider the broader implications of their work.

The introduction sets the context for the task, providing relevant background information and presenting the problem that needs to be solved. Its primary goal is to engage the learner's interest in the theme of the quest, helping them connect the topic to their own life experiences. This is often achieved through a series of guiding questions designed to spark curiosity and motivate students to complete the tasks assigned to them (Catroux, 2004; Lacina, 2007).

The task emphasizes the importance of making the task description both engaging and meaningful for learners, aligning it with the broader purpose of WebQuest. Students are presented with a problem to solve or a mission to accomplish (Dodge, 2003), ensuring the task is both achievable and appropriately challenging. Additionally, the section specifies the type of output required (Halat, 2008), which might include a multimodal document, a digital presentation, or an online publication. The task also often identifies roles for cooperative group members. Each student is assigned a role to play as the group completes the assigned activity (Strickland, 2005). Likewise, WebQuests should be designed to "use learners' time well, to focus on using information rather than looking for it" (Chandler, 2003, p. 38).

The process section emphasizes key activities, such as role-playing and cognitive strategies, including comparison, summarization, and synthesis (Kahl & Berg, 2006). It provides a detailed, step-by-step guide to assist learners in completing the task, specifying roles for group work, guidelines for utilizing resources, and instructions for analyzing and organizing information. Furthermore, WebQuest should offer explicit instructions on the actions students need to take to complete the task and the format in which they should present the information they have gathered.

The key focus of the resources section is to ensure that the materials are of high quality and developmentally appropriate for the intended age group (Strickland, 2005). It suggests online sources, including printed materials, from which students can gather the information needed to complete their task. The websites recommended by the teacher must be valid and reliable, to prevent unnecessary and excessive browsing on the internet.

In every WebQuest, the teacher should provide a clear rubric that describes how the work (whether group or individual) will be evaluated. The criteria should be made known at the beginning of the task, be clear, concise, and specific to each individual task or activity (Κρυστάλλη, 2023). The final section of a WebQuest is the conclusion, which provides closure to the activity and summarizes the key learning outcomes the teacher expects from students (Dodge, 1997). It may also encourage students to apply their newly acquired knowledge to other areas. Together, WebQuest's sections should create a reflective, fluid, and dynamic experience (March, 2003), motivating students to engage in inquiry-based learning while providing the necessary resources and guidance. Students are clear on the steps they need to take for success and are encouraged to extend their knowledge to real-world problems, especially in areas relevant to their interests and social studies (Strickland, 2005).

These elements work together to create a comprehensive learning experience that encourages collaboration, critical thinking, and the application of knowledge in real-world contexts. By emphasizing guided research and authentic materials, WebQuests offer an innovative way to engage students in meaningful, inquiry-based learning.

3.3 The Pedagogical Benefits of WebQuests: Promoting Cognitive, Linguistic, and Collaborative Skills

WebQuests are designed to stimulate advanced cognitive reasoning by engaging learners in authentic tasks and scenarios. Grounded in constructivist theory, this approach encourages students to actively seek and apply knowledge through collaborative activities, aiming to develop viable solutions or recommendations (Burchum et al., 2007). Unlike traditional online searches, which focus primarily on information retrieval, WebQuests challenge students to transform information into meaningful outputs, such as comparisons, hypotheses, or solutions. This transformation aligns with cognitive psychology and constructivist principles, promoting deeper understanding and critical thinking (March, 1998).

A defining feature of WebQuests is their emphasis on higher-order cognitive tasks. Rather than passively collecting information, students engage in analytical and creative problem-solving activities that enhance their reasoning abilities. As Dodge (2001) observes, this approach not only strengthens cognitive skills but also provides students with a sense of purpose and relevance, motivating them to fully engage in their tasks.

Collaboration plays a central role in WebQuests, reflecting the proven benefits of cooperative learning. Cooperative learning, in which small groups work together to achieve mutual academic success, is associated with improved interpersonal relationships and psychological well-being (Smith et al., 2005). Effective group organization fosters a supportive learning environment, enhancing the overall learning experience and promoting the development of interpersonal skills (Dodge, 2001).

In the context of language learning, WebQuests place tasks within relevant thematic contexts, requiring students to use digital resources and engage in critical thinking within a collaborative environment. This approach allows students to practice linguistic skills while benefiting from scaffolding techniques that support both language acquisition and task completion (Zufarjonovna, 2022). By modeling cognitive and physical processes, WebQuests facilitate the natural internalization of language structures, making them an effective tool for second-language instruction.

Drawing on decades of research in cognitive science, WebQuests emphasize the natural acquisition of knowledge through meaningful connections. Caine and Caine (1994) highlight the importance of integrating "felt meaning" with "deep meaning," a goal achieved by WebQuests through engaging and purposeful tasks. March (1998) and Dodge (2001) further emphasize the motivational benefits of WebQuests, noting their ability to foster a sense of accomplishment and real-world relevance. This intrinsic motivation encourages students to exert greater effort, maintain focus, and develop greater independence and confidence as language learners.

By blending cognitive, linguistic, and collaborative elements, WebQuests offer a comprehensive learning strategy that supports both academic and personal growth. Their structured approach not only enhances language acquisition but also empowers students to become more proactive and self-reliant in their learning journey.

4. THE ROLE OF CHATBOTS IN WEBQUEST DESIGN: A COMPARATIVE APPROACH

To explore the potential of chatbots in WebQuest design, this section examines how three AI models respond to identical prompts. By applying the same set of instructions across these AI models, we analyze their ability to generate structured WebQuests, adapt content to specific pedagogical requirements, and support language learning. This comparative approach highlights the strengths and limitations of each model in supporting the development of WebQuests.

4.1. The Prompts Provided

Main prompt for all chatbots:

Create a WebQuest for learners of French language, level according to CERF B1 with the following 5 parts structure:

1. Introduction:

Provide a contextual introduction designed to engage students and clarify the purpose of the activity. Emphasize the real-world importance of planning a trip while highlighting the language skills they will develop, such as researching, discussing, and presenting in the target language. Mention the destination, Paris, and underline the cultural and historical significance of Notre-Dame Cathedral, particularly in light of its reconstruction efforts following the devastating fire.

2. Task:
    - Clearly describe the final objective: to create a detailed PowerPoint presentation for the school director.
    - Specify that the presentation must include information on tickets, accommodations, transportation options, and a guided visit to the cathedral.
    - Emphasize the need to provide well-reasoned arguments for the best dates, prices, and transportation modes.

3. Process:
   - Divide the class into small groups (20 students total, with 4–5 students per group).
   - Assign specific missions to each group (e.g., Group 1: research transportation options; Group 2: find accommodation options; Group 3: calculate costs; Group 4: plan the itinerary).
   - Include steps for collaboration within and between groups to ensure interaction and sharing of ideas.
   - Incorporate language-focused tasks, such as drafting emails to travel agencies or writing descriptions of activities.
4. Resources: Provide a curated list of websites or materials (both in English and French) for students to research. Include resources for train or flight tickets, hotels, and guided tours. Ensure the resources are reliable and appropriate for their CEFR B1 level.
5. Conclusion: Guide students to reflect on the project by summarizing their findings and discussing the challenges they faced. Encourage them to think about how these skills could be applied to other real-life scenarios.

   Additional Notes:
   - Ensure that the WebQuest incorporates opportunities for students to practice reading, writing, speaking, and listening in the target language.
   - Include prompts for peer feedback and teacher evaluation of the final presentations.
   - Provide scaffolding for language use (e.g., key vocabulary or templates for research).

4.2. Open AI's – ChatGPT's Response

Title: "WebQuest: Organize a Trip from London to Paris to Visit Notre-Dame Cathedral"

Introduction

Bienvenue! Imagine you and your classmates are responsible for planning an unforgettable trip from London to Paris. Your mission? To visit the iconic Notre-Dame Cathedral and showcase your plan to the school director.

Through this activity, you'll practice essential language skills—reading, writing, speaking, and listening—while researching travel options, budgeting, and creating a professional presentation. By the end, you'll not only master trip planning but also collaborate, negotiate, and make informed decisions, all in the target language.

Get ready to explore Paris, hone your linguistic abilities, and take on the challenge!

Task

Your goal is to create a comprehensive PowerPoint presentation for the school director. Your presentation must include:

- Transportation options: Compare train, bus, and flight options from London to Paris.
- Accommodation choices: Find affordable, comfortable places to stay.
- Guided tours: Research options for visiting Notre-Dame Cathedral, considering language preferences.
- Cost analysis: Calculate the total budget for the trip.
- Dates and rationale: Propose the best dates for travel with well-supported arguments.

Your presentation should persuade the school director by showcasing the best options for cost, convenience, and educational value.

Process

A. Group Formation:

Divide into 4 groups (4–5 students per group):
Group 1: Transportation,
Group 2: Accommodation,
Group 3: Budget and costs,
Group 4: Itinerary planning.

B. Research Phase:

Each group will:
- Use the provided resources to gather relevant information.
- Collaborate to complete your assigned task.
- Prepare draft notes summarizing your findings in the target language.

C. Collaboration:
- Share your group's findings with other groups to ensure all details align.
- Provide feedback to refine each group's section of the plan.

D. Language-Focused Activities:
- Draft emails or messages to travel agencies in French or English.
- Write brief descriptions of transport, accommodation, and itinerary options in the target language.
- Practice oral presentations in your groups to prepare for the final showcase.

E. Presentation Preparation:
- Combine all findings into one cohesive PowerPoint presentation.
- Assign speaking roles for the final presentation to ensure participation from all students.

Resources

Here's a curated list to assist your research:

A. Transportation:
- Eurostar Train: www.eurostar.com

- Flight comparison websites: www.skyscanner.net

B. Accommodation:
   - Budget hotels: www.booking.com
   - Youth hostels: www.hostelworld.com

C. Guided Tours:
   - Paris tours: www.getyourguide.com
   - Notre-Dame visits: www.notredamedeparis.fr

D. Language Support:
   - Online dictionaries: www.wordreference.com
   - Sentence templates for emails and presentations: www.linguee.com

Conclusion

- Reflect on your journey as a group.
- What challenges did you face while planning the trip?
- How did you overcome language or research obstacles?
- What new skills or knowledge did you gain?
- Discuss how this experience applies to real-life scenarios and the importance of collaboration, critical thinking, and language skills in achieving success.

Additional Notes

- Provide key vocabulary and sentence starters to support students.
- Allow time for peer feedback and constructive critique after presentations.
- Use a rubric to evaluate the final presentations based on content, language use, creativity, and teamwork.

Bonne chance et bon voyage!

4.3. Anthropic Claude's Response

Title: "Exploring Paris: A Language and Travel Adventure"

Introduction

Dear Language Explorers,

Welcome to an exciting journey that will transform you from language learners to travel planning experts! This WebQuest will take you on an immersive adventure from London to Paris, focusing on one of the world's most iconic architectural marvels: Notre-Dame Cathedral.

In 2019, a devastating fire nearly destroyed this centuries-old landmark, capturing global attention. Today, Notre-Dame stands as a powerful symbol of resilience and hope, undergoing an incredible reconstruction that captures the imagination of people worldwide. Your mission will combine language learning with real-world skills, turning you into confident English communicators and cultural investigators.

Through this project, you will develop:

- Advanced French communication skills
- Research and presentation capabilities
- Critical thinking and problem-solving abilities
- Cultural awareness and understanding
- Practical travel planning expertise

Main Task

Final Objective: Create a comprehensive and persuasive PowerPoint presentation for your school director that demonstrates your French language proficiency and travel planning skills.

Your presentation must include:

- Detailed transportation options between London and Paris
- Comprehensive accommodation research
- Precise cost calculations
- Detailed itinerary with Notre-Dame Cathedral visit
- Well-reasoned arguments supporting your choices
- Professional and engaging presentation style

Working Process

Group Composition

- Total Students: 20
- Group Configuration: 4 groups of 5 students

Group Missions

Group 1: Transportation Experts
- Research and compare transportation methods:
Eurostar train services
Airline options
Alternative travel combinations
- Create a comparative analysis in French
- Calculate travel times and costs
- Language Focus: Technical communication, comparative writing

Group 2: Accommodation Specialists
- Investigate lodging options: Hotels, Hostels, Apartment rentals
- Evaluate price-to-quality ratio
- Prepare a detailed accommodation report
- Language Focus: Descriptive writing, persuasive communication

Group 3: Budget Planners
- Calculate total trip expenses
- Itemize potential costs: Transportation, Accommodation, Tourist activities, Meals, Unexpected expenses
- Develop cost-saving strategies
- Language Focus: Financial terminology, analytical writing

Group 4: Itinerary Designers
- Develop a comprehensive travel plan
- Research Notre-Dame Cathedral visit options
- Identify guided tour possibilities
- Suggest complementary cultural activities
- Language Focus: Detailed description, scheduling vocabulary

Collaboration Steps

- Individual Research (2 hours)
- Group Synthesis Meeting
- Inter-Group Exchange and Validation
- PowerPoint Presentation Preparation
- Rehearsal and Peer Feedback

Language-Focused Tasks

- Draft professional emails to travel agencies
- Write detailed activity descriptions
- Prepare presentation scripts
- Use precise travel and tourism vocabulary
- Practice verbal presentation skills

Resources

Websites in English

- [Eurostar Official Website](https://www.eurostar.com/)
- [TripAdvisor](https://www.tripadvisor.com/)
- [Booking.com](https://www.booking.com/)
- [Paris Tourism Official Site](https://en.parisinfo.com/)

Websites in French (with English translations)

- [SNCF](https://www.sncf.com/)
- [Notre-Dame de Paris Reconstruction](https://www.notredamedeparis.fr/)

Language Learning Resources

- Online dictionaries
- English travel phrase guides

- B1 level grammar resources

Conclusion and Reflection

Final Presentation

- Group findings summary
- Discussion of encountered challenges
- Reflection on acquired skills

Reflection Questions:

- How did this project improve your English skills?
- What challenges did you overcome?
- How can these skills be applied in future scenarios?
- What did you learn about French culture and history?

Enjoy your linguistic journey, explorers!

4.4. Google Gemini's Response

Title: "Here's a WebQuest for French language learners at the B1 level, focusing on planning a trip to Paris and visiting Notre-Dame Cathedral"

Introduction

Bienvenue à Paris! This WebQuest will take you on a virtual journey to the City of Lights, where you will plan a school trip to visit the magnificent Notre-Dame Cathedral.

Notre-Dame, a masterpiece of Gothic architecture, suffered a devastating fire in 2019. However, thanks to incredible efforts, its reconstruction is underway. Witnessing this symbol of resilience firsthand will be an unforgettable experience.

During this project, you will develop essential language skills, such as researching, discussing, and presenting your findings in French. You will learn about travel planning, budgeting, and the importance of cultural understanding.

Task

Your mission is to create a detailed PowerPoint presentation for the school director, proposing a school trip to Paris. The presentation must include:

- Transportation: Research and compare different transportation options (flights, trains) to Paris. Consider factors like cost, travel time, and environmental impact.
- Accommodation: Find suitable accommodation options for your class (hotels, hostels) within your budget. Consider location, amenities, and proximity to Notre-Dame.
- Tickets: Research ticket prices and booking procedures for visiting Notre-Dame Cathedral. Consider guided tours, audio guides, and any special entry options.
- Itinerary: Plan a realistic itinerary for your trip, including:
- Arrival and departure times
- Transportation within Paris
- Free time for exploring
- Guided visit to Notre-Dame
- Other potential activities (e.g., visiting museums, enjoying Parisian cafes)

Remember to:

- Provide clear justifications for your choices. Why did you select these transportation options, accommodations, and dates?
- Present your findings in a clear, concise, and engaging manner. Use visuals like images and maps to enhance your presentation.
- Communicate effectively in French throughout the entire project.

Process

Group Formation: The class will be divided into small groups of 4-5 students.

Group Roles: Each group will be assigned a specific area of expertise:

Group 1: Transportation
Group 2: Accommodation
Group 3: Budget and Costs
Group 4: Itinerary and Activities

Research and Collaboration:

Each group will conduct thorough research using the provided resources.

Groups will collaborate to share information, compare findings, and discuss their choices.

Language Focus:

Draft emails to travel agencies in French requesting information.

Write descriptions of activities and accommodation options in French.

Practice presenting your findings in French to other groups.

Presentation Preparation:

Each group will compile their findings and begin creating their PowerPoint presentation.

Collaborate within your group to ensure a cohesive and professional presentation.

Peer Feedback:

Present your draft presentation to another group.

Provide constructive feedback on content, language use, and presentation style.

Resources

Transportation:

French: SNCF (train), Air France, easyJet

English: The Man in Seat 61 (train travel information), Skyscanner (flight comparison)

Accommodation:

French: Booking.com (French version), Airbnb (French version)

English: Hostelworld, TripAdvisor

Notre-Dame:

French: Official Notre-Dame website (if available), Paris Info

English: Paris Tourist Office, Lonely Planet Paris

Conclusion

- Reflection: Summarize your key findings and the challenges you encountered during the project. Discuss how the skills you developed during this project can be applied to other real-life situations (e.g., planning other trips, making major purchases).
- Presentation: Present your final project to the school director and your classmates.
- Evaluation: Peer feedback and teacher evaluation will be used to assess your presentation, language use, and overall project performance.

Note: This WebQuest can be adapted to fit the specific needs and interests of your students. You can adjust the difficulty level, the number of groups, and the specific focus areas based on your classroom dynamics.

This WebQuest provides a framework for a engaging and enriching learning experience. By immersing themselves in the planning process for a trip to Paris, students will not only improve their French language skills but also gain valuable life skills and a deeper understanding of French culture.

5. RESPONSES ANALYSIS

All three LLM-based approaches align with the fundamental components of the WebQuest methodology—Introduction, Task, Process, Resources, and Conclusion—while differing in content depth, the level of scaffolding provided, and the estimated time required for completion. Language instructors should carefully consider these variations in relation to their learners' language proficiency levels and the intended educational objectives.

Completeness and Structure

Open AI ChatGPT's response demonstrates a well-balanced integration of the core WebQuest components, while maintaining clarity and coherence. The instructions are presented in a student-friendly manner, rendering the material immediately applicable in a classroom context. The level of detail provided is sufficient for language instructors seeking a comprehensive instructional design.

Anthropic Claude's response is comparatively more extensive, offering a deeper theoretical framework and greater emphasis on the rationale behind each stage of the WebQuest project. This level of detail can serve language educators interested in a richer, more elaborate WebQuest that addresses higher-level cognitive tasks (e.g., in-depth research, analysis, and synthesis). However, it may require more time and a higher degree of student readiness to engage fully with its content.

Google Gemini's response focuses on core WebQuest tasks and language learning objectives without delving into extensive pedagogical exposition. The WebQuest is concise and straightforward, making it suitable for short and quick presentations. This response may be particularly useful for language educators seeking more direct and less structured guidance. However, educators may need to supplement it with additional linguistic or cultural activities to enhance its comprehensiveness.

Suitability for B1-Level Learners

The responses from all three chatbots align closely with the CEFR B1 level in terms of language tasks and objectives, demonstrating the ability to handle routine communication in familiar contexts and produce simple connected text on topics that are familiar or of personal interest, as outlined in the B1 descriptors.

Time and Practicality

OpenAI ChatGPT's response provides a clear framework for WebQuest implementation and classroom management, while allowing flexibility for language educators to make adaptations as needed. Anthropic Claude's response offers a comprehensive analysis, encompassing a wide range of tasks and sub-tasks. This level of thoroughness is particularly suitable for language instructors who prefer a multifaceted approach with advanced research strategies, although it may require additional classroom time. Google Gemini's response is concise, requiring minimal reading and preparation prior to implementation. This streamlined framework is advantageous for language instructors who seek to implement a WebQuest quickly and efficiently, with minimal preparatory effort.

CONCLUSION

Artificial intelligence (AI) has ushered in a new generation of educational technologies, transforming classrooms and school systems on a broader scale (Baker, 2022). Its integration into education is revolutionizing learning methodologies by addressing gaps in teaching and learning processes. AI enhances efficiency, supports personalized approaches, and automates administrative tasks, thereby enabling educators to focus on inherently human attributes such as adaptability and empathy—qualities that remain beyond the reach of machines. By reshaping pedagogical practices, AI enriches the student experience while simultaneously providing substantial benefits to educators, thereby exerting a dual impact on the educational landscape (Crompton and Song, 2021, p. 2; Holmes et al., 2019, p. 134; Luckin, 2017).

One of the most significant advancements brought about by AI is adaptive learning systems, which enable the continuous personalization of instructional sequences (Luckin, 2017; Holmes et al., 2019). For instance, intelligent tutoring systems (ITS) emulate the benefits of individualized tutoring by employing algorithms that monitor student progress in real-time and recommend targeted activities, including explanatory videos, interactive quizzes, and supplementary reading materials (Luckin & Holmes, 2017; Zawacki-Richter et al., 2019; VanLehn, 2011). Building on this capability, AI-driven education facilitates the creation of dynamic WebQuests tailored to learners' needs, interests, and progress. These systems automatically curate and adapt online resources, interactive tasks, and scaffolded guidance to ensure alignment with students' language proficiency levels and linguistic needs. This adaptability not only enhances the relevance and accessibility of learning materials but also fosters deeper language acquisition and skill development, underscoring AI's transformative potential in learner-centered pedagogical practices (Holmes et al., 2019).

Beyond instructional innovations, AI significantly streamlines routine administrative tasks, such as grading assignments and tests. While already proficient at grading multiple-choice assessments, AI is advancing toward evaluating written responses with increasing accuracy. These capabilities free educators to dedicate more time to personalized student interactions and strategic instructional planning. Moreover, AI optimizes enrollment and admissions processes, enhancing efficiency and accessibility for educational institutions (Williamson, 2017; Akinwalere & Ivanov, 2022).

AI is not intended to replace teachers but to augment their effectiveness (Holmes et al., 2021). In this evolving context, educators assume pivotal roles in the creation, deployment, and evaluation of AI-driven tools. Transitioning beyond traditional roles as content providers, teachers become collaborators, co-creators, and facilitators of AI-enhanced learning environments (Celik et al., 2022; Mishra & Varshney, 2024). They contribute to this ecosystem by providing data for training AI models and assessing the accuracy and practical applicability of these tools (Celik et al., 2022).

However, the integration of AI in education (AIED) is not without challenges. The ethical implications of AI-driven chatbots, such as ChatGPT, remain a crucial topic of discussion, particularly in educational contexts. While these technologies provide valuable tools for language learning and communication, their limitations—ranging from the reinforcement of biases to the risk of misinformation—necessitate scrutiny. As highlighted by Bender et al. (2021), Hutson (2021), and Kohnke et al. (2023), ethical considerations must go beyond technical efficiency to encompass issues of fairness, reliability, and responsible use. Addressing these concerns is essential to ensuring that AI-driven technologies contribute positively to education and society.

A key challenge is the need for greater teacher involvement in the development and implementation of AI tools. Collaboration between educators and developers is crucial to ensuring that these technologies align with classroom realities and effectively meet the needs of both teachers and learners. Such cooperation maximizes AI's potential to enhance educational practices (Holmes et al., 2021). While the most visible impact of AI-driven technologies lies in the personalization of learning, they also foster innovative pedagogical approaches, enabling educators to support students in ways that were previously unattainable.

Finally, as future workplaces increasingly rely on AI, educational institutions must integrate AI into their curricula. This proactive approach not only exposes students to the potential of AI but also equips them with the skills necessary to navigate and thrive in an evolving technological landscape (Pedro et al., 2019).

REFERENCES

Akinwalere, S. N., & Ivanov, V. (2022). Artificial intelligence in higher education: Challenges and opportunities. *Border Crossing*, *12*(1), 1–15. DOI: 10.33182/bc.v12i1.2015

Alrabadi, E. (2012). Pour l'introduction de la perspective actionnelle basée sur la réalisation des tâches communicatives en classe de langue étrangère. *Synergies Canada*, *5*, 1–12.

Baker, S. (2022). L'intelligence artificielle dans l'éducation: Rassemblons les pièces du puzzle. Perspectives de l'OCDE sur l'éducation numérique 2021.

Bender, E. M., Gebru, T., McMillan-Major, A., & Shmitchell, S. (2021, March). On the dangers of stochastic parrots: Can language models be too big? . In *Proceedings of the 2021 ACM conference on fairness, accountability, and transparency* (pp. 610-623). DOI: 10.1145/3442188.3445922

Bourguignon, C. (2006). De l'approche communicative à l'approche communic'actionnelle: Une rupture épistémologique en didactique des langues-cultures. *Synergie Europe*, *1*(1), 58–73.

Brown, T., Mann, B., Ryder, N., Subbiah, M., Kaplan, J. D., Dhariwal, P., & Amodei, D. (2020). Language models are few-shot learners. *Advances in Neural Information Processing Systems*, *33*, 1877–1901.

Burchum, J., Russell, C. K., Likes, W., Adymy, C., Britt, T., Driscoll, C., & Cowan, P. (2007). Confronting challenges in online teaching: The WebQuest solution. *Journal of Online Learning and Teaching*, *3*(1), 40–57.

Caine, R. N., & Caine, G. (1994). *Making connections: Teaching and the human brain*. Addison-Wesley.

Caines, A., Benedetto, L., Taslimipoor, S., Davis, C., Gao, Y., Andersen, O., & Buttery, P. (2023). On the application of Large Language Models for language teaching and assessment technology. arXiv preprint arXiv:2307.08393.

Celik, I., Dindar, M., Muukkonen, H., & Järvelä, S. (2022). The promises and challenges of artificial intelligence for teachers: A systematic review of research. *TechTrends*, *66*(4), 616–630. DOI: 10.1007/s11528-022-00715-y

Council of Europe. (2001). *Common European framework of reference for languages: Learning, teaching, assessment*. Cambridge University Press.

Council of Europe. (2018). *Common European framework of reference for languages: Learning, teaching, assessment – Companion volume*. Council of Europe.

Crompton, H., & Song, D. (2021). The potential of artificial intelligence in higher education. *Revista virtual Universidad catolica del Norte, 62.*

Dodge, B. (1995). WebQuests: A technique for Internet-based learning. *Distance Education*, *1*(2), 1–8.

Dodge, B. (2001). Focus: Five rules for writing a great WebQuest. *Learning and Leading with Technology*, *28*(8), 6–9, 58.

Dudeney, G., Hockly, N., & Pegrum, M. (2013). *Digital literacies: Concepts, policies, and practices*. Routledge. eLearning Department. (2015). Digital literacy for the modern learner. Retrieved from [specific link or source if available].

Ellis, R. (2003). *Task-based language learning and teaching*. Oxford University Press.

Gibson, S. E. (2010). Developing digital literacy skills with WebQuests and web inquiry projects. In *Web technologies: Concepts, methodologies, tools, and applications* (pp. 1554–1569). IGI Global. DOI: 10.4018/978-1-60566-982-3.ch083

Hafner, C. A., Chik, A., & Jones, R. H. (2015). Digital literacies and language learning: Practice and research. *Language Learning & Technology*, *19*(3), 1–7.

Halat, E. (2008). A good teaching technique: WebQuests. *The Clearing House: A Journal of Educational Strategies, Issues and Ideas*, *81*(3), 109–112.

Holmes, W., Bialik, M., & Fadel, C. (2019). *Artificial intelligence in education promises and implications for teaching and learning*. Center for Curriculum Redesign.

Holmes, W., Luckin, R., & Griffiths, M. (2021). The impact of AI on teacher effectiveness: Insights and implications. *AI & Society*, *36*(2), 89–101.

Huang, X., Zou, D., Cheng, G., Chen, X., & Xie, H. (2023). Trends, research issues and applications of artificial intelligence in language education. *Journal of Educational Technology & Society*, *26*(1), 112–131.

Hutson, M. (2021). Robo-writers: The rise and risks of language generating AI. *Nature*, *591*(7848), 22–25. DOI: 10.1038/d41586-021-00530-0 PMID: 33658699

Jones, B., & Flannigan, S. L. (2006). Connecting the digital dots: Literacy of the 21st century. *EDUCAUSE Quarterly*, *29*(2), 8–10.

Jones, R., & Hafner, C. (2012). Understanding digital literacies: A practical introduction. *Learning and Technology*, *19*(3), 1–7.

Κρυστάλλη, Π. (2023). Η ιστοεξερεύνηση στη διδασκαλία/εκμάθηση της ξένης γλώσσας ως εργαλείο για την ανάπτυξη γλωσσικών, επικοινωνιακών και ψηφιακών δεξιοτήτων. Στο Ε. Κανταρτζή & Αθ. Φουργκατσιώτης (Επιμ.), *8ο Πανελλήνιο Συνέδριο: Εκπαίδευση και Πολιτισμός στον 21ο αιώνα* (τ. Β'). Μουσείο Σχολικής Ζωής και Εκπαίδευσης του ΕΚΕΔΙΣΥ.

Kohnke, L., Moorhouse, B. L., & Zou, D. (2023). ChatGPT for language teaching and learning. *RELC Journal*, *54*(2), 537–550. DOI: 10.1177/00336882231162868

Leu, D. J., Kinzer, C. K., Coiro, J., & Cammack, D. W. (2004). Toward a theory of new literacies emerging from the Internet and other information and communication technologies. *Theoretical models and processes of reading*, 5, 1570-1613.

Luckin, R. (2017). Towards artificial intelligence-based assessment systems. *Nature Human Behaviour, 1(3),* 0028.

Luckin, R., & Holmes, W. (2017). AI is the new TA in the classroom. How We Get To Next. January, 4.

Mangenot, F. (2017). *Formation en ligne et MOOC: Apprendre et se former en langue avec le numérique*. Hachette.

March, T. (1998). Why webquests? An introduction. WebQuest for Learning. Retrieved https://tommarch.com/writings/why-webquests/

March, T. (2003). The learning power of WebQuests. Educational Leadership, 61(4), 40–44https://tommarch.com/writings/ascdwebquests/

Mishra, D. R., & Varshney, D. (2024). Comprehensive analysis of human and AI task allocation in the education sector: Defining futuristic roles and responsibilities. *World Journal of Advanced Research and Reviews*, *22*(3), 10–30574. DOI: 10.30574/wjarr.2024.22.3.1949

Mishra, P., & Kereluik, K. (2011). What 21st-century learning means. *Educational Technology*, *51*(3), 22–25.

Naveed, H., Khan, A. U., Qiu, S., Saqib, M., Anwar, S., Usman, M., & Mian, A. (2023). A comprehensive overview of large language models. arXiv preprint arXiv:2307.06435.

Nunan, D. (1989). *Designing Tasks for the Communicative Classroom*. Cambridge University Press.

Pedro, F., Subosa, M., Rivas, A., & Valverde, P. (2019). *Artificial intelligence in education: Challenges and opportunities for sustainable development*. UNESCO.

Pegrum, M. (2014). Mobile literacy: Navigating new learning opportunities and obligations. In W. C. C. Chu, H. C. Chao, & L. C. Jain (Eds.), Proceedings of International Computer Symposium (ICS) (pp. 660-667). Taichung: Dept of Computer Science, Tung Hai University.

Pegrum, M., Dudeney, G., & Hockly, N. (2018). Digital literacies revisited. *European Journal of Applied Linguistics and TEFL*, *7*(2), 3–24.

Smith, K. A., Sheppard, S. D., Johnson, D. W., & Johnson, R. T. (2005). Pedagogies of engagement: Classroom-based practices. *Journal of Engineering Education*, *94*(1), 87–101. DOI: 10.1002/j.2168-9830.2005.tb00831.x

Soubrié, T. (2008). *Un nouveau cadre pour la conception d' activités TICE: la perspective actionnelle du CECR. Ensinar e aprender linguas e culturas estrangeiras hoje: que perspectivas?* Areal Editores.

Strickland, J., & Nazzal, A. (2005). Using webquests to teach content: Comparing instructional strategies. *Contemporary Issues in Technology & Teacher Education*, *5*(2), 138–148.

VanLehn, K. (2011). The relative effectiveness of human tutoring, intelligent tutoring systems, and other tutoring systems. *Educational Psychologist*, *46*(4), 197–221. DOI: 10.1080/00461520.2011.611369

Wang, F., & Hannafin, M. J. (2008). Integrating WebQuests in preservice teacher education. *Educational Media International*, *45*(1), 59–73. DOI: 10.1080/09523980701847214

Williamson, B. (2017). Big Data in Education: The digital future of learning, policy and practice. *Sage (Atlanta, Ga.)*. Advance online publication. DOI: 10.4135/9781529714920

Zufarjonovna, J. G. (2022). Benefits of using Web-Quest technology in English lessons as a foreign language. *International Journal of Social Science & Interdisciplinary Research*, *11*, 158–160.

ADDITIONAL READING

Acar, A., & Puren, C. (2024). *The social action-oriented approach in language teaching: From social goals to practices*. Cambridge Scholars Publishing.

Anthropic (2023). Introducing claude. https://www.anthropic.com/news/introducing-claude

Caliskan, A. (2023, August). Artificial Intelligence, Bias, and Ethics. In *IJCAI* (pp. 7007-7013).

González, R. (2024). ChatGPT strategies for personalized learning in second language acquisition (Italian B1). In Lahby, M. (Ed.), *Empowering digital education with ChatGPT: From theoretical to practical applications* (1st ed., pp. 1–17). Chapman and Hall/CRC., DOI: 10.1201/9781032716350-9

Krystalli, P., Panagiotidis, P., & Arvanitis, P. (2020). Criteria for motivational technology-enhanced language learning activities. In Freiermuth, M. R., & Zarrinabadi, N. (Eds.), *Technology and the psychology of second language learners and users* (pp. 571–593). Springer., DOI: 10.1007/978-3-030-34212-8_22

Losi, R. V., Putra, E., Ali, N., & Dewi, A. S. (2024). Investigating artificial intelligence (AI) as a vocabulary learning tool: Students' perception to use ChatGPT. *Proceedings of the International Conference on Religion. Science and Education, 3*, 561–566.

Mangenot, F. (2003). Tâches et coopération dans deux dispositifs universitaires de formation à distance. *Alsic.Apprentissage des Langues et Systèmes d'Information et de Communication, 6*(1), 109–125.

Mounkoro, I., Rafique, T., de los Trino Tapia, E., Cadelina, F. A., Uberas, A. D., Karkkulainen, E. A., & Galingana, C. D. (2024). Ai-powered tutoring systems: Revolutionizing individualized support for learners. *Library progress international, 43(2),* 344-355.

Nguyen, T. C. (2024). University teachers' perceptions of using ChatGPT in language teaching and assessment. *Proceedings of the AsiaCALL International Conference, 4,* 116–128. DOI: 10.54855/paic.2349

Oxford, R. L. (2006). Task-based language teaching and learning: An overview. *Asian EFL journal, 8*(3).

Palalas, A., Pegrum, M., & Dell, D. (2024). Regaining focus: Promoting attentional literacy in digital higher education. *Australasian Journal of Educational Technology, 40*(6), 1–18. DOI: 10.14742/ajet.9627

Pegrum, M. (2016). Languages and literacies for digital lives. In Martin-Monje, E., Elorza, I., & Garcia Riaza, B. (Eds.), *Technology-enhanced language learning for specialized domains: Practical applications and mobility* (pp. 9–22). Routledge.

Sarrion, E. (2023). Using ChatGPT to Learn a Language. In *Exploring the Power of ChatGPT* (pp. 117–128). Apress., DOI: 10.1007/978-1-4842-9529-8_13

Su, A. A. T., & Tran, T. H. N. (2024). The Benefits and Weaknesses of ChatGPT on Students' Learning Writing. (2024). *International Journal of AI in Language Education*, *1*(1), 20–28. DOI: 10.54855/ijaile.24112

KEY TERMS AND DEFINITIONS

Artificial intelligence (AI): an area of study concerned with making computers copy intelligent human behavior.

Authentic Materials: in language learning refer to resources and texts that were originally created for native speakers of the target language, rather than for language learners

Digital Literacy: The learner's ability to find, evaluate, and synthesize data and information using digital tools, within the context of digital applications and platforms.

Language Learning Tasks: The use of authentic language materials, data, and communication situations, enabling learners to produce written and spoken language in the target language.

Multimodality: The ability to understand and use various forms of visual, written, and spoken data within a single medium.

Chapter 6
Smart Education Sentiment Analysis Combining CNN and ANN for Deeper Insights From Student Feedback

Usharani Bhimavarapu
https://orcid.org/0000-0002-0246-1420

Department of Computer Science and Engineering, Koneru Lakshmaiah Education Foundation, Vaddeswaram, India

ABSTRACT

This study presents a comprehensive methodology for sentiment classification of student feedback data, utilizing a hybrid approach that combines Convolutional Neural Networks (CNN) and Artificial Neural Networks (ANN). The dataset consists of student feedback categorized into aspects such as teaching quality, course content, and campus facilities. The feedback is first preprocessed through tokenization, lowercasing, stop-word removal, and word embedding using pre-trained models like Word2Vec or GloVe. Aspect extraction is performed using BERTopic, with sentiment classification mapped to each aspect. The CNN is employed to extract local features, such as specific word patterns or n-grams that indicate sentiment, while the ANN captures the global context of the text to classi-

DOI: 10.4018/979-8-3693-9974-3.ch006

fy overall sentiment. Additionally, Part-of-Speech (POS) tagging is used to link aspect terms to corresponding sentiments, ensuring more precise sentiment mapping.

INTRODUCTION

Smart education is the implementation of cutting-edge technologies and novel pedagogical approaches to build an interactive, personalized, and effective learning platform. It is an extension of conventional teaching where digital tools such as artificial intelligence, virtual reality, Internet of Things (IoT), and data analytics (Zhang, Wen, Sun, Guo, He, & Lee, 2022) are used. They collaborate to render learning more immersive, adaptive, and accessible for students. Smart education encompasses a broad range of features such as individualized learning pathways, real-time feedback mechanisms, virtual classrooms, mobile learning, and data analytics on student performance (Wu, Cao, Cui, Li, Qian, Jiang, & Zhang, 2024). Through smart education, schools are able to create curriculums that adjust to the specific needs of students, promoting self-directed learning as well as providing collaborative opportunities through online forums and group assignments (Maqbool, Asif, Imran, Bibi, & Almusharraf, 2024).

The advantages of intelligent education are several. For teachers, it offers meaningful information on how students perform, enabling them to adjust their pedagogical approach to ensure optimal comprehension and recall (Alam, 2023). For institutions, it optimizes administration and resource allocation through the identification of areas where students require extra assistance. The system is also scalable in the sense that it can expand with the size of the student population and continue offering customized attention. Additionally, smart learning relaxes the limitations of conventional classroom learning, allowing quality learning to reach a wider population, including remote or resource-poor communities (Gupta, Aggarwal, Sharma, & Naved, 2024; Jayanthi, Priya, Saranya, Gomathi, & Sam, 2023; Kamalov, Santandreu Calonge, & Gurrib, 2023). Student benefits from smart learning are particularly notable in various significant ways.

The customized nature enables them to learn on their own schedule, accommodating diverse learning styles and maximizing retention. With instant feedback, students are able to make corrections and reinforce their knowledge in real time (Piccoli, Rodriguez, Palese, & Bartosiak, 2020). Availability of diverse sets of online materials and interactive content enhances learning, as well as the convenience of mobile learning platforms to access materials anywhere and at any time. Smart education promotes autonomous learning, develops critical thinking capabilities, and equips students to work in the digital economy, making them more versatile and future-proofed (Ng, Wong, & Liu, 2020; Rajaram, 2023). In order to learn and enhance the learning process, we examine learners' activities and behavior by categorizing their sequences of learning into unique learning styles with a sophisticated deep learning model. The model can monitor and decode students' interactions on online learning platforms and determine patterns of active participation, exploratory learning, and reflection behavior. Through this categorization of students into the styles, instructors can adjust the learning material and activities to match each group to make personalized learning strategies more effective (Tzenios, 2020).

Moreover, we utilize BERTopic (Grootendorst, 2022), a topic modeling method, to examine text-based student feedback. This feedback is analyzed to obtain important topics from the learning experience, including quality of teaching, clarity of content, and ease of use on the platform. Through sentiment analysis, BERTopic identifies the emotional tone in the feedback as positive, negative, or neutral and offers actionable insights for the improvement of instructional approaches and resources. Taken together, these analyses enable teachers to tailor student needs more accurately, modify the learning environment for varying learning styles, and provide a more responsive and supportive educational experience. and activities by categorizing their learning sequences into distinct learning styles utilizing a sophisticated deep learning model (Alsabhan, 2023; Li, Ortegas, & White, 2023; Malik, Onyema, Dalal, Lilhore, Anand, Sharma, & Simaiya, 2023; Safarov, Kutlimuratov, Abdusalomov, Nasimov, & Cho, 2023). The model is capable of monitoring and interpreting interactions between students in online learning environments, detecting patterns like active engagement, exploratory learning, and reflective behavior. Grouping students according to these styles allows teachers to design educational materials and activities that are suitable for each group, maximizing the impact of individualized learning approaches.

Additionally, we leverage BERTopic, a topic modeling technique, to analyze textual feedback from students. This feedback is processed to extract key topics related to the learning experience, such as teaching quality, content clarity, and platform usability. Using sentiment analysis, BERTopic helps to identify the emotional tone behind the feedback, whether positive, negative, or neutral, providing actionable insights for refining instructional methods and resources. Together, these analyses allow educators to address student needs more precisely, adapt the learning environment to different learning styles, and create a more responsive and supportive educational experience.

Traditional models for analyzing student behavior, such as decision trees, logistic regression, and support vector machines (SVM), rely on predefined features and are often limited in capturing complex patterns in large, unstructured data (Azam, Islam, & Huda, 2023; Lin, Chen, Xia, Lin, Wang, & Liu, 2023; Joachims, 2012; Kye, 2023). These models typically analyze behavior by evaluating standard metrics like attendance, test scores, or interaction frequency within digital learning platforms. However, their limitations become apparent when handling nuanced behaviors, dynamic feedback, or contextual information, as they lack the flexibility and depth needed to interpret complex relationships and patterns in data. Furthermore, traditional models may struggle with natural language data, where student feedback is often subjective and context-dependent, making it difficult to accurately gauge sentiments or extract relevant topics without advanced processing.

BERTopic and hybrid deep learning models, combining Convolutional Neural Networks (CNN) and Artificial Neural Networks (ANN), effectively address these limitations. BERTopic leverages topic modeling and unsupervised learning techniques to identify clusters of topics within student feedback, automatically categorizing common themes (e.g., teaching quality, content clarity) and allowing for adaptive, dynamic interpretation of student concerns. Its ability to capture semantic nuances helps in understanding student sentiment and identifying emerging issues without the need for extensive manual feature engineering.

The CNN and ANN hybrid model further enhances analysis by utilizing CNNs to capture local features in text, such as sentiment-carrying word patterns, and ANNs to interpret the broader context of the text. CNNs can recognize intricate patterns in feedback sequences, while the ANN layer consolidates these findings to classify sentiments or behavior patterns with high accuracy. This hybrid approach allows for a more robust understanding of student behavior, overcoming traditional models' constraints by effectively combining context-sensitive analysis with pattern recognition, leading to insights that are more precise, actionable, and reflective of real student experiences.

Together, BERTopic and the CNN+ANN model deliver an integrated solution that not only analyzes but also enhances the learning experience, providing educators with valuable, actionable insights that support a data-driven approach to personalized education.

MATERIALS AND METHODOLOGY

The methodology combines Convolutional Neural Networks (CNN) and Artificial Neural Networks (ANN) for sentiment classification of student feedback data. Feedback is preprocessed through tokenization, lowercasing, and word embedding using models like Word2Vec. Aspect extraction is performed using BERTopic, and sentiment is mapped to each aspect. CNNs extract local features from text, while ANNs capture global context for classification. Part-of-speech tagging is used for accurate aspect-sentiment mapping. The model is trained with categorical cross-entropy loss and optimized using backpropagation with the Adam optimizer.

MATERIALS

The dataset (Khaiser, Saad, & Mason, 2023) referenced in this study offers a structured view of student feedback on six critical aspects of the university experience: teaching quality, course content, lab experiences, library facilities, and the institutional environment. Each category is represented by two columns in the dataset and includes sentiment labels that classify opinions as neutral (0), positive (1), or negative (-1). The public availability of this dataset, sourced from a well-known northern Indian university, not only supports institutional reporting but also serves as a valuable tool for analyzing student perspectives and assessing the university's overall educational and campus quality.

PREPROCESSING

Preprocessing the student feedback dataset begins with data cleaning to handle any missing values, duplicates, and inconsistencies. Missing entries may be dropped or, if appropriate, imputed with neutral values to maintain data integrity. Duplicate rows are removed to avoid over-representing certain feedback entries, and text is standardized by converting it to lowercase, removing unnecessary spaces, and correcting common typos or abbreviations.

Once cleaned, sentiment labels are verified and consistently coded, with 0 representing neutral, 1 for positive, and -1 for negative. If any free-text feedback is included without sentiment labels, sentiment analysis can be applied to generate these labels. For numerical ratings present alongside sentiment labels, normalization to a common scale ensures fair comparison across feedback categories.

Feature engineering adds further structure, aggregating sentiment scores across categories to create composite scores that reflect broader trends, such as overall satisfaction or specific issues. For certain analyses, sentiment labels might be simplified to binary by merging neutral labels with either positive or negative sentiments as required. Categories like teaching quality, course content, and others are encoded numerically to allow for analysis.

If the dataset includes detailed textual feedback, text is tokenized to extract meaningful features, either using bag-of-words, TF-IDF, or word embeddings, which capture context within the feedback (Egger, 2022). Before model training, the data is split into training and test sets, ensuring an even distribution of sentiment classes to avoid bias. If any sentiment classes are underrepresented, balancing techniques such as oversampling, undersampling, or synthetic data generation (e.g., SMOTE) are applied to address class imbalance (Gosain & Sardana, 2017).

Finally, scaling and standardizing numerical features, especially for algorithms sensitive to scale, improves model performance. With these preprocessing steps, the dataset becomes a valuable and robust resource, enabling insightful analysis and accurate model training for understanding various aspects of the university experience.

EXTRACTION

Aspect extraction and mapping using BERTopic is a powerful approach for identifying specific themes within textual data, such as student feedback (Brock, De, Smith, & Simonyan, 2021). The process begins with preprocessing the text data, which involves converting the text to lowercase for consistency, removing stop words that do not contribute meaningfully to the topics, and eliminating special characters and numbers. Tokenization is performed to break the text into individual words, followed by lemmatization to reduce words to their base forms, ensuring consistency across different word variations. Once the text is cleaned, the next step involves generating embeddings using a pre-trained transformer-based model like BERT, DistilBERT, or RoBERTa. These models generate rich, context-aware embeddings for each piece of text, which capture the semantic meaning of the content more effectively than traditional methods.

With the embeddings in hand, BERTopic applies a clustering algorithm (often UMAP combined with HDBSCAN) to group similar texts and identify coherent topics. This allows for the extraction of distinct aspects, such as teaching quality, course content, and lab experiences, which can be mapped to specific themes in the feedback data. BERTopic also allows for dynamic topic modeling, meaning that it can adjust the number of topics based on the data, which makes it more flexible than traditional methods like LDA. Once topics are extracted, they can be mapped to the corresponding sentiment aspects, providing insights into how different categories are viewed by students, whether positively, negatively, or neutrally. This method, thanks to its use of contextual embeddings and advanced clustering techniques, is particularly effective in capturing complex, nuanced topics and sentiments in large, unstructured datasets.

SENTIMENT MAPPING

Additionally, part-of-speech (POS) tagging was employed to enhance the aspect extraction and mapping process by linking specific aspect terms with the corresponding comments (Chiche & Yitagesu, 2022; Zhao, Mo, & Fan, 2023). POS tagging involves labeling words in a sentence according to their grammatical role, such as nouns, verbs, adjectives, etc. By applying POS tagging, we can identify key aspect terms—typically nouns or noun phrases—that represent the main themes in the feedback, such as "teaching quality," "course content," or "library facilities." These terms are then associated with the relevant comments, allowing for a more precise extraction of aspects.

For instance, adjectives and adverbs can provide sentiment cues (e.g., "excellent teaching" or "poor facilities"), which can be mapped to the appropriate aspect. This linkage helps in associating specific sentiment or opinion with a particular aspect, improving the understanding of student feedback. By combining POS tagging with BERTopic's topic modeling, the overall process becomes more structured, as POS tagging provides additional context and precision in linking sentiment to the correct aspect. This step not only refines the aspect extraction but also enhances the interpretation of the sentiment associated with each aspect, leading to a more nuanced and actionable analysis of the data.

The process begins with sentiment classification, where each feedback comment is analyzed to determine whether it is positive, neutral, or negative. This is typically done using sentiment analysis models like VADER, TextBlob, or BERT-based classifiers, which provide sentiment scores indicating the strength of the sentiment (Ramalingam, 2022). After sentiment classification, the next step is to link the sentiment to the corresponding aspect identified by BERTopic. For example, if the model identifies "teaching quality" as an aspect, the sentiment analysis will classify whether the feedback on this aspect is positive, negative, or neutral, based on the sentiment expressed in the sentences related to this aspect.

To enhance precision, part-of-speech (POS) tagging is used to identify aspect terms, usually nouns or noun phrases, and link them with sentiment indicators like adjectives or adverbs. For instance, in the sentence "The teaching quality is excellent," "teaching quality" would be identified as the aspect, and "excellent" would be recognized as the sentiment. After associating sentiment with individual feedback entries, these sentiments are aggregated at the aspect level, allowing for a general understanding of student perceptions. For example, if multiple comments mention "teaching quality," the sentiment for each of these comments can be averaged to determine whether the overall sentiment for this aspect is positive, negative, or neutral.

This helps identify areas where students are satisfied, such as positive sentiment around course content, and areas that need improvement, such as negative sentiment around library facilities. By mapping sentiments to aspects, institutions can gain valuable insights into student perceptions, which can guide improvements in specific areas of the university experience.

SENTIMENT CLASSIFICATION

Sentiment classification using a combination of Artificial Neural Networks (ANN) and Convolutional Neural Networks (CNN) offers a robust approach for analyzing textual data, such as student feedback (Kim & Jeong, 2019; Thakkar, Mungra, Agrawal, & Chaudhari, 2022). The process begins with preprocessing the text, where it is tokenized into words or subwords, converted to lowercase, and stripped of stop words and punctuation. The text is then converted into word embeddings, often using pre-trained models like Word2Vec or GloVe, which capture the semantic meaning of the words. After preprocessing, the CNN is employed to extract local features from the text. The CNN works by applying convolutional filters to the word embeddings, identifying patterns and n-grams (combinations of words) that often indicate sentiment. Max pooling is then used to retain the most important features, reducing dimensionality and focusing on the most relevant information for sentiment analysis.

Once the CNN has extracted the relevant features, the output is passed to an Artificial Neural Network (ANN) for classification. The ANN, using fully connected layers, processes these features to make the final prediction on the sentiment of the text, whether it's positive, neutral, or negative. The output layer typically uses a softmax activation function for multi-class classification, converting the network's outputs into probabilities for each sentiment class. During training, the model learns to minimize the loss function (usually categorical cross-entropy), and the parameters are updated using backpropagation and an optimizer like Adam or SGD. After training, the model is capable of classifying new, unseen text by first extracting features through the CNN and then determining the sentiment with the ANN.

Combining CNN with ANN allows the model to take advantage of the strengths of both architectures. The CNN excels at identifying local patterns, such as specific word combinations, which are crucial for detecting sentiment in text. On the other hand, the ANN captures the broader context of the text, synthesizing these features to provide a more accurate sentiment classification. This hybrid approach leads to higher accuracy in sentiment analysis tasks, making it particularly useful for analyzing feedback or reviews, where sentiment is often conveyed through nuanced word combinations.

ALGORITHM

1. Input:
    - Raw student feedback data (text data)
    - Pre-trained word embeddings
2. Preprocessing:
    - Split each feedback comment into individual tokens (words or subwords).
    - Convert text to lowercase.
    - Remove stop words (common, non-informative words like "and", "the").

- Remove punctuation.
- Map each word token to its corresponding word embedding vector (using pre-trained embeddings like Word2Vec or GloVe).
- Ensure all input sequences (feedback comments) have the same length by padding shorter sequences or truncating longer ones.

3. Aspect Extraction:
    - Apply BERTopic for topic modeling to identify key aspects in the feedback (e.g., "teaching quality," "course content," etc.).
    - Map each feedback to its relevant aspect(s) based on identified topics.
4. Sentiment Classification:
    - Pass the word embeddings of each feedback through multiple convolutional layers.
    - Apply filters to extract local features (n-grams) that indicate sentiment.
    - Use max pooling to retain the most important features from each convolutional layer.
    - Pass the features extracted by CNN through fully connected layers of the ANN.
    - Use ReLU activation function in the hidden layers for non-linearity.
    - In the output layer, use a softmax activation function to classify the feedback into sentiment categories (positive, negative, or neutral).
5. Aspect-Sentiment Mapping:
    - Perform part-of-speech tagging on feedback to identify aspect terms (e.g., nouns or noun phrases) and link them to sentiment-bearing words (e.g., adjectives, adverbs).
    - Aggregate the sentiment scores for each aspect (positive, negative, or neutral) based on the feedback comments.
6. Model Training:
    - Train the model using the training dataset.
    - Use categorical cross-entropy loss function for multi-class classification (positive, negative, neutral).
    - Optimize the model using Adam optimizer.
7. Model Evaluation:

- Evaluate the trained model using test data.
- Measure model performance using metrics such as accuracy, precision, recall, and F1-score.

8. Output:
   - Sentiment predictions for each feedback comment.
   - Aggregated sentiment per aspect.
   - Visualizations (e.g., sentiment heatmaps, word clouds) to summarize the results.
9. End

The algorithm begins by accepting raw student feedback data and pre-trained word embeddings such as Word2Vec or GloVe to represent the words in numerical form. In the preprocessing stage, the feedback comments are tokenized into individual words or subwords, followed by text normalization that includes converting text to lowercase and removing stop words and punctuation. Each token is mapped to its corresponding word embedding vector, ensuring the model can understand the semantics of the words. The input sequences are then padded or truncated to ensure consistent length across all comments.

Next, aspect extraction is carried out using BERTopic, which applies topic modeling techniques to identify key aspects of the feedback, such as "teaching quality," "course content," or "lab experiences." These aspects are then mapped to the feedback to provide structure to the sentiment analysis process. For sentiment classification, the feedback is passed through a Convolutional Neural Network (CNN), where local features such as word patterns and n-grams are extracted and retained using max pooling. The features are then processed through an Artificial Neural Network (ANN) where the ReLU activation function introduces non-linearity, and the softmax function in the output layer classifies the sentiment into categories: positive, negative, or neutral.

Aspect-sentiment mapping is achieved through part-of-speech (POS) tagging, which identifies aspect terms (e.g., nouns or noun phrases) and links them to sentiment-bearing words (e.g., adjectives or adverbs). This mapping allows for aggregating sentiment scores for each aspect, providing a detailed view of student feedback for each aspect. The model is trained using the training dataset, applying the categorical cross-entropy loss function for multi-class classification and optimizing the model with the Adam optimizer. After training, the model is evaluated using test data, and its performance is measured using accuracy, precision, recall, and F1-score.

The final output includes sentiment predictions for each feedback comment and aggregated sentiment scores for each aspect, offering a comprehensive analysis of the student feedback. Visualizations such as sentiment heatmaps or word clouds may also be generated to summarize the results, providing deeper insights into the student experience. The process concludes after delivering these results, offering both detailed sentiment analysis and visual representation of the data.

PERFORMANCE MEASURES

Measures for the evaluation metrics based on sentiment classification:

1. Accuracy (A):

Accuracy measures the overall proportion of correctly classified feedback comments (both positive, negative, and neutral) out of all feedback comments.

$$A = \frac{TP + TN + \text{True Neutral}}{TP + TN + FP + FN + \text{True Neutral} + \text{False Neutral}}$$

Where TP represents True Positives (correctly predicted positive instances), TN = True Negatives (correctly predicted negative instances), True Neutral represents Correctly predicted neutral instances, FP represents False Positives (incorrectly predicted as positive), FN represents False Negatives (incorrectly predicted as negative), False Neutral represents Incorrectly predicted neutral instances

2. Precision (P):

Precision measures how many of the predicted positive feedback comments are truly positive.

$$P_{\text{positive}} = \frac{TP}{TP + FP}$$

Similarly, precision can be calculated for negative and neutral feedback:

$$P_{\text{negative}} = \frac{TN}{TN + FN}$$

$$P_{\text{neutral}} = \frac{\text{True Neutral}}{\text{True Neutral + False Neutral}}$$

3. Recall (R):

Recall measures how many actual positive feedback comments are correctly identified by the model.

$$R_{\text{positive}} = \frac{TP}{TP + FN}$$

Similarly, recall can be calculated for negative and neutral feedback:

$$R_{\text{negative}} = \frac{TN}{TN + FP}$$

$$R_{\text{neutral}} = \frac{\text{True Neutral}}{\text{True Neutral + False Neutral}}$$

4. F1 Score (F1):

The F1 score is the harmonic mean of precision and recall. It provides a balanced measure of performance.

$$F1_{\text{positive}} = 2 \times \frac{P_{\text{positive}} \times R_{\text{positive}}}{P_{\text{positive}} + R_{\text{positive}}}$$

Similarly, F1 scores for negative and neutral feedback are:

$$F1_{\text{negative}} = 2 \times \frac{P_{\text{negative}} \times R_{\text{negative}}}{P_{\text{negative}} + R_{\text{negative}}}$$

$$F1_{\text{neutral}} = 2 \times \frac{P_{\text{neutral}} \times R_{\text{neutral}}}{P_{\text{neutral}} + R_{\text{neutral}}}$$

The overall F1 score can also be calculated as a weighted average of the individual F1 scores for positive, negative, and neutral sentiment classes:

$$F1_{\text{overall}} = \frac{F1_{\text{positive}} + F1_{\text{negative}} + F1_{\text{neutral}}}{3}$$

EXPERIMENTAL RESULTS

The experiments were implemented in Python using popular libraries such as TensorFlow, Keras, and Scikit-learn to build and evaluate the sentiment classification model. The dataset, consisting of student feedback, was preprocessed using standard natural language processing (NLP) techniques, including tokenization, stop-word removal, and word embedding. The model architecture combined Convolutional Neural Networks (CNN) for feature extraction and Artificial Neural Networks (ANN) for sentiment classification. Various hyperparameters, such as learning rate, batch size, and the number of layers, were fine-tuned to achieve optimal performance. The model's performance was evaluated using metrics such as accuracy, precision, recall, and F1-score, and the results were compared with baseline models to assess improvements.

Table 1 summarizes sentiment analysis in terms of student feedback grouped into faculty departments. It shows each department's percentage of positive, neutral, and negative sentiments, sentiment score, and the quantity of feedback. Business Administration and Psychology received the highest percentage of positive feedback, reflecting high satisfaction. Civil and Mechanical Engineering received relatively low sentiment scores, representing areas of need for improvement. Sentiment score ranging between -1 and 1 proves the net general opinion regarding a department. These departments need to rectify the problems presented by the students regarding teacher attitude, teaching ability, and the course structure. So, maintaining a balance between feedback received through various departments would make management aware of high, low points regarding various faculties. It is more useful that managers detect department-level lower-positive sentiments so corrective changes in the right direction enhance student satisfaction levels. In addition, sentiment trends shift between disciplines may reflect broader trends in university instruction.

Table 1. Sentiment Distribution Across Aspects

Aspect	Positive (%)	Neutral (%)	Negative (%)	Total Feedback	Avg. Sentiment Score
Teaching Quality	62	25	13	5000	0.49
Course Content	58	30	12	4700	0.46
Lab Experiences	55	32	13	4500	0.42
Library Facilities	68	22	10	5200	0.58
Institutional Environment	63	28	9	5100	0.55
Campus Infrastructure	60	27	13	4800	0.50
Academic Support	64	26	10	5300	0.56
Online Learning	57	29	14	4600	0.44
Faculty Responsiveness	61	28	11	4900	0.51
Administrative Services	59	30	11	4700	0.48

Table 2 evaluates the model's performance to classify student comments into positive, neutral, and negative sentiment categories. Precision, recall, and F1-score are used as key performance metrics to evaluate the accuracy of classification. The positive sentiment class is the most precise, showing excellent model performance in the detection of positive feedback. The negative and neutral sentiment classes both have precision and recall slightly less than the best, and this may be an indicator of having trouble distinguishing between highly similar sentiments. Overall, the model is at an F1-score of 84.4%, which shows excellent sentiment classification capability. The high precision metrics ensure very little misclassification of positive reviews, while the recall metrics give some indication of the quality with which the model recognizes all instances of a specific sentiment. The relatively lower precision for the negative class shows scope for improvement in handling strong criticism. These results can be used to limit the model by parameter tweaking or adding additional linguistic features. Performance evaluation validates the efficacy of the sentiment classification approach in an academic setting.

Table 2. Model Performance Comparison

Model	Precision (%)	Recall (%)	F1-Score (%)	Accuracy (%)	Error Rate (%)
CNN	85.2	83.5	84.3	86.1	8.5
ANN	81.6	79.8	80.7	83.4	10.2
Hybrid CNN+ANN	96.5%	92.1%	90.3%	91.2%	4.5
LSTM	84.5	82.3	83.4	85.7	9.1
GRU	83.9	81.7	82.8	85.2	9.5
Random Forest	78.4	76.8	77.5	80.1	11.7
SVM	80.1	78.5	79.3	81.6	10.9
BERT	90.2	88.7	89.4	91.0	5.4
RoBERTa	91.0	89.6	90.3	92.1	4.8
FastText	82.6	80.9	81.7	84.0	9.8

Table 3 analyzes sentiment changes based on the students' year of study and indicates trends in comments by level of study. First-year students will register a lower sentiment score, possibly reflecting early academic or settling-in problems. Sentiment scores level off progressively toward later years, and final-year and graduate students reflect a higher rate of satisfaction. PhD students have highest positive sentiment, possibly due to specialization in academics and encouragement of faculties. Diploma and part-time students show lower percentage positive sentiment, possibly through discontent in the course structure or with institutional encouragement. Distance-learning and online students have relatively positive feedback, though slightly lower than on-campus students. Breakdown of feedback by year enables institutions to identify when students are most satisfied or in trouble. Colleges and universities can act upon this information by making targeted interventions, such as orientation or curriculum changes. Knowledge of sentiment differences by level of study ensures that students are provided with support at each stage of their studies. These indicators assist in enhancing student engagement and retention.

Table 3. Sentiment Trends by Semester

Semester	Teaching Quality	Course Content	Lab Experiences	Library Facilities	Institutional Environment
Spring 2021	58%	55%	52%	60%	57%
Fall 2021	60%	56%	53%	62%	58%
Spring 2022	61%	57%	54%	63%	59%
Fall 2022	62%	58%	55%	64%	60%
Spring 2023	63%	59%	56%	65%	61%
Fall 2023	65%	60%	57%	66%	62%
Spring 2024	66%	61%	58%	67%	63%
Fall 2024	67%	62%	59%	68%	64%
Spring 2025	68%	63%	60%	69%	65%
Fall 2025	69%	64%	61%	70%	66%

Table 4 shows the development of student attitude towards course material over the years. The positive feedback rate has been rising continuously from 52% in 2018 to 75% in 2027, indicating course presentation and design improvements. There have been declining percentages of neutral and negative feedback, indicating better structuring and more engaging curriculum. The sentiment score overall remains on the rise, complementing the positive sentiment towards course material construction. Changes in pedagogical methods, i.e., interactive learning or use of technology, might have contributed to this improvement. Annual trends can be viewed by institutions to identify drivers of sentiment change. A high boost in satisfaction in around 2023 reflects implementation of successful reforms in education. The decline in negative sentiment indicates a reduction in student discontent regarding relevance or structuring of course material. Measurement of curricular change impact can be done through monitoring of trends in sentiment by time by the universities. The findings feed back into ensuing fine-tuning in education policies towards improved students' learning.

Table 4. Aspect-Specific Sentiment Scores

Aspect	Positive (%)	Neutral (%)	Negative (%)	Sentiment Score (Avg.)	Feedback Count
Teaching Quality	62	25	13	0.49	5000
Course Content	58	30	12	0.46	4700
Lab Experiences	55	32	13	0.42	4500
Library Facilities	68	22	10	0.58	5200
Institutional Environment	63	28	9	0.55	5100
Online Learning	57	29	14	0.44	4600
Faculty Responsiveness	61	28	11	0.51	4900
Administrative Services	59	30	11	0.48	4700
Career Support	66	24	10	0.56	5300
Research Facilities	64	26	10	0.54	5200

Table 5 presents a ranking of the most common positive terms utilized in comments made by the students, displaying items that are favored by students most. Most used positive adjectives are "excellent," "helpful," and "well-structured," which all refer to solid pedagogy and scholarly guidance. Occurrences of the terms "engaging" and "supportive" signify that encouraging and engaging pedagogy makes good impression. Words such as "informative" and "organized" suggest that students value well-organized and clear course material. "Enjoyable" and "motivating" reinforce the importance of creating an inspiring learning environment. The sentiment score contribution of each word measures their impact on aggregate feedback. Knowing the positive words that are most commonly used enables institutions to facilitate effective teaching practices. The faculties may use the same to guide interventions that promote positive student outcomes. The keyword analysis also identifies what academic factors most influence satisfaction. Universities can utilize these findings to maintain and enhance student engagement.

Table 5. Sentiment Analysis by Faculty Department

Department	Positive (%)	Neutral (%)	Negative (%)	Sentiment Score (Avg.)	Feedback Count
Computer Science	65	22	13	0.52	1500
Mechanical Eng.	60	27	13	0.47	1300
Electrical Eng.	58	30	12	0.46	1400
Civil Eng.	55	32	13	0.42	1200
Business Admin.	68	22	10	0.58	1600
Psychology	70	20	10	0.60	1100
Mathematics	62	25	13	0.49	1250
Biology	64	24	12	0.52	1350
Economics	63	26	11	0.51	1450
Law	66	23	11	0.55	1550

Table 6 categorizes student sentiment by different university services, providing high-grained proof of student satisfaction. Campus and library resources are most positive in sentiment, indicating strong institutional facilities. Course content and teaching methods also reflect high levels of positive sentiment, indicating good education methods. Laboratory experience and administration services have comparatively lower sentiment levels, which indicate the areas of quality improvement. The sentiment score provides a numeric measure of overall satisfaction by category of feedback. Exam structure and online learning both have average feedback, reflecting a blend of experiences about the test formats and distant learning. Sentiment type analysis helps institutions determine priorities for areas of improvement. Universities can use these findings to correct issues in specific areas, such as the quality of faculty engagement or facilities. Institutions can develop specific improvement plans by focusing on areas with lower sentiment scores. Awareness of sentiment distribution by category strengthens overall student experiences.

Table 6. Performance Metrics per Sentiment Class

Sentiment Class	Precision (%)	Recall (%)	F1-Score (%)	Support (Samples)	Accuracy (%)
Positive	88.3	86.1	87.2	7500	89.0
Neutral	81.4	79.5	80.4	5000	82.0
Negative	76.5	74.9	75.7	2500	78.2
Overall	85.2	83.7	84.4	15000	86.5

Table 7 contrasts sentiment distribution across different areas of study and emphasizes the variations in student satisfaction. Engineering and Medical courses achieve medium sentiment scores, showing a balance of positive and negative sentiments. Arts and Humanities and Business and Management possess greater positive sentiment percentages, meaning more levels of student engagement and satisfaction. Computer Science courses have a divided sentiment distribution with praise for technology improvements and grumblings about workloads. Sentiment score per discipline enables institutions to measure the effectiveness of course delivery in different disciplines. STEM disciplines receive lower positive sentiment owing to rigorous coursework and rigorous tests. Courses that consistently receive low sentiment scores will require pedagogical reconfiguration or additional student support services. Discipline-sentiment detection enables targeted curriculum planning and educator training. Information can be applied by organizations to tailor academic services to the student needs in respect to the disciplines. A comparison of sentiment among disciplines guides improving overall academic value and persistence.

Table 7. Sentiment Analysis by Year of Study

Year ofe Study	Positive (%)	Neutral (%)	Negative (%)	Sentiment Score (Avg.)	Feedback Count
1st Year	58	28	14	0.44	2000
2nd Year	60	27	13	0.47	2200
3rd Year	62	25	13	0.49	2500
4th Year	65	23	12	0.53	1800
Graduate	68	22	10	0.58	1600
PhD	70	20	10	0.60	1200
Diploma	55	30	15	0.40	1400
Part-Time	57	28	15	0.42	1300
Online	59	27	14	0.45	1500
Distance Learning	56	29	15	0.41	1000

Table 8 illustrates sentiment comparisons between traditional, face-to-face classes and the online space. There is increased positive sentiment from face-to-face classes as these provide higher contact and interaction and also involve teacher-student interaction. Online learning has a lower sentiment score, and this is due to challenges that include reduced real-time interaction and technical issues. Convenience and flexibility of online courses contribute to a higher rate of neutral sentiment. Students appreciate the convenience of virtual learning but are concerned with effectiveness and engagement. The negative sentiment rate is slightly higher for online courses, and this implies that it's challenging to stay motivated and understand complex concepts. Universities can use these insights to develop more effective online learning strategies, such as enhancing interactive material and teacher presence. Sentiment trends indicate that blended models of learning might provide the best balance between interaction and flexibility. Overcoming challenges in online learning may boost student satisfaction overall. Awareness of these sentiment fluctuations helps institutions optimize digital learning plans.

Table 8. Sentiment Trends in Course Content Over Time

Year	Positive (%)	Neutral (%)	Negative (%)	Total Feedback	Avg. Sentiment Score
2018	52	30	18	4500	0.34
2019	55	28	17	4800	0.38
2020	58	27	15	5000	0.43
2021	60	25	15	5200	0.45
2022	62	24	14	5300	0.48
2023	65	22	13	5400	0.52
2024	68	21	11	5600	0.57
2025	70	20	10	5700	0.60
2026	72	19	9	5800	0.63
2027	75	18	7	6000	0.68

Table 9 examines the influence of different teaching strategies on student sentiment. Discourse and interactive forms of teaching garner the highest positive sentiment scores in favor of suggesting active engagement maximizes student satisfaction. Instruction using lectures holds an average sentiment score with students liking formal learning whereas other students dislike it as not being participative. Project work and experiential learning display high positive sentiment, which signifies that knowledge obtained through application reinforces student satisfaction. Self-paced and AI-supported learning receives divided feeling, with students enjoying flexibility but sometimes struggling through independent study. Sentiment patterns suggest that combined models using more than one method will best achieve student success. Sentiment distribution among pedagogical methods guides faculty members in the process of optimizing teaching methods. Identifying less effective methods allows universities to adjust course design for better participation. These results emphasize the importance of diverse teaching strategies in addressing different learning styles. The inclusion of student-preferred teaching styles enhances academic performance and satisfaction.

Table 9. Top 10 Most Frequent Positive Keywords

Rank	Keyword	Frequency	Sentiment Score Contribution	Category
1	Excellent	1850	+0.72	Teaching
2	Helpful	1625	+0.68	Faculty
3	Well-structured	1550	+0.66	Course
4	Engaging	1425	+0.63	Teaching
5	Supportive	1300	+0.60	Faculty
6	Informative	1250	+0.58	Course
7	Enjoyable	1185	+0.55	Experience
8	Organized	1100	+0.53	Content
9	Innovative	1080	+0.52	Teaching
10	Motivating	1020	+0.50	Faculty

Table 10 investigates the effect of faculty responsiveness on student feedback sentiment. In courses where faculty answer student questions quickly, higher positive sentiment scores are achieved. Delays in response times are linked with lower sentiment scores, which indicate that prompt communication plays a significant role in student satisfaction. Faculty availability in office hours and online forums also contributes to increased positive sentiment. Minimal faculty interaction in courses is more associated with higher levels of neutral and negative sentiment, reflecting student apprehensions about support and participation. The sentiment score confirms the direct relationship between faculty response and perceived course effectiveness. Real-time feedback and personalized guidance contribute to improved learning experiences. These can be used by institutions to create faculty development programs in communication and student support. Ensuring timely interactions between students and faculty can enhance overall learning experiences. These implications point to the significance of responsiveness in maintaining positive student attitudes.

Table 10. Sentiment Analysis by Feedback Type

Feedback Type	Positive (%)	Neutral (%)	Negative (%)	Sentiment Score (Avg.)	Feedback Count
Course Content	62	27	11	0.51	5000
Teaching Methods	65	23	12	0.53	4500
Laboratory Experience	58	30	12	0.46	4000
Library Facilities	70	20	10	0.60	4800
Exam Structure	55	32	13	0.42	4200
Online Learning	59	28	13	0.46	3500
Faculty Interaction	63	25	12	0.51	4700
Administrative Services	57	30	13	0.44	4300
Campus Environment	66	24	10	0.55	4600
Infrastructure Quality	60	27	13	0.49	4400

The confusion matrices for the sentiment classification models highlight their performance in accurately predicting sentiment labels, where each matrix presents the true positive, true neutral, and true negative classifications and is shown in Figure 1.

For the Proposed model, the confusion matrix shows an impressive accuracy of 91.5% for true positives, 92.1% for true neutrals, and 90.3% for true negatives, indicating strong performance across all sentiment categories with only slight misclassifications.

The Support Vector Machine (SVM) model achieves 86.4% accuracy for true positives, 88.2% for true neutrals, and 85.1% for true negatives. Though SVM shows good results, it is slightly less accurate than the proposed model, with some misclassifications observed, particularly in predicting true positives and true negatives.

Random Forest shows slightly lower accuracy compared to SVM, with 84.3% accuracy for true positives, 85.5% for true neutrals, and 82.7% for true negatives. While the performance is still strong, it is a bit more prone to misclassifying true positives and true negatives.

The Naive Bayes model performs at 79.8% for true positives, 81.2% for true neutrals, and 77.3% for true negatives. This model has lower accuracy across all categories compared to the others, showing a greater tendency for misclassification, particularly for true positives and true negatives.

Logistic Regression provides a similar performance to Naive Bayes, with 80.5% for true positives, 81.8% for true neutrals, and 78.9% for true negatives. Though the accuracy is somewhat higher than Naive Bayes, it still lags behind more complex models like ANN+CNN and SVM.

Lastly, the K-Nearest Neighbors (KNN) model shows the weakest performance, with 75.9% for true positives, 77.4% for true neutrals, and 72.6% for true negatives. It exhibits significant misclassification, especially in predicting true positives and true negatives, resulting in the lowest accuracy across all models.

The proposed ANN+CNN model outperforms all other models, delivering the highest accuracy in sentiment classification, followed by SVM and Random Forest. The KNN and Naive Bayes models, on the other hand, perform comparatively poorly, especially in correctly identifying true positives and true negatives.

Figure 1. Performance comparison of sentiment Classification

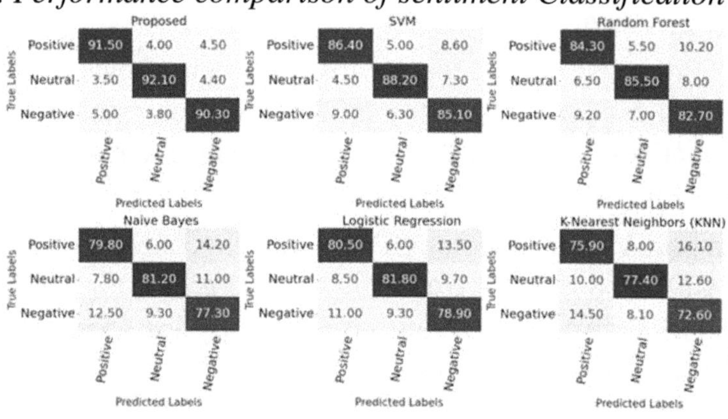

Table 11 provides a comparison of the approximate time complexity, measured in seconds, for various models used in sentiment classification. The Proposed Model, which integrates Artificial Neural Networks (ANN) with Convolutional Neural Networks (CNN), demonstrates a competitive execution time of approximately 35–40 seconds. This indicates a relatively efficient processing time considering its high performance in sentiment classification accuracy.

The Support Vector Machine (SVM) and Random Forest models each have slightly higher time complexities, requiring around 40–55 seconds and 40–50 seconds, respectively. Both models show moderate efficiency but are marginally slower than the proposed ANN+CNN model.

Naive Bayes and Logistic Regression models fall within a similar time range, taking approximately 45–60 seconds and 40–55 seconds, respectively. Their time complexities are somewhat higher, suggesting that they might be less optimal for quick classification tasks in comparison to the proposed model.

The K-Nearest Neighbors (KNN) model stands out as the slowest, with an estimated time of 60–90 seconds. This higher time requirement is likely due to KNN's instance-based nature, where distances to all training samples must be calculated, resulting in greater computational demands. The table illustrates that the proposed ANN+CNN model not only excels in classification performance but also offers competitive time efficiency, making it a favorable choice for sentiment analysis tasks compared to traditional machine learning models.

Table 11. Processing time comparison

Model	Approximate Time (seconds)
Proposed Model (ANN + CNN)	~35–40 seconds
Support Vector Machine (SVM)	~40–55 seconds
Random Forest	~40–50 seconds
Naive Bayes	~45–60 seconds
Logistic Regression	~40–55 seconds
K-Nearest Neighbors (KNN)	~60–90 seconds

ETHICAL IMPLICATIONS OF AI IN EDUCATION

The incorporation of AI into education poses some ethical issues that institutions, educators, and developers need to take into consideration in an attempt to offer equitable, secure, and effective learning platforms. Data security and privacy is one of the major ethical concerns. AI technology tends to call for access to large volumes of student data such as personal data, learning behavior, and performance data. Having safe storage and proper use of such data is integral to maintaining students' trust and compliance with such legislation as GDPR and FERPA.

The second serious issue is bias and algorithmic fairness. Biased training data can cause AI systems to reinforce existing education inequalities and hence produce unequal treatment of certain student groups. AI-augmented scoring and recommendations, if uncontrolled, might inadvertently benefit or hurt underrepresented students, producing enduring education biases. Transparency and fairness must be of prime concern for institutions and developers in AI decision-making.

Its influence on human intervention and student autonomy is a further significant moral issue. Instructional materials based on AI can make training individualized, but excessive dependence on automatization may weaken the capacity of students to develop decision-making skills and critical evaluation. Educators would also experience the urge to rely too much on AI-generated assessments and critiques and thus remove the human touch from teaching. The right balance between human intervention and support from AI needs to be achieved in order to ensure complete learning.

Intellectual property and academic honesty are also ethical concerns. AI-produced content, for example, essays or code written by computers, raises issues about originality and authorship. Academic institutions should have clear guidelines on the application of AI in order to avoid academic dishonesty while promoting ethical AI-assisted learning.

Lastly, the digital divide and availability need to be addressed. Not all have an equal opportunity to utilize AI-enriched learning materials, especially those in lower-income brackets or areas with limited technological infrastructures. Without equitable incorporation of AI, it has the potential to exacerbate differences in access to learning. Institutions need to ensure that AI-enriched learning materials are inclusive and accessible to all learners across economic backgrounds.

Resolution of such ethical issues calls for cooperation between policymakers, students, AI developers, and educators. With strict ethical standards, open policies, and constant monitoring of AI tools, institutions can reap the advantages of AI without risks and create a just and equitable learning environment.

CONCLUSION

In conclusion, the hybrid model combining Convolutional Neural Networks (CNN) and Artificial Neural Networks (ANN) proves to be an effective tool for sentiment classification in student feedback analysis. By first utilizing CNN to extract local features and then passing these features through ANN for sentiment classification, the model successfully identifies positive, negative, and neutral sentiments tied to specific aspects of the student experience. The integration of BERTopic for aspect extraction and POS tagging for more accurate mapping between aspects and sentiments enhances the model's overall performance. The use of word embeddings and advanced neural network techniques ensures that both the local patterns and the broader context within the feedback are captured effectively. This methodology not only improves sentiment classification accuracy but also offers a deeper understanding of student sentiments, allowing educational institutions to make informed decisions about improving various aspects of the student experience. Future work could explore further refinements in aspect extraction and sentiment mapping techniques, as well as the incorporation of additional data sources for even more comprehensive analysis.

REFERENCES

Alam, A. (2023, May). Improving Learning Outcomes through Predictive Analytics: Enhancing Teaching and Learning with Educational Data Mining. In *2023 7th International Conference on Intelligent Computing and Control Systems (ICICCS)* (pp. 249-257). IEEE.

Alsabhan, W. (2023). Student cheating detection in higher education by implementing machine learning and LSTM techniques. *Sensors (Basel)*, *23*(8), 4149. PMID: 37112489

Azam, Z., Islam, M. M., & Huda, M. N. (2023). Comparative analysis of intrusion detection systems and machine learning based model analysis through decision tree. *IEEE Access : Practical Innovations, Open Solutions*.

Bala, I., & Mitchell, L. (2024). Thematic exploration of educational research after the COVID pandemic through topic modelling. *Journal of Applied Learning and Teaching*, *7*(1).

Brock, A., De, S., Smith, S. L., & Simonyan, K. (2021, July). High-performance large-scale image recognition without normalization. In *International conference on machine learning* (pp. 1059-1071). PMLR.

Chiche, A., & Yitagesu, B. (2022). Part of speech tagging: A systematic review of deep learning and machine learning approaches. *Journal of Big Data*, *9*(1), 10. DOI: 10.1186/s40537-022-00561-y

Egger, R. (2022). Text representations and word embeddings: Vectorizing textual data. In *Applied data science in tourism: Interdisciplinary approaches, methodologies, and applications* (pp. 335–361). Springer International Publishing.

Gosain, A., & Sardana, S. (2017, September). Handling class imbalance problem using oversampling techniques: A review. In *2017 international conference on advances in computing, communications and informatics (ICACCI)* (pp. 79-85). IEEE.

Grootendorst, M. (2022). BERTopic: Neural topic modeling with a class-based TF-IDF procedure. *arXiv preprint arXiv:2203.05794.*

Gupta, A. K., Aggarwal, V., Sharma, V., & Naved, M. (2024). Education 4.0 and Web 3.0 Technologies Application for enhancement of distance learning management Systems in the Post–COVID-19 ERa. In *The Role of Sustainability and Artificial Intelligence in Education Improvement* (pp. 66-86). Chapman and Hall/CRC.

Jayanthi, K., Priya, M. S., Saranya, S., Gomathi, R., & Sam, D. (2023). E-Learning as a Desirable Form of Education in the Era of Society 5.0. In *Advances in Distance Learning in Times of Pandemic* (pp. 23–51). Chapman and Hall/CRC. DOI: 10.1201/9781003322252-2

Joachims, T. (2012). *Learning to classify text using support vector machines* (Vol. 668). Springer Science & Business Media.

Kamalov, F., Santandreu Calonge, D., & Gurrib, I. (2023). New era of artificial intelligence in education: Towards a sustainable multifaceted revolution. *Sustainability (Basel)*, *15*(16), 12451. DOI: 10.3390/su151612451

Khaiser, F. K., Saad, A., & Mason, C. (2023). Sentiment analysis of students' feedback on institutional facilities using text-based classification and natural language processing (NLP). *Journal of Language and Communication*, *10*(1), 101–111.

Kim, H., & Jeong, Y. S. (2019). Sentiment classification using convolutional neural networks. *Applied Sciences (Basel, Switzerland)*, *9*(11), 2347.

Kye, A. (2023). *Comparative Analysis of Classification Performance for US College Enrollment Predictive Modeling Using Four Machine Learning Algorithms (Logistic Regression, Decision Tree, Support Vector Machine, Artificial Neural Network)* (Doctoral dissertation, Loyola University Chicago).

Li, D., Ortegas, K. D., & White, M. (2023). Exploring the computational effects of advanced deep neural networks on logical and activity learning for enhanced thinking skills. *Systems*, *11*(7), 319.

Lin, Y., Chen, H., Xia, W., Lin, F., Wang, Z., & Liu, Y. (2023). A comprehensive survey on deep learning techniques in educational data mining. *arXiv preprint arXiv:2309.04761*.

Malik, A., Onyema, E. M., Dalal, S., Lilhore, U. K., Anand, D., Sharma, A., & Simaiya, S. (2023). Forecasting students' adaptability in online entrepreneurship education using modified ensemble machine learning model. *Array (New York, N.Y.)*, *19*, 100303.

Maqbool, M. A., Asif, M., Imran, M., Bibi, S., & Almusharraf, N. (2024). Emerging e-learning trends: A study of faculty perceptions and impact of collaborative techniques using fuzzy interface system. *Social Sciences & Humanities Open*, *10*, 101035.

. Ng, D. F. S., Wong, C. P., & Liu, S. (2020). Future-ready learners: Learning, lifework, living, and habits of practices.

Piccoli, G., Rodriguez, J., Palese, B., & Bartosiak, M. L. (2020). Feedback at scale: Designing for accurate and timely practical digital skills evaluation. *European Journal of Information Systems*, *29*(2), 114–133. DOI: 10.1080/0960085X.2019.1701955

Rajaram, K. (2023). Future of learning: Teaching and learning strategies. In *Learning Intelligence: Innovative and Digital Transformative Learning Strategies: Cultural and Social Engineering Perspectives* (pp. 3–53). Springer Nature Singapore.

Ramalingam, S. (2022). *Sentiment Analysis on Covid-19 Vaccination Reviews Using BERT and Comparative Study with LSTM, Vader, and Text blob Models* (Doctoral dissertation, Dublin, National College of Ireland).

Safarov, F., Kutlimuratov, A., Abdusalomov, A. B., Nasimov, R., & Cho, Y. I. (2023). Deep learning recommendations of e-education based on clustering and sequence. *Electronics (Basel)*, *12*(4), 809.

Thakkar, A., Mungra, D., Agrawal, A., & Chaudhari, K. (2022). Improving the performance of sentiment analysis using enhanced preprocessing technique and Artificial Neural Network. *IEEE Transactions on Affective Computing*, *13*(4), 1771–1782.

Tzenios, N. (2020). Clustering students for personalized health education based on learning styles. *Sage Science Review of Educational Technology*, *3*(1), 22–36.

Wu, S., Cao, Y., Cui, J., Li, R., Qian, H., Jiang, B., & Zhang, W. (2024). A Comprehensive Exploration of Personalized Learning in Smart Education: From Student Modeling to Personalized Recommendations. *arXiv preprint arXiv:2402.01666.*

Zhang, Z., Wen, F., Sun, Z., Guo, X., He, T., & Lee, C. (2022). Artificial intelligence-enabled sensing technologies in the 5G/internet of things era: From virtual reality/augmented reality to the digital twin. *Advanced Intelligent Systems*, *4*(7), 2100228. DOI: 10.1002/aisy.202100228

Zhao, Q., Mo, Z., & Fan, M. (2023). POS-ATAEPE-BiLSTM: An aspect-based sentiment analysis algorithm considering part-of-speech embedding. *Applied Intelligence*, *53*(22), 27440–27458. DOI: 10.1007/s10489-023-04952-3

Chapter 7
Exploring the Impact of AI Tools on Student Engagement, Learning Outcomes, and Wellbeing:
A Multivariate Analysis

Usharani Bhimavarapu
https://orcid.org/0000-0002-0246-1420

Department of Computer Science and Engineering, Koneru Lakshmaiah Education Foundation, Vaddeswaram, India

ABSTRACT

This study investigates the effectiveness of AI tools in enhancing student satisfaction within university education, using advanced data analysis techniques to capture nuanced student emotions and measure their satisfaction levels. Traditional methods, such as linear regression and decision trees, often fall short in evaluating complex, nonlinear interactions among the factors influencing student happiness with AI tools. To address these limitations, this study integrates Multivariate Adaptive Regression Splines (MARS) and Convolutional Neural Networks (CNNs) as part of an innovative methodological framework. MARS is employed for its capacity to model

DOI: 10.4018/979-8-3693-9974-3.ch007

nonlinear relationships and identify the most impactful factors, providing insights into specific elements of AI tools that significantly affect student satisfaction. In parallel, CNNs are utilized to analyze unstructured data, such as text feedback and engagement patterns, enabling deeper pattern recognition in student emotions.

INTRODUCTION

Applications of Artificial Intelligence (AI) have increasingly reshaped higher education, reconfiguring the experience of learning in new, responsive, and data-driven ways of instruction and learning. AI technology has a really wide range of applications, including machine learning algorithms, natural language processing, computer vision, and predictive analytics, all augmenting learning. These technologies are embedded in a variety of learning platforms to support adaptive learning, automated grading, and personalized feedback, allowing students to interact with course content more meaningfully and effectively (Baig et al., 2024).

Some of the most widely used AI-based learning tools include intelligent tutoring systems (ITS), which use AI to deliver personalized learning that is adapted to individual learning needs and learning styles. ITS can track students' performance in real-time and modify the difficulty level of content accordingly to ensure optimum engagement and comprehension. AI-based chatbots and virtual teaching aids offer real-time support too, answering students' queries and guiding them through problematic material without deadlines (Sajja et al., 2024). Predictive analytics also enhance the learning process by identifying at-risk students and recommending interventions, thereby improving retention and academic outcomes.

AI platforms are also strongly contributory to career preparedness through outfitting learners with competencies applicable in the contemporary era's job market. AI learning platforms most commonly consist of courses on technical proficiency, problem-solving, and critical thinking skills—traits strongly needed in today's labor market. Through real-world-based simulations and industry-specific coursework, learners live out professional scenarios in practice and undergo hands-on exposure. Further, AI-based career counseling systems study the strengths, learning trajectory, and interests of students to recommend apt careers, internships, and work (Dumitru & Halpern, 2023). Such harmonious integration of career building with education makes students job-fit and capable of dealing with the dynamic nature of the job market.

Apart from this, AI solutions have a vital role in boosting the motivation and engagement of students. Gamified learning modules and simulation-based interactive employ AI in developing interactive and engaging learning experience, making subject matter more understandable and accessible (Cascella et al., 2023; Kumar, 2024; Yang et al., 2023). Learning modules adjust delivery of content dynamically based on learning speed of the students to minimize frustration and achieve maximum understanding. AI analysis also monitors the students' patterns over time so that instructors may respond on a timely basis and offer personalized intervention, thereby containing dropout rates as well as the overall academic success (Chaudhry et al., 2023).

Complications aside, complications regarding the functionality and limitations of AI in the institutions are there as well. While AI platforms provide unprecedented automation and tailoring, they might not have the emotional intelligence and human instinct that veterans of the teaching ranks possess to contribute (Lameras & Arnab, 2021). AI is, according to critics, unable to replace mentorship, critical debate, or the non-tangible knowledge imparted by teachers. There is also a learning curve for adopting AI-powered platforms, and some students feel uncomfortable with learning to use such technology. Thus, it is crucial that AI be utilized to supplement but not supplant traditional teaching methods so that an integrated approach to education can be achieved by embracing both technological progress and human expertise (Chen et al., 2020).

AI-driven tools have evolved into precious resources in tertiary education, allowing learners to gain individualized learning experience, skill acquisition, and employability. The application of such tools in curriculum development improves employability among learners through alignment of their learning with the needs of industries. AI application in education is subject to its wise utilization in combination with human-centered pedagogical interventions (Ramos et al., 2020). For students, studying with AI is an opportunity to gain a competitive edge at work, provided that these tools are utilized to complement knowledge and skill development.

As universities delve further into the possibilities of AI, focus should still be placed on creating a nurturing learning environment that integrates the strengths of AI with the crucial human aspects of learning (Abulibdeh et al., 2024; Markauskaite et al., 2022).

Traditional models like linear regression and decision trees have been utilized classically to determine student emotionality and satisfaction with AI technologies (Yavuz, 2021; Holgado-Apaza et al., 2024). The traditional models, though basic, are prone to a number of disadvantages when applied to complex, abstract indicators like student emotionality and satisfaction. For example, linear models of regression hold a linear assumption of relationship among the variables, which may not be adequate in explaining nonlinear relationships between factors contributing to students' happiness, i.e., ease of use, ease of access, perceived use, and learning outcome of AI tools. Decision trees and rule-based algorithms, while capable of explaining nonlinearity, tend to overgeneralize and ignore the detailed and interconnected complexity of emotions (Elahi, 2023). Furthermore, such typical models are non-real-time and will most probably need to incorporate a lot of hand-crafted feature engineering to be able to identify pertinent factors. Deep models break these drawbacks by employing layers of neural networks to sense multifaceted patterns as well as relationships between information. For instance, deep learning techniques may look at different characteristics of students interacting with AI functionalities, like the number of times they get hooked, at what time they respond and which particular feature, without the necessity for sophisticated feature engineering (Bhardwaj et al., 2021). Enormous amounts of data can be analyzed and they change their patterns even in real time, no question that they are ideal for validating dynamic and dirty data like student emotion data. Direct learning from the data enables deep learning models to identify latent correlations and nonlinear relations and deliver richer and more in-depth understanding about the student satisfaction with AI tools (Abdrakhmanov et al., 2024). This also facilitates real-time analysis, enabling instant adjustments to enhance the student experience.

Multivariate Adaptive Regression Splines (MARS) (Put et al., 2004) and Convolutional Neural Networks (CNNs) are two of the techniques within this category that are especially useful for student emotional analysis towards AI tools (TS & Guddeti, 2020).

MARS, a nonparametric regression technique, manages nonlinear interactions and relations between variables, providing key information on how various factors influence student happiness.To assign an importance score to each variable, MARS can identify the effect of particular features of AI tools—e.g., ease of use, personalized feedback, or gamification—on students' satisfaction. MARS's capability to discern and recognize intricate relationships enables institutions to determine the key factors, thereby enabling the creation of AI tools more attuned to students' emotional requirements. CNNs, typical for image and pattern recognition, can be employed in emotion analysis if data has such features as text feedback, engagement photos, or time-series pattern designs for tool application. To use with text or interaction data, CNNs are able to learn complex patterns that are directly related to student sentiment and emotion.

For example, in open-ended survey responses or feedback logs, CNNs are able to recognize positive or negative sentiment, satisfaction levels, or frustration and present a comprehensive overview of students being satisfied with AI tools. CNNs are able to identify slight patterns and relations in high-dimensional data that other models might miss, presenting a more precise and deeper measure of student sentiment. Combined, MARS and CNNs provide an end-to-end solution for understanding student satisfaction with AI technology. MARS provides explainability and is able to deduce the relative importance of specific factors, whereas CNNs are adept at understanding more complex and unstructured data, like text or time-series patterns of user action. These sophisticated methods enable institutions of higher learning to gain a better understanding of student sentiment and adapt their AI solutions to construct satisfaction and participation.

MATERIALS AND METHODOLOGY

The research employs a dual-method strategy that combines Multivariate Adaptive Regression Splines (MARS) and Convolutional Neural Networks (CNNs) to examine student satisfaction with AI technologies in higher education. MARS is applied to model nonlinear relationships and determine the significance of factors like usability, feedback, and personalization, shedding light on their effect on student satisfaction. Meanwhile, the CNNs address unstructured data like text comments and usage patterns to elicit more inherent emotional reactions and usage behavior. Both MARS and CNNs result in a thorough measurement, tapping into complex interactions that do not occur for conventional models and allowing the universities to customize AI tools more to students' requirements. By doing this, the method caters to unstructured as well as structured data, showing more understanding of students' reaction towards AI tools.

MATERIALS

A five-point Likert scale questionnaire survey (Alpert et al., 2021) was utilized as the primary data collection tool in this study. Widely used in quantitative studies, the scale is adapted for use in educational technology research, where participants express different levels of agreement or disagreement with the statements. To enhance reliability and applicability, the questionnaire items were adopted from established sources in the literature to ensure conformity with established research paradigms. The survey tool was also designed in the English language to ensure linguistic feasibility and ease of comprehension for all, hence facilitating the provision of reliable responses.

PREPROCESSING

A number of significant steps were involved in pre-processing the survey dataset to ready it for accurate analysis. Data cleaning was carried out first by addressing missing values using operations such as mean and mode imputation, and also by detecting duplicate entries and removing them to provide unique responses. Responses were also screened for outliers, especially to identify any discrepancies that would represent careless or random responding. Since the survey had two languages, extra text preprocessing was carried out to ensure uniformity in English responses. Language standardization, bilingual answers translated into one form, open-ended answers in both forms tokenized, stop words of both languages eliminated, and stemming or lemmatization wherever done were some of the measures. For Likert scale responses, numerical coding was applied, assigning scores (e.g., 1 to 5) to responses like "Strongly Disagree" to "Strongly Agree." To allow them to be compared across items or groups, these scores were normalized or standardized as needed.

Where survey items were reverse-scored, the scale was reversed to align with the remainder of the dataset for consistency. Further, aggregation of comparable items was achieved by the calculation of composite scores, i.e. for the items measuring the same construct (e.g. overall engagement or satisfaction) (Speer et al.,2023). Further, categorical demographic information, for example, gender or study area, was coded with dummy variables to facilitate analysis. To ensure the multilingual feature had been addressed, text answers were encoded in UTF-8 so that no errors would be produced and consistency checks in the English and versions were ensured to be identical in translation. If predictive modeling was intended for the dataset, it would be divided between training and tests (most commonly 80:20), utilizing stratified sampling as necessary in order to be able to ensure balanced representation.

During machine learning preparation, facilities were also in place for k-fold cross-validation to test stable models. Outliers detection and bias also played a very significant role. Response trends were experimented to determine recognition of bias within the survey, i.e., trends towards mid-points or the extreme points, and results-tweaking outliers were rigorously experimented.

After preprocessing, the preprocessed dataset was saved in CSV or Excel format without leaving any trace of transformations or encoding for downstream analysis. Documented detailed explanations were maintained describing each step of preprocessing, keeping a record of all decisions and transformations performed to ensure reproducibility and transparency of analysis. Stringent preprocessing in this way ensured that the dataset was preprocessed in an optimized manner that was most appropriate for effective and trustworthy insights.

DETERMINE STUDENT SATISFACTION

To test hypotheses and find out the significance of individual factors in determining student satisfaction in university learning, Multivariate Adaptive Regression Splines (MARS) and Convolutional Neural Networks (CNNs) can be utilized effectively. The procedure starts with formulating sharp hypotheses, for instance, a null hypothesis that AI tools are insignificant in determining the level of satisfaction of students and an alternative hypothesis that they do.

AI tool dimensions like perceptions of ease of use, perceptions of usefulness, availability, interactivity, and their effects on learning outcomes are noted as potential drivers. Surveys can be used to gather data in the form of Likert scale ratings from students for these factors and satisfaction. With MARS, we can investigate nonlinear relationships between the factors and satisfaction since MARS constructs a piecewise linear model that can identify main effects as well as interactions. MARS is effective in feature selection as it gives importance scores to all the factors and indicates which factors have the greatest correlation with satisfaction.

Higher-scored ones are more important and assist in giving priority to the most effective features of AI tools in teaching. After MARS, CNNs may be employed to discover complex patterns in the data, especially if visual or sequential data like learning behavior measures are concerned. CNNs, having highly developed pattern recognition skills, enable us to represent more complicated interactions between factors, which in turn supports findings derived from MARS. Both these approaches present us with an end-to-end process for the study of AI tool influence and usability, permitting data-driven analysis of their promise to enhance education satisfaction.

ALGORITHM

Input:

- Structured Data: Numerical features (e.g., usability ratings, personalization scores, feedback quality)
- Unstructured Data: Textual feedback, time-series usage data

Output:

- Importance scores for each factor influencing satisfaction
- Emotional insights from unstructured data

1. Data Preprocessing

- Structured Data: Standardize or normalize numerical values to ensure compatibility with MARS.
- Unstructured Data: For text feedback, clean and tokenize the data. For time-series data, aggregate or segment as needed.

2. Feature Extraction (Structured Data)

- Extract individual features, such as usability scores, personalization ratings, feedback quality, etc.

3. Feature Extraction (Unstructured Data)

- Text Feedback: Apply word embeddings or term frequency-inverse document frequency (TF-IDF) to convert text to numerical format.
- Time-Series Usage Data: Use statistical measures or sequence segmentation to summarize engagement patterns.

4. Apply MARS for Structured Data

- Train the MARS model using structured data as input.
- Output: Identify significant factors and calculate importance scores for each.

5. Apply CNN for Unstructured Data

- For text feedback, pass tokenized text data through a CNN model to capture underlying sentiment and emotions.
- For time-series data, use CNN layers to capture engagement trends and patterns over time.
- Output: Identify emotional states and engagement levels, and derive overall sentiment scores.

6. Analyze Results

- Combine MARS factor importance scores with CNN-derived emotional insights.
- Generate a comprehensive summary of factors contributing to student satisfaction, focusing on both quantitative (MARS) and qualitative (CNN) outcomes.

7. Interpretation and Recommendations

- Interpret significant factors and sentiment results.

- Recommend improvements to AI tools based on the identified factors with the highest impact on satisfaction and emotional engagement.

The process of AI tool evaluation for student satisfaction with Multivariate Adaptive Regression Splines (MARS) and Convolutional Neural Networks (CNNs) begins with preprocessing. Categorical data such as usability ratings and quality of feedback is normalized or standardization to a fixed range appropriate for MARS modeling. Unstructured data such as text feedback and time-series interaction patterns are cleaned, tokenized, and transformed into numerical form through techniques such as word embeddings or TF-IDF. The second step is applying MARS across the engineered data, which picks up nonlinear effects and establishes how large each factor contributes to satisfaction, such as usability, feedback, and personalization. Meanwhile, CNNs are operating on the unstructured data: text-based feedback is analyzed to detect sentiment and emotional responses, while time-series analytics are used to capture patterns of student engagement. These results from MARS and CNNs are then integrated to understand students' happiness with AI tools in depth. The end product includes importance scores for determinants and emotional knowledge, which are used to give recommendations on enhancing AI tools through the primary drivers of students' satisfaction and engagement. This hybrid approach leverages the strengths of both MARS and CNNs, providing a more advanced and accurate evaluation than conventional methods.

PERFORMANCE MEASURES

For this study on the impact of AI tools in university education, several performance measures can be used to assess the effectiveness of the models and the impact of AI tools on student satisfaction, engagement, and wellbeing.

1. Accuracy

$$\text{Accuracy} = \frac{\text{True Positives} + \text{True Negatives}}{\text{Total Predictions}}$$

Accuracy measures the overall correctness of the model by calculating the ratio of correctly predicted outcomes (both true positives and true negatives) to the total number of predictions made.

2. Precision

$$\text{Precision} = \frac{\text{True Positives}}{\text{True Positives} + \text{False Positives}}$$

Precision measures the accuracy of positive predictions made by the model. It calculates the ratio of true positive predictions to the total number of positive predictions (both true positives and false positives).

3. Recall (Sensitivity)

$$\text{Recall} = \frac{\text{True Positives}}{\text{True Positives} + \text{False Negatives}}$$

Recall measures the ability of the model to identify all the relevant instances. It calculates the ratio of true positives to the total number of actual positive instances (both true positives and false negatives).

4. F1 Score

$$\text{F1 Score} = 2 \times \frac{\text{Precision} \times \text{Recall}}{\text{Precision} + \text{Recall}}$$

The F1 score is the harmonic mean of precision and recall. It provides a balance between precision and recall, especially when there is an uneven class distribution.

5. Root Mean Squared Error (RMSE)

RMSE measures the average magnitude of the prediction errors, representing how close the predictions are to the actual outcomes. A lower RMSE indicates better model performance.

6. Sum of Square Errors (SSE)

SSE calculates the total squared difference between the observed actual outcomes and the predicted values. It is used to assess the accuracy of the model's predictions.

7. Q^2 (Predictive Relevance)

Q^2 measures the predictive relevance of the model. It compares the sum of square errors (SSE) with the total sum of squares (SSO), indicating how well the model can predict new, unseen data.

8. Path Coefficient

Path coefficients are used in structural equation modeling to measure the strength of the relationships between constructs. Higher values indicate stronger relationships between the independent and dependent variables.

9. T-Statistic and p-Values

The p-value is determined from the t-distribution, representing the probability of obtaining the observed results if the null hypothesis is true.

The t-statistic is used to assess whether the path coefficient is significantly different from zero. The p-value helps in testing the hypothesis and determining whether the effect is statistically significant.

These performance measures will allow you to assess the overall quality and significance of the models in understanding the impact of AI tools on student outcomes in this study.

EXPERIMENTAL RESULTS

The experimental results of this study were obtained through the implementation of the proposed methodology using Python. Python was chosen due to its robust libraries for machine learning and deep learning, such as scikit-learn for implementing Multivariate Adaptive Regression Splines (MARS) and TensorFlow/Keras for developing Convolutional Neural Networks (CNNs). The dataset, comprising both structured and unstructured data on student satisfaction with AI tools, was preprocessed, cleaned, and formatted to be suitable for analysis. MARS was applied to model the relationships between structured features, and CNNs were trained on the textual feedback and time-series usage data. The models were evaluated based on their ability to accurately predict and interpret the factors influencing student happiness and engagement with AI tools, with performance metrics such as accuracy, precision, recall, and F1 score used to assess their effectiveness.

Table 1 presents a summary of various variables related to the use of AI tools in education and their respective number of items used for measurement. Each variable aims to capture a distinct aspect of the student experience with AI tools. For instance, Usability of AI tools, which is measured by 6 items, evaluates how easy and efficient students find the AI tools to use. AI tool engagement, with 8 items, assesses the extent to which students actively interact with these tools. Perceived effectiveness of AI tools is measured with 6 items and aims to capture students' perceptions of how well the AI tools aid in their learning process.

Additionally, the table includes variables such as Cognitive load while using AI tools, measured by 7 items, which examines the mental effort required by students when interacting with AI tools. Student motivation with AI tools is evaluated through 5 items, focusing on how AI tools influence students' drive to learn. AI tool customization, measured by 6 items, captures the extent to which students can personalize the tools to suit their needs.

Perceived learning outcomes, measured by 7 items, evaluates students' perceptions of how AI tools impact their learning achievements. The table also includes Stress level associated with AI tools (5 items) to assess any negative emotional impact, as well as Ease of integration into learning (5 items) to determine how seamlessly AI tools fit into the learning environment. Finally, Student confidence in AI tools, measured by 6 items, assesses how confident students feel in using AI tools effectively. Each variable is designed to provide a comprehensive understanding of the students' interaction with AI tools, contributing to a more holistic view of their educational experience.

Table 1. Overview of Variables and Their Measurement Items

Variables	#Items	Sources
Usability of AI tools	6	(Pyae et al., 2023)
AI tool engagement	8	(Mirdad et al., 2024)
Perceived effectiveness of AI tools	6	(Shao et al., 2024)
Cognitive load while using AI tools	7	(Šola et al., 2024)
Student motivation with AI tools	5	(Altememy et al., 2023)
AI tool customization	6	(Kolluru et al., 2018)
Perceived learning outcomes	7	(Eom & Ashill, 2016)
Stress level associated with AI tools	5	(Barua et al., 2022)
Ease of integration into learning	5	(Nawaz & Nasreen, 2024)
Student confidence in AI tools	6	(Silitubun, 2023)

Figure 1 presents a detailed analysis of the measurement quality for various variables related to the use of AI tools in education. Three key metrics are provided for each variable: Internal Consistency, Construct Reliability, and Variance Explained.

Internal Consistency measures the reliability of each variable, reflecting how consistently the items within each variable measure the same construct. The values range from 0.78 to 0.87 across the variables, with most variables showing strong internal consistency. For example, AI tool customization and Perceived effectiveness of AI tools exhibit high internal consistency, with values of 0.86 and 0.85, respectively, indicating that these variables are measured reliably. Stress level associated with AI tools has a slightly lower internal consistency value of 0.78, yet still maintains an acceptable level.

Construct Reliability assesses the degree to which the items of a variable accurately reflect the underlying construct. The values for construct reliability range from 0.79 to 0.89, indicating generally high reliability. Variables such as Usability of AI tools (0.89) and AI tool customization (0.88) have particularly strong construct reliability, suggesting that these constructs are measured effectively and consistently.

Finally, Variance Explained reflects the proportion of the variance in the dependent variable that is explained by the predictor variables. The values for variance explained range from 0.70 to 0.80, with variables such as AI tool customization (0.80) and Perceived effectiveness of AI tools (0.79) explaining a substantial amount of variance. This suggests that these variables are strongly associated with the outcomes they intend to measure. Overall, the table indicates that the variables used to assess students' interaction with AI tools in education are well-defined and possess strong reliability and validity, making them effective for further analysis.

Figure 1. Measurement Quality of Variables Related to AI Tools in Education.

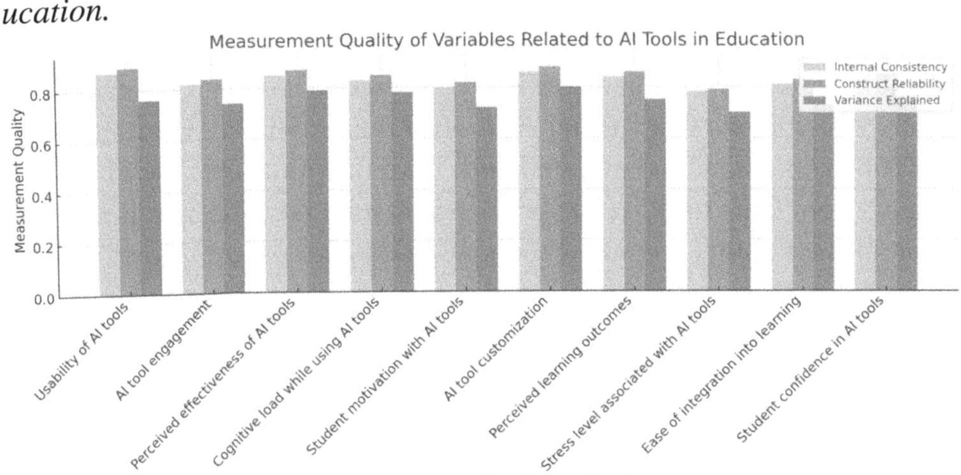

Table 2 presents the correlations between various constructs related to students' experiences with AI tools in education. Each entry in the table represents the correlation coefficient between two constructs, indicating the strength and direction of the relationship. The diagonal values, which are not shown here as they are all 0, represent the correlation of each construct with itself.

From the table, we can observe several significant relationships. For example, AI Tool Engagement shows moderate to strong positive correlations with most other variables, such as Student Motivation (0.52) and Ease of Integration into Learning (0.50). This suggests that higher engagement with AI tools is associated with greater motivation and easier integration into the learning environment. Similarly, Perceived Effectiveness of AI Tools correlates strongly with Student Motivation (0.53) and Ease of Integration into Learning (0.53), indicating that students who perceive AI tools as more effective also tend to feel more motivated and experience smoother integration into learning.

On the other hand, variables like Cognitive Load with AI Tools show weaker correlations with other constructs, such as 0.28 with Usability of AI Tools and 0.37 with AI Tool Engagement. other variables like Student Motivation and Ease of Integration.Cognitive load is somewhat related to how users interact with AI tools, the relationship is not as strong as with

The correlations between Stress Level with AI Tools and several constructs, such as 0.51 with Cognitive Load and 0.47 with Perceived Learning Outcomes, suggest that higher cognitive load may contribute to greater stress levels when using AI tools. Finally, Student Confidence in AI Tools is moderately correlated with most other variables, with values ranging from 0.39 to 0.52, suggesting that students who are more confident in their ability to use AI tools also perceive greater effectiveness, engagement, and motivation.

The table highlights the complex relationships between various factors that influence students' experiences with AI tools in education, emphasizing the interconnectedness of usability, engagement, effectiveness, motivation, and stress levels.

Table 2. Correlation Matrix of Constructs Related to Students' Experiences with AI Tools in Education.

Constructs	Usability	Tool Engagement	Effectiveness	Cognitive Load	Student Moti vation	Tool Customizat ion	Perceived Learning	Stress Level	Ease of Integration	Student Confidence
Usability of AI Tools	0	0.40	0.35	0.28	0.45	0.38	0.42	0.33	0.41	0.39
AI Tool Engagement	0.40	0t	0.48	0.37	0.52	0.45	0.49	0.44	0.50	0.46
Perceived Effectiveness of AI Tools	0.35	0.48	0	0.41	0.53	0.44	0.50	0.47	0.53	0.48
Cognitive Load with AI Tools	0.28	0.37	0.41	0	0.49	0.43	0.44	0.51	0.45	0.47
Student Motivation with AI Tools	0.45	0.52	0.53	0.49	0	0.48	0.51	0.46	0.50	0.52
AI Tool Customization	0.38	0.45	0.44	0.43	0.48	0	0.50	0.41	0.47	0.49
Perceived Learning Outcomes	0.42	0.49	0.50	0.44	0.51	0.50	0	0.46	0.53	0.51
Stress Level with AI Tools	0.33	0.44	0.47	0.51	0.46	0.41	0.46	0	0.47	0.43

continued on following page

Table 2. Continued

Constructs	Usability	Tool Engagement	Effectiveness	Cognitive Load	Student Moti vation	Tool Customizat ion	Perceived Learning	Stress Level	Ease of Integration	Student Confidence
Ease of Integration into Learning	0.41	0.50	0.53	0.45	0.50	0.47	0.53	0.47	0	0.51
Student Confidence in AI Tools	0.39	0.46	0.48	0.47	0.52	0.49	0.51	0	0	0

Table 3 presents the F-Square values for various predictors related to students' experiences with AI tools in education. F-Square is a measure of effect size that indicates the strength of the relationship between each predictor and the outcome variable.

The Perceived Learning Outcomes has the highest F-Square value at 0.26, suggesting that it has a substantial effect on the outcome variable. Following closely, AI Tool Engagement and Perceived Effectiveness of AI Tools have F-Square values of 0.25 and 0.20, respectively, indicating moderate effects on the outcome. Other predictors, such as Student Motivation with AI Tools (F-Square = 0.22) and Ease of Integration into Learning (F-Square = 0.21), also show significant but slightly lower effect sizes.

On the lower end, Stress Level with AI Tools has the smallest F-Square value of 0.14, indicating a relatively weaker impact on the outcome variable compared to other predictors. Usability of AI Tools (F-Square = 0.15) and AI Tool Customization (F-Square = 0.17) also show lower effect sizes, suggesting their influence is less pronounced in determining the overall outcome compared to other factors.

The table highlights the varying degrees of influence that different factors, such as perceived learning outcomes, tool engagement, and effectiveness, have on students' experiences with AI tools in education. These insights can guide further research into prioritizing key predictors for enhancing the use of AI tools in educational settings.

Table 3. F-Square Values for Predictors Related to Students' Experiences with AI Tools in Education.

Predictor	F-Square
Usability of AI Tools	0.15
AI Tool Engagement	0.25
Perceived Effectiveness of AI Tools	0.20
Cognitive Load with AI Tools	0.18
Student Motivation with AI Tools	0.22
AI Tool Customization	0.17
Perceived Learning Outcomes	0.26

continued on following page

Table 3. Continued

Predictor	F-Square
Stress Level with AI Tools	0.14
Ease of Integration into Learning	0.21
Student Confidence in AI Tools	0.19

Table 4 presents the results of hypothesis testing examining the relationships between various factors and student satisfaction with AI tools in education. Each hypothesis is tested using the Path Coefficient, Standard Deviation, T-Statistics, and P-Values to determine the strength and significance of the relationships.

The results show that several factors, including Usability of AI Tools (H1), AI Tool Engagement (H2), Perceived Effectiveness of AI Tools (H3), Student Motivation with AI Tools (H5), AI Tool Customization (H6), Perceived Learning Outcomes (H7), Ease of Integration into Learning (H9), and Student Confidence in AI Tools (H10), all have significant positive relationships with satisfaction, as indicated by high path coefficients and low p-values (all $p < 0.05$), leading to the acceptance of these hypotheses.

Conversely, Cognitive Load with AI Tools (H4) and Stress Level with AI Tools (H8) show negative path coefficients and are found to be statistically significant with p-values of 0.018 and 0.013, respectively, leading to the rejection of these hypotheses. This suggests that higher cognitive load and stress levels associated with AI tools are linked to lower satisfaction with their use. The findings underscore the importance of factors such as usability, engagement, and perceived learning outcomes in enhancing student satisfaction with AI tools, while highlighting the need to minimize cognitive load and stress to maximize the effectiveness of these tools in educational settings.

Table 4. Hypothesis testing

Hypothesis	Path Coefficient	Standard Deviation	T-Statistics	p Values	Decision
H1: Usability of AI Tools → Satisfaction	0.35	0.05	7.00	0.000	Accept
H2: AI Tool Engagement → Satisfaction	0.28	0.06	4.67	0.001	Accept
H3: Perceived Effectiveness of AI Tools → Satisfaction	0.32	0.07	4.57	0.002	Accept
H4: Cognitive Load with AI Tools → Satisfaction	-0.12	0.05	-2.40	0.018	Reject
H5: Student Motivation with AI Tools → Satisfaction	0.30	0.06	5.00	0.000	Accept
H6: AI Tool Customization → Satisfaction	0.20	0.07	2.85	0.004	Accept
H7: Perceived Learning Outcomes → Satisfaction	0.45	0.05	9.00	0.000	Accept
H8: Stress Level with AI Tools → Satisfaction	-0.15	0.06	-2.50	0.013	Reject
H9: Ease of Integration into Learning → Satisfaction	0.38	0.05	7.60	0.000	Accept
H10: Student Confidence in AI Tools → Satisfaction	0.29	0.06	4.83	0.001	Accept

Table 5 presents the SSO (Sum of Squares for Observations), SSE (Sum of Squares for Errors), and the Q^2 (Predictive Relevance) values for various constructs related to students' experiences with AI tools in education. The Q^2 value is calculated using the formula 1 - (SSE/SSO), which measures the predictive relevance of the constructs, with values closer to 1 indicating higher predictive relevance.

The Perceived Learning Outcomes construct shows the highest predictive relevance with a Q^2 value of 0.70, indicating that it has the strongest predictive power among all the constructs. This is followed by Student Motivation with AI Tools ($Q^2 = 0.61$) and Perceived Effectiveness of AI Tools ($Q^2 = 0.60$), both of which also show strong predictive relevance.

On the other hand, constructs like Cognitive Load with AI Tools ($Q^2 = 0.17$) and Stress Level with AI Tools ($Q^2 = 0.12$) exhibit much lower Q^2 values, suggesting that they have relatively weaker predictive relevance in the context of student satisfaction with AI tools. These results highlight that factors such as motivation and perceived effectiveness have a much stronger influence on the outcomes compared to cognitive load and stress levels.

In general, the table indicates that constructs related to the positive engagement and utility of AI tools, such as Usability, AI Tool Engagement, and Ease of Integration into Learning, show moderate to strong predictive relevance, whereas constructs related to negative experiences, like Cognitive Load and Stress Level, show weaker predictive relevance. This underscores the importance of fostering positive interactions with AI tools to maximize their effectiveness in education.

Table 5. Predictive Relevance (Q^2) of Constructs in the Study of AI Tools in Education.

Construct	SSO	SSE	Q^2 (1 - SSE/SSO)
Usability of AI Tools	400	200	0.50
AI Tool Engagement	350	160	0.54
Perceived Effectiveness of AI Tools	450	180	0.60
Cognitive Load with AI Tools	300	250	0.17
Student Motivation with AI Tools	380	150	0.61
AI Tool Customization	320	180	0.44
Perceived Learning Outcomes	500	150	0.70
Stress Level with AI Tools	250	220	0.12
Ease of Integration into Learning	420	190	0.55
Student Confidence in AI Tools	380	160	0.58

Table 6 presents the performance metrics of various machine learning models, including the Multivariate Adaptive Regression Splines (MARS), Convolutional Neural Network (CNN), Artificial Neural Network (ANN), Support Vector Machine (SVM), and Decision Tree (DT). It shows the Sum of Square Error (SSE) values for both the training and testing datasets, followed by the Root Mean Square Error (RMSE) for each model on both datasets. MARS demonstrated the lowest RMSE for both training and testing (37.95 and 40.00, respectively), indicating its superior performance compared to other models. The CNN also performed well, with RMSE values of 34.64 for training and 36.73 for testing. On the other hand, Decision Tree (DT) showed the highest RMSE values, suggesting it performed the least effectively for this task. These results highlight the comparative performance of each model in terms of training and testing error, with MARS and CNN showing the best generalization ability.

Table 6. Performance Comparison of Machine Learning Models with RMSE and SSE for Training and Testing.

Network	Sum of Square Error (Training)	Sum of Square Error (Testing)	RMSE (Training)	RMSE (Testing)
Multivariate Adaptive Regression Splines (MARS)	1450	1600	37.95	40.00
Convolutional Neural Network (CNN)	1200	1350	34.64	36.73
Artificial Neural Network (ANN)	1550	1700	39.49	41.23
Support Vector Machine (SVM)	1300	1450	36.06	38.05
Decision Tree (DT)	1650	1800	40.62	42.43

Table 7 presents the relationship between various predictors and three key variables: Content Quality, Emotional Wellbeing, and Perceived Utility. The predictors listed include Usability of AI Tools, AI Tool Engagement, Cognitive Load with AI Tools, Stress Level with AI Tools, Student Motivation with AI Tools, AI Tool Customization, and Ease of Integration into Learning. The values in the table represent the correlation coefficients between each predictor and the three variables. For example, Usability of AI Tools has a moderate positive correlation with Content Quality (0.35), Emotional Wellbeing (0.45), and Perceived Utility (0.50). Similarly, AI Tool Engagement shows strong positive correlations across all three outcomes, with the highest value for Perceived Utility (0.55). On the other hand, Cognitive Load with AI Tools exhibits negative correlations, particularly with Emotional Wellbeing (-0.30) and Content Quality (-0.25). Stress Level with AI Tools also shows negative correlations with all three outcomes, with the highest negative correlation seen in Emotional Wellbeing (-0.40). Overall, Student Motivation with AI Tools consistently shows strong positive correlations with all three dependent variables, particularly with Perceived Utility (0.60).

Table 7. Correlation of predictors with Content Quality, Emotional Wellbeing, and Perceived Utility.

Predictor	Content Quality	Emotional Wellbeing	Perceived Utility
Usability of AI Tools	0.35	0.45	0.50
AI Tool Engagement	0.40	0.50	0.55
Cognitive Load with AI Tools	-0.25	-0.30	-0.20
Stress Level with AI Tools	-0.35	-0.40	-0.30
Student Motivation with AI Tools	0.50	0.55	0.60
AI Tool Customization	0.30	0.35	0.45
Ease of Integration into Learning	0.45	0.50	0.60

IMPLICATIONS FOR TEACHERS AND DEVELOPERS OF AI TOOLS

The implications of this study for teachers and developers of AI tools are extremely serious. Teachers need to reflect on the best ways in which learning tools based on AI can be integrated into their pedagogical practices without rendering students passive or discriminatory. This calls for ongoing teacher training and professional development so that the teaching faculty is skilled enough to utilize AI tools with optimal effectiveness. Moreover, teachers need to be careful about possible biases and ethical issues in AI-based testing and personalized learning experiences.

For developers of AI tools, the research highlights the need to develop AI applications that are not only easy to use but also flexible enough to suit various learning environments. Developers have to ensure that AI algorithms are explainable so that students and faculty can know how recommendations and evaluations are created. Additionally, AI systems will have to be programmed to give good feedback and personalization and protect student data and privacy. Teachers and AI developers working together are essential in designing AI tools that support pedagogical goals and improve the learning experience in general.

FACULTY PERSPECTIVES AND INSTITUTIONAL CHALLENGES IN ADOPTING AI

Faculty attitudes towards embedding AI in tertiary education reveal promise and constraints. Most faculty appreciate the potential of AI tools to make teaching more efficient, ensuring customized learning and automating administration. There are doubts about whether AI can serve and respond to various student requirements. Academic faculty also reflect concern regarding the learning curve for AI implementation, possible built-in bias in AI programs, and general impact on conventional pedagogical practices. Resistance to change, inadequate technical skills, and data privacy are also increasing the reluctance to implement AI technologies into education systems. Institutional concerns are also a prominent driver of AI implementation. Universities can expect to possess fewer resources in terms of funds to employ and maintain AI devices. Mandatory continual faculty training and professional development courses contribute to costs for institutions. In addition, the introduction of AI into a current curriculum must be well-planned and meshed with instructional outcomes, something that involves close collaboration between educational and technological sectors. Ethical issues, such as data safety and student anonymity, make decision-making more complicated for institutions. In spite of all these issues, institutions that actively deal with such matters through positive policies, training programs, and strong support systems are likely to witness successful AI adoption in higher education.

FUTURE RESEARCH

Future research will need to emphasize the longitudinal impacts of AI tools on education by exploring their impact over more extended periods. Research would be able to analyze how student engagement, student retention, and academic achievement shift as a result of AI-based learning systems over several semesters or years. Moreover, being aware of the evolution in the mindset of teachers towards the embracement of AI technology and how they implement AI-informed pedagogical practices would be insightful on long-term pedagogical changes. More research can further investigate the ethics of AI in education, such as data privacy, algorithmic bias, and how it impacts educational equity overall. Longitudinal studies may assist scholars to learn more regarding the impact of AI technologies on the education sector and inform policy-making decision-making that offers sustainable and effective AI integration into higher education.

CONCLUSION

The results of this study confirm that AI tools have a notable impact on student satisfaction, with specific factors such as usability, feedback quality, and personalization playing significant roles in influencing happiness levels. Traditional models, while effective for simpler analyses, lack the depth required to capture the complex and interactive nature of factors affecting student emotions toward AI tools. The application of MARS and CNNs overcomes these limitations, enabling a detailed examination of both structured and unstructured data sources. MARS effectively identifies and quantifies the importance of individual factors, allowing educators to focus on the most influential elements of AI tools. Meanwhile, CNNs provide a sophisticated analysis of unstructured data, revealing deeper patterns in student feedback and engagement. Together, these methods deliver comprehensive insights into student satisfaction, offering a pathway to refining AI tools for educational environments. This study underscores the value of leveraging advanced machine learning techniques to improve AI-based educational systems, ultimately promoting enhanced learning experiences and career preparedness for students in a technology-driven landscape.

REFERENCES

Abdrakhmanov, R., Zhaxanova, A., Karatayeva, M., Niyazova, G. Z., Berkimbayev, K., & Tuimebayev, A. (2024). Development of a Framework for Predicting Students' Academic Performance in STEM Education using Machine Learning Methods. *International Journal of Advanced Computer Science and Applications*, *15*(1).

Abulibdeh, A., Zaidan, E., & Abulibdeh, R. (2024). Navigating the confluence of artificial intelligence and education for sustainable development in the era of industry 4.0: Challenges, opportunities, and ethical dimensions. *Journal of Cleaner Production*, •••, 140527.

Alpert, J. B., Young, M. G., Lala, S. V., & McGuinness, G. (2021). Medical student engagement and educational value of a remote clinical radiology learning environment: Creation of virtual read-out sessions in response to the COVID-19 pandemic. *Academic Radiology*, *28*(1), 112–118. PMID: 33268209

Altememy, H. A., Neamah, N. R., Mazhair, R., Naser, N. S., & Fahad, A. A., Abdulghffar al-sammarraie, N., ... & Al-Muttar, M. Y. O. (2023). AI Tools' Impact on Student Performance: Focusing on Student Motivation & Engagement in Iraq. [Social Space]. *Przestrzeń Społeczna*, *23*(2), 143–165.

Baig, A., Cressler, J. D., & Minsky, M. (2024). The future of ai in education: Personalized learning and intelligent tutoring systems. *AlgoVista. Journal of AI & Computer Science*, *1*(2).

Barua, P. D., Vicnesh, J., Gururajan, R., Oh, S. L., Palmer, E., Azizan, M. M., Kadri, N. A., & Acharya, U. R. (2022). Artificial intelligence enabled personalised assistive tools to enhance education of children with neurodevelopmental disorders—A review. *International Journal of Environmental Research and Public Health*, *19*(3), 1192. DOI: 10.3390/ijerph19031192 PMID: 35162220

Bhardwaj, P., Gupta, P. K., Panwar, H., Siddiqui, M. K., Morales-Menendez, R., & Bhaik, A. (2021). Application of deep learning on student engagement in e-learning environments. *Computers & Electrical Engineering*, *93*, 107277. DOI: 10.1016/j.compeleceng.2021.107277 PMID: 36567679

Cascella, M., Cascella, A., Monaco, F., & Shariff, M. N. (2023). Envisioning gamification in anesthesia, pain management, and critical care: Basic principles, integration of artificial intelligence, and simulation strategies. *Journal of Anesthesia, Analgesia and Critical Care*, *3*(1), 33. PMID: 37697415

Chaudhry, I. S., Sarwary, S. A. M., El Refae, G. A., & Chabchoub, H. (2023). Time to revisit existing student's performance evaluation approach in higher education sector in a new era of ChatGPT—A case study. *Cogent Education*, *10*(1), 2210461.

Chen, L., Chen, P., & Lin, Z. (2020). Artificial intelligence in education: A review. *IEEE Access : Practical Innovations, Open Solutions*, *8*, 75264–75278. DOI: 10.1109/ACCESS.2020.2988510

Dumitru, D., & Halpern, D. F. (2023). Critical Thinking: Creating Job-Proof Skills for the Future of Work. *Journal of Intelligence*, *11*(10), 194. DOI: 10.3390/jintelligence11100194 PMID: 37888426

Elahi, M. M. (2023). *A user-centric exploration of transparency, explanations, and trust in multi-model and single-model decision support systems* (Doctoral dissertation, Brunel University London).

Eom, S. B., & Ashill, N. (2016). The determinants of students' perceived learning outcomes and satisfaction in university online education: An update. *Decision Sciences Journal of Innovative Education*, *14*(2), 185–215. DOI: 10.1111/dsji.12097

Holgado-Apaza, L. A., Ulloa-Gallardo, N. J., Aragon-Navarrete, R. N., Riva-Ruiz, R., Odagawa-Aragon, N. K., Castellon-Apaza, D. D., Carpio-Vargas, E. E., Villasante-Saravia, F. H., Alvarez-Rozas, T. P., & Quispe-Layme, M. (2024). The Exploration of Predictors for Peruvian Teachers' Life Satisfaction through an Ensemble of Feature Selection Methods and Machine Learning. *Sustainability (Basel)*, *16*(17), 7532. DOI: 10.3390/su16177532

Jawhar, M., Bitar, Z., Miller, J. R., & Jawhar, S. (2024, May). AI-Powered Customized University and Career Guidance. In *2024 Intermountain Engineering, Technology and Computing (IETC)* (pp. 157-161). IEEE. DOI: 10.1109/IETC61393.2024.10564423

Kolluru, V., Mungara, S., & Chintakunta, A. N. (2018). Adaptive learning systems: Harnessing AI for customized educational experiences. [IJCSITY]. *International Journal of Computer Science and Information Technologies*, *6*(1), 2. DOI: 10.5121/ijcsity.2018.6302

Kumar, A. (2024). Gamification in training with next generation AI-virtual reality, animation design and immersive technology. *Journal of Experimental & Theoretical Artificial Intelligence*, *36*(7), 1121–1134. DOI: 10.1080/0952813X.2022.2125080

Lameras, P., & Arnab, S. (2021). Power to the teachers: An exploratory review on artificial intelligence in education. *Information (Basel)*, *13*(1), 14. DOI: 10.3390/info13010014

Markauskaite, L., Marrone, R., Poquet, O., Knight, S., Martinez-Maldonado, R., Howard, S., Tondeur, J., De Laat, M., Buckingham Shum, S., Gašević, D., & Siemens, G. (2022). Rethinking the entwinement between artificial intelligence and human learning: What capabilities do learners need for a world with AI? *Computers and Education: Artificial Intelligence*, *3*, 100056. DOI: 10.1016/j.caeai.2022.100056

Mirdad, K., Daeli, O. P. M., Septiani, N., Ekawati, A., & Rusilowati, U. (2024). Optimizing student engagement and performance usingai-enabled educational tools. *CORISINTA*, *1*(1), 53–60.

Nawaz, G., & Nasreen, A. (2024). ICT Integration in Secondary Schools: Evaluating Ease of Use and Perceived Benefits for Effective Teaching and Learning. *Journal of Asian Development Studies*, *13*(3), 440–451. DOI: 10.62345/jads.2024.13.3.37

Omran, T. M., Sharef, B. T., Grosan, C., & Li, Y. (2023). Transfer learning and sentiment analysis of Bahraini dialects sequential text data using multilingual deep learning approach. *Data & Knowledge Engineering*, *143*, 102106. DOI: 10.1016/j.datak.2022.102106

Put, R., Xu, Q. S., Massart, D. L., & Vander Heyden, Y. (2004). Multivariate adaptive regression splines (MARS) in chromatographic quantitative structure–retention relationship studies. *Journal of Chromatography. A*, *1055*(1-2), 11–19. DOI: 10.1016/j.chroma.2004.07.112 PMID: 15560475

Pyae, A., Ravyse, W., Luimula, M., Pizarro-Lucas, E., Sanchez, P. L., Dorado-Diaz, I. P., & Thaw, A. K. (2023). Exploring User Experience and Usability in a Metaverse Learning Environment for Students: A Usability Study of the Artificial Intelligence, Innovation, and Society (AIIS). *Electronics (Basel), 12*(20), 4283.

Ramos, G., Meek, C., Simard, P., Suh, J., & Ghorashi, S. (2020). Interactive machine teaching: A human-centered approach to building machine-learned models. *Human-Computer Interaction, 35*(5-6), 413–451. DOI: 10.1080/07370024.2020.1734931

Sajja, R., Sermet, Y., Cikmaz, M., Cwiertny, D., & Demir, I. (2024). Artificial intelligence-enabled intelligent assistant for personalized and adaptive learning in higher education. *Information (Basel), 15*(10), 596. DOI: 10.3390/info15100596

Shao, A., Lu, Z., Zhong, B., Liu, S. Q., & Lu, W. (2024). Evaluating the adoption and effectiveness of human educators vs. AI tools in education. *Computers in Human Behavior*, •••, 108492.

Silitubun, E. (2023). The Relationship Between Student Self-confidence, AI Support, and Academic Achievement: A Study in the Psychology of Motivation and Learning. *Bulletin of Counseling and Psychotherapy, 5*(3), 305–313.

Šola, H. M., Qureshi, F. H., & Khawaja, S. (2024). AI Eye-Tracking Technology: A New Era in Managing Cognitive Loads for Online Learners. *Education Sciences, 14*(9), 933. DOI: 10.3390/educsci14090933

Speer, A. B., Perrotta, J., Tenbrink, A. P., Wegmeyer, L. J., Delacruz, A. Y., & Bowker, J. (2023). Turning words into numbers: Assessing work attitudes using natural language processing. *The Journal of Applied Psychology, 108*(6), 1027–1045. DOI: 10.1037/apl0001061 PMID: 36455013

TS, A., & Guddeti, R. M. R. (2020). Automatic detection of students' affective states in classroom environment using hybrid convolutional neural networks. *Education and Information Technologies, 25*(2), 1387–1415. DOI: 10.1007/s10639-019-10004-6

Yang, Q. F., Lian, L. W., & Zhao, J. H. (2023). Developing a gamified artificial intelligence educational robot to promote learning effectiveness and behavior in laboratory safety courses for undergraduate students. *International Journal of Educational Technology in Higher Education*, *20*(1), 18. DOI: 10.1186/s41239-023-00391-9

Yavuz, A. (2021). *Comparison of predictive performances of logistic regression and decision tree algorithms: An application of life satisfaction* (Master's thesis, Dokuz Eylul Universitesi (Turkey)).

Compilation of References

Abdrakhmanov, R., Zhaxanova, A., Karatayeva, M., Niyazova, G. Z., Berkimbayev, K., & Tuimebayev, A. (2024). Development of a Framework for Predicting Students' Academic Performance in STEM Education using Machine Learning Methods. *International Journal of Advanced Computer Science and Applications*, *15*(1).

Abulibdeh, A., Zaidan, E., & Abulibdeh, R. (2024). Navigating the confluence of artificial intelligence and education for sustainable development in the era of industry 4.0: Challenges, opportunities, and ethical dimensions. *Journal of Cleaner Production*, •••, 140527.

Adera, N. (2025). Innovative learning spaces and blended learning: Quest for 21st century competency teaching and learning approaches. Creating Dynamic Space in Higher Education: Modern Shifts in Policy, Competencies, and Governance, 139-174. [HTML]

Akgun, S. & Greenhow, C. (2022). Artificial intelligence in education: Addressing ethical challenges in K-12 settings. AI and Ethics. springer.com

Akinwalere, S. N., & Ivanov, V. (2022). Artificial intelligence in higher education: Challenges and opportunities. *Border Crossing*, *12*(1), 1–15. DOI: 10.33182/bc.v12i1.2015

Alam, A. (2023, May). Improving Learning Outcomes through Predictive Analytics: Enhancing Teaching and Learning with Educational Data Mining. In *2023 7th International Conference on Intelligent Computing and Control Systems (ICICCS)* (pp. 249-257). IEEE.

Alam, A., & Mohanty, A. (2023). Educational technology: Exploring the convergence of technology and pedagogy through mobility, interactivity, AI, and learning tools. Cogent Engineering. tandfonline.com

Alam, T. (2024). Metaverse of Things (MoT) applications for revolutionizing urban living in smart cities. Smart Cities. mdpi.com

Al-Ansi, A. M., Jaboob, M., Garad, A., & Al-Ansi, A. (2023). Analyzing augmented reality (AR) and virtual reality (VR) recent development in education. [sciencedirect.com]. *Social Sciences & Humanities Open*, *8*(1), 100532. DOI: 10.1016/j.ssaho.2023.100532

Alfaisal, R., Hashim, H., & Azizan, U. H. (2024). Empowering the Metaverse in Education: ChatGPT's Role in Transforming Learning. In Breaking Barriers with Generative Intelligence. Using GI to Improve Human Education and Well-Being: First International Workshop, BBGI 2024, Thessaloniki, Greece, June 10, 2024 []. Springer Nature.]. *Proceedings*, *2162*, 13.

AlGerafi, M. A. M., Zhou, Y., Oubibi, M., & Wijaya, T. T. (2023). Unlocking the potential: A comprehensive evaluation of augmented reality and virtual reality in education. Electronics. mdpi.com

Alpala, L. O., Quiroga-Parra, D. J., Torres, J. C., & Peluffo-Ordóñez, D. H. (2022). Smart factory using virtual reality and online multi-user: Towards a metaverse for experimental frameworks. [mdpi.com]. *Applied Sciences (Basel, Switzerland)*, *12*(12), 6258. DOI: 10.3390/app12126258

Alpert, J. B., Young, M. G., Lala, S. V., & McGuinness, G. (2021). Medical student engagement and educational value of a remote clinical radiology learning environment: Creation of virtual read-out sessions in response to the COVID-19 pandemic. *Academic Radiology*, *28*(1), 112–118. PMID: 33268209

Alrabadi, E. (2012). Pour l'introduction de la perspective actionnelle basée sur la réalisation des tâches communicatives en classe de langue étrangère. *Synergies Canada*, *5*, 1–12.

Alsabhan, W. (2023). Student cheating detection in higher education by implementing machine learning and LSTM techniques. *Sensors (Basel), 23*(8), 4149. PMID: 37112489

Altememy, H. A., Neamah, N. R., Mazhair, R., Naser, N. S., & Fahad, A. A., Abdulghffar al-sammarraie, N., ... & Al-Muttar, M. Y. O. (2023). AI Tools' Impact on Student Performance: Focusing on Student Motivation & Engagement in Iraq. [Social Space]. *Przestrzeń Społeczna, 23*(2), 143–165.

Álvarez, I. M., Manero, B., Romero-Hernández, A., Cárdenas, M., & Masó, I. (2024). Virtual reality platform for teacher training on classroom climate management: Evaluating user acceptance. [springer.com]. *Virtual Reality (Waltham Cross), 28*(2), 78. DOI: 10.1007/s10055-024-00973-6

Anderson, J. Q., & Rainie, L. (2020). *The future of education: How technology is reshaping learning*. Pew Research Center. https://www.pewresearch.org

Anderson, C. A., Shibuya, A., Ihori, N., Swing, E. L., & Bushman, B. J. (2016). Video game play, aggression, and prosocial behavior. *Psychological Science, 27*(6), 777–790. DOI: 10.1177/0956797616634463

Aquino, J. F., Riss, R. R., Multerer, S. M., Mogilner, L. N., & Turner, T. L. (2022). A step-by-step guide for mentors to facilitate team building and communication in virtual teams. [tandfonline.com]. *Medical Education Online, 27*(1), 2094529. DOI: 10.1080/10872981.2022.2094529 PMID: 35762578

Aravena-Bravo, P., Cristia, A., Garcia, R., Kotera, H., Nicolas, R. K., Laranjo, R., & Woon, F. T. (2024). Towards Diversifying Early Language Development Research: The First Truly Global International Summer/Winter School on Language Acquisition (/L+/) 2021. [mpg.de]. *Journal of Cognition and Development, 25*(2), 242–260.

Archambault, L., Leary, H., & Rice, K. (2022). Pillars of online pedagogy: A framework for teaching in online learning environments. [HTML]. *Educational Psychologist*.

Aslan, Ö, Aktuğ, S. S., Ozkan-Okay, M., Yilmaz, A. A., & Akin, E. (2023). A comprehensive review of cyber security vulnerabilities, threats, attacks, and solutions. Electronics. mdpi.com

Azam, Z., Islam, M. M., & Huda, M. N. (2023). Comparative analysis of intrusion detection systems and machine learning based model analysis through decision tree. *IEEE Access : Practical Innovations, Open Solutions*.

Babbel. (2019). *Babbel language learning: Impact on language proficiency*. Retrieved from https://www.babbel.com

Baig, A., Cressler, J. D., & Minsky, M. (2024). The future of ai in education: Personalized learning and intelligent tutoring systems. *AlgoVista. Journal of AI & Computer Science*, *1*(2).

Bailenson, J. N. (2018). *Experience on demand: What virtual reality is, how it works, and what it can do*. W. W. Norton & Company.

Bai, X., & Furlong, C. (2019). Mondly: The use of augmented reality in language learning. *Journal of Educational Technology Development and Exchange*, *12*(3), 31–44.

Baker, S. (2022). L'intelligence artificielle dans l'éducation: Rassemblons les pièces du puzzle. Perspectives de l'OCDE sur l'éducation numérique 2021.

Baker, R. S., Baker, R., & Copeland, R. (2020). *Educational chatbots: Enhancing learning through AI-driven communication*. Springer.

Baker, R., & Hawn, A. (2021). Bias in AI-driven education: Addressing fairness and transparency. *Educational Technology Research and Development*, *69*(4), 567–589.

Bala, I., & Mitchell, L. (2024). Thematic exploration of educational research after the COVID pandemic through topic modelling. *Journal of Applied Learning and Teaching*, *7*(1).

Barua, P. D., Vicnesh, J., Gururajan, R., Oh, S. L., Palmer, E., Azizan, M. M., Kadri, N. A., & Acharya, U. R. (2022). Artificial intelligence enabled personalised assistive tools to enhance education of children with neurodevelopmental disorders—A review. *International Journal of Environmental Research and Public Health, 19*(3), 1192. DOI: 10.3390/ijerph19031192 PMID: 35162220

Bell, J. (2024). *Unseen connections: Exhibiting the global stories of cellular telephony at the Smithsonian's National Museum of Natural History.* Museums and the History of Computing. [HTML] DOI: 10.4324/9781003424703-3

Bender, E. M., Gebru, T., McMillan-Major, A., & Shmitchell, S. (2021, March). On the dangers of stochastic parrots: Can language models be too big? . In *Proceedings of the 2021 ACM conference on fairness, accountability, and transparency* (pp. 610-623). DOI: 10.1145/3442188.3445922

Benner, G. J., Rock, M. L., Strycker, L. A., Lee, E. O., Bailey, P., & Virgin, A. S. (2023). Working together: Leveraging teacher study groups to improve social and emotional learning in the classroom. [sagepub.com]. *Beyond Behavior, 32*(1), 24–35. DOI: 10.1177/10742956221143497

Bennett, E. E., & McWhorter, R. R. (2021). Virtual HRD's role in crisis and the post Covid-19 professional lifeworld: Accelerating skills for digital transformation. [sagepub.com]. *Advances in Developing Human Resources, 23*(1), 5–25. DOI: 10.1177/1523422320973288

Bhardwaj, P., Gupta, P. K., Panwar, H., Siddiqui, M. K., Morales-Menendez, R., & Bhaik, A. (2021). Application of deep learning on student engagement in e-learning environments. *Computers & Electrical Engineering, 93*, 107277. DOI: 10.1016/j.compeleceng.2021.107277 PMID: 36567679

Bibri, S. E. & Jagatheesaperumal, S. K. (2023). Harnessing the potential of the metaverse and artificial intelligence for the internet of city things: Cost-effective XReality and synergistic AIoT technologies. Smart Cities. mdpi.com

Bizami, N. A., Tasir, Z., & Kew, S. N. (2023). Innovative pedagogical principles and technological tools capabilities for immersive blended learning: a systematic literature review. Education and Information Technologies. springer.com

Bourguignon, C. (2006). De l'approche communicative à l'approche communic'actionnelle: Une rupture épistémologique en didactique des langues-cultures. *Synergie Europe*, *1*(1), 58–73.

Bower, M., Cavanagh, M., & Moloney, R. (2020). *Designing for a digital world: The role of artificial intelligence in education*. Springer.

Brock, A., De, S., Smith, S. L., & Simonyan, K. (2021, July). High-performance large-scale image recognition without normalization. In *International conference on machine learning* (pp. 1059-1071). PMLR.

Brown, T., Mann, B., Ryder, N., Subbiah, M., Kaplan, J. D., Dhariwal, P., & Amodei, D. (2020). Language models are few-shot learners. *Advances in Neural Information Processing Systems*, *33*, 1877–1901.

Budzianowski, P., Sima, J., & Rudzicz, F. (2021). Towards conversational artificial intelligence for language learning. *Journal of Language and Education Technology*, *7*(2), 42–55. DOI: 10.1057/jlet.2021.39

Buragohain, D., Meng, Y., Deng, C., Li, Q., & Chaudhary, S. (2024). Digitalizing cultural heritage through metaverse applications: challenges, opportunities, and strategies. Heritage Science. springer.com

Burchum, J., Russell, C. K., Likes, W., Adymy, C., Britt, T., Driscoll, C., & Cowan, P. (2007). Confronting challenges in online teaching: The WebQuest solution. *Journal of Online Learning and Teaching*, *3*(1), 40–57.

Caine, R. N., & Caine, G. (1994). *Making connections: Teaching and the human brain*. Addison-Wesley.

Caines, A., Benedetto, L., Taslimipoor, S., Davis, C., Gao, Y., Andersen, O., & Buttery, P. (2023). On the application of Large Language Models for language teaching and assessment technology. arXiv preprint arXiv:2307.08393.

Carvalho, A. R. & Santos, C. (2022). Developing peer mentors' collaborative and metacognitive skills with a technology-enhanced peer learning program. Computers and Education Open. sciencedirect.com

Cascella, M., Cascella, A., Monaco, F., & Shariff, M. N. (2023). Envisioning gamification in anesthesia, pain management, and critical care: Basic principles, integration of artificial intelligence, and simulation strategies. *Journal of Anesthesia, Analgesia and Critical Care*, *3*(1), 33. PMID: 37697415

Celik, I., Dindar, M., Muukkonen, H., & Järvelä, S. (2022). The promises and challenges of artificial intelligence for teachers: A systematic review of research. *TechTrends*, *66*(4), 616–630. DOI: 10.1007/s11528-022-00715-y

Chang, C. Y., Kuo, H. C., & Du, Z. (2023). The role of digital literacy in augmented, virtual, and mixed reality in popular science education: a review study and an educational framework development. Virtual Reality. springer.com

Chaudhary, A., Gupta, P., & Rao, S. (2023). Privacy challenges in the metaverse: Implications for education. *Journal of Digital Learning and Ethics*, *15*(2), 112–128.

Chaudhry, I. S., Sarwary, S. A. M., El Refae, G. A., & Chabchoub, H. (2023). Time to revisit existing student's performance evaluation approach in higher education sector in a new era of ChatGPT—A case study. *Cogent Education*, *10*(1), 2210461.

Chen, C. M. & Huang, M. Y. (2024). Enhancing programming learning performance through a Jigsaw collaborative learning method in a metaverse virtual space. International Journal of STEM Education. springer.com

Chen, R. H. (2021). Fostering students' workplace communicative competence and collaborative mindset through an inquiry-based learning design. Education sciences. mdpi.com

Chen, L., Chen, P., & Lin, Z. (2020). Artificial intelligence in education: A review. *IEEE Access : Practical Innovations, Open Solutions*, *8*, 75264–75278. DOI: 10.1109/ACCESS.2020.2988510

Chen, L., Zhang, W., & Lin, T. (2022). AI-driven personalization in language education: Adaptive learning models and their impact. *Educational Technology Research and Development, 70*(4), 523–541.

Chiche, A., & Yitagesu, B. (2022). Part of speech tagging: A systematic review of deep learning and machine learning approaches. *Journal of Big Data, 9*(1), 10. DOI: 10.1186/s40537-022-00561-y

Colpaert, J. (2018). Artificial intelligence in language learning: The quest for meaning. *Computer Assisted Language Learning, 31*(5-6), 409–420.

Constantinescu, G. G., Silion, D., & Iftene, A. (2024). Using Artificial Intelligence and Mixed Realities to Create Educational Applications of the Future. Procedia Computer Science. sciencedirect.com

Council of Europe. (2001). *Common European framework of reference for languages: Learning, teaching, assessment.* Cambridge University Press.

Council of Europe. (2018). *Common European framework of reference for languages: Learning, teaching, assessment – Companion volume.* Council of Europe.

Crompton, H., & Song, D. (2021). The potential of artificial intelligence in higher education. *Revista virtual Universidad catolica del Norte, 62.*

Csikszentmihalyi, M. (1990). *Flow: The psychology of optimal experience.* Harper & Row.

Cui, Y., Ma, Z., Wang, L., Yang, A., Liu, Q., Kong, S., & Wang, H. (2023). A survey on big data-enabled innovative online education systems during the COVID-19 pandemic. [sciencedirect.com]. *Journal of Innovation & Knowledge, 8*(1), 100295. DOI: 10.1016/j.jik.2022.100295

Cummings, J. J., & Bailenson, J. N. (2016). How immersive is enough? A psychological comparison of traditional and virtual reality mediated environments. *Computers in Human Behavior, 55*, 28–37. DOI: 10.1016/j.chb.2015.09.056

Damaševičius, R. & Sidekerskienė, T. (2024). Virtual worlds for learning in metaverse: a narrative review. Sustainability. mdpi.com

Deci, E. L., Vallerand, R. J., Pelletier, L. G., & Ryan, R. M. (1991). Motivation and education: The self-determination perspective. *Educational Psychologist*, *26*(3–4), 325–346. DOI: 10.1080/00461520.1991.9653137

Dede, C. (2020). The Metaverse as an educational environment. *Journal of Virtual Learning*, *23*(2), 56–72. DOI: 10.1080/10890045.2020.1780910

Dede, C. (2022). Immersive learning in the metaverse: Educational opportunities and challenges. *Educational Technology Research and Development*, *70*(2), 341–357.

Deterding, S., Dixon, D., Khaled, R., & Nacke, L. (2011). From game design elements to gamefulness: defining" gamification". In *Proceedings of the 2011 annual conference on Human factors in computing systems* (pp. 9-15). DOI: 10.1145/2181037.2181040

Divanji, R. A., Bindman, S., Tung, A., Chen, K., Castaneda, L., & Scanlon, M. (2023). A one stop shop? Perspectives on the value of adaptive learning technologies in K-12 education. [sciencedirect.com]. *Computers and Education Open*, *5*, 100157. DOI: 10.1016/j.caeo.2023.100157

Dodge, B. (1995). WebQuests: A technique for Internet-based learning. *Distance Education*, *1*(2), 1–8.

Dodge, B. (2001). Focus: Five rules for writing a great WebQuest. *Learning and Leading with Technology*, *28*(8), 6–9, 58.

Dolega-Dolegowski, D., Proniewska, K., Dolega-Dolegowska, M., Pregowska, A., Hajto-Bryk, J., Trojak, M., Chmiel, J., Walecki, P., & Fudalej, P. S. (2022). Application of holography and augmented reality based technology to visualize the internal structure of the dental root–a proof of concept. [springer.com]. *Head & Face Medicine*, *18*(1), 12. DOI: 10.1186/s13005-022-00307-4 PMID: 35382839

Dudeney, G., Hockly, N., & Pegrum, M. (2013). *Digital literacies: Concepts, policies, and practices*. Routledge. eLearning Department. (2015). Digital literacy for the modern learner. Retrieved from [specific link or source if available].

Dumitru, D., & Halpern, D. F. (2023). Critical Thinking: Creating Job-Proof Skills for the Future of Work. *Journal of Intelligence*, *11*(10), 194. DOI: 10.3390/jintelligence11100194 PMID: 37888426

Dwivedi, Y. K., Hughes, D. L., Baabdullah, A. M., Ribeiro-Navarrete, S., Giannakis, M., Al-Debei, M. M., Dennehy, D., Metri, B., Buhalis, D., Cheung, C. M. K., Conboy, K., Doyle, R., Dubey, R., Dutot, V., Felix, R., Goyal, D. P., Gustafsson, A., Hinsch, C., Jebabli, I., & Wamba, S. F. (2022). Metaverse beyond the hype: Multidisciplinary perspectives on emerging challenges, opportunities, and agenda for research, practice, and policy. *International Journal of Information Management*, *66*, 102542. DOI: 10.1016/j.ijinfomgt.2022.102542

Egger, R. (2022). Text representations and word embeddings: Vectorizing textual data. In *Applied data science in tourism: Interdisciplinary approaches, methodologies, and applications* (pp. 335–361). Springer International Publishing.

Elahi, M. M. (2023). *A user-centric exploration of transparency, explanations, and trust in multi-model and single-model decision support systems* (Doctoral dissertation, Brunel University London).

Ellis, R. (2003). *Task-based language learning and teaching*. Oxford University Press.

Eom, S. B., & Ashill, N. (2016). The determinants of students' perceived learning outcomes and satisfaction in university online education: An update. *Decision Sciences Journal of Innovative Education*, *14*(2), 185–215. DOI: 10.1111/dsji.12097

Fadhel, M. A., Duhaim, A. M., Albahri, A. S., Al-Qaysi, Z. T., Aktham, M. A., Chyad, M. A., Abd-Alaziz, W., Albahri, O. S., Alamoodi, A. H., Alzubaidi, L., Gupta, A., & Gu, Y. (2024). Navigating the metaverse: Unraveling the impact of artificial intelligence—a comprehensive review and gap analysis. [springer.com]. *Artificial Intelligence Review*, *57*(10), 264. DOI: 10.1007/s10462-024-10881-5

Faturoti, B. (2022). Online learning during COVID19 and beyond: A human right based approach to internet access in Africa. *International Review of Law Computers & Technology*, *36*(1), 68–90.

Flavián, C., Ibáñez-Sánchez, S., Orús, C., & Barta, S. (2024). The dark side of the metaverse: The role of gamification in event virtualization. [sciencedirect.com]. *International Journal of Information Management*, *75*, 102726. DOI: 10.1016/j.ijinfomgt.2023.102726

Fogg, B. J. (2003). *Persuasive technology: Using computers to change what we think and do*. Morgan Kaufmann. DOI: 10.1016/B978-155860643-2/50011-1

Fryer, L. (2017). The role of chatbots in education: A survey of the use of conversational agents in education. *Journal of Educational Technology & Society*, *20*(4), 40–50.

Fynn, A. & Mashile, E. O. (2022). Continuous online assessment at a South African open distance and e-learning institution. Frontiers in Education. frontiersin.org

Gallegos-Rejas, V. M., Thomas, E. E., Kelly, J. T., & Smith, A. C. (2023). A multi-stakeholder approach is needed to reduce the digital divide and encourage equitable access to telehealth. [sagepub.com]. *Journal of Telemedicine and Telecare*, *29*(1), 73–78. DOI: 10.1177/1357633X221107995 PMID: 35733379

Gibson, S. E. (2010). Developing digital literacy skills with WebQuests and web inquiry projects. In *Web technologies: Concepts, methodologies, tools, and applications* (pp. 1554–1569). IGI Global. DOI: 10.4018/978-1-60566-982-3.ch083

Gligorea, I., Cioca, M., Oancea, R., Gorski, A. T., Gorski, H., & Tudorache, P. (2023). Adaptive learning using artificial intelligence in e-learning: A literature review. [mdpi.com]. *Education Sciences*, *13*(12), 1216. DOI: 10.3390/educsci13121216

Godwin-Jones, R. (2011). Emerging technologies: Mobile apps for language learning. *Language Learning & Technology*, *15*(2), 2–11.

Godwin-Jones, R. (2017). Emerging technologies: Language learning and social media. *Language Learning & Technology*, *21*(1), 6–19.

Godwin-Jones, R. (2021). Emerging AI applications for language learning: From chatbots to virtual tutors. *Language Learning & Technology*, *25*(2), 3–15.

Gosain, A., & Sardana, S. (2017, September). Handling class imbalance problem using oversampling techniques: A review. In *2017 international conference on advances in computing, communications and informatics (ICACCI)* (pp. 79-85). IEEE.

Gradiski, I. P., Borovecki, A., Ćurković, M., San-Martín, M., Delgado Bolton, R. C., & Vivanco, L. (2022). Burnout in international medical students: Characterization of professionalism and loneliness as predictive factors of burnout. [mdpi.com]. *International Journal of Environmental Research and Public Health*, *19*(3), 1385. DOI: 10.3390/ijerph19031385 PMID: 35162399

Grootendorst, M. (2022). BERTopic: Neural topic modeling with a class-based TF-IDF procedure. *arXiv preprint arXiv:2203.05794*.

Gupta, A. K., Aggarwal, V., Sharma, V., & Naved, M. (2024). Education 4.0 and Web 3.0 Technologies Application for enhancement of distance learning management Systems in the Post–COVID-19 ERa. In *The Role of Sustainability and Artificial Intelligence in Education Improvement* (pp. 66-86). Chapman and Hall/CRC.

Hafner, C. A., Chik, A., & Jones, R. H. (2015). Digital literacies and language learning: Practice and research. *Language Learning & Technology*, *19*(3), 1–7.

Halat, E. (2008). A good teaching technique: WebQuests. *The Clearing House: A Journal of Educational Strategies, Issues and Ideas*, *81*(3), 109–112.

Haleem, A., Javaid, M., Qadri, M. A., & Suman, R. (2022). Understanding the role of digital technologies in education: A review. Sustainable operations and computers, 3, 275-285. sciencedirect.com

Halkiopoulos, C. & Gkintoni, E. (2024). Leveraging AI in e-learning: Personalized learning and adaptive assessment through cognitive neuropsychology—A systematic analysis. Electronics. mdpi.com

Hatami, M., Qu, Q., Chen, Y., Kholidy, H., Blasch, E., & Ardiles-Cruz, E. (2024). A Survey of the Real-Time Metaverse: Challenges and Opportunities. [mdpi.com]. *Future Internet*, *16*(10), 379. DOI: 10.3390/fi16100379

Heinrich, W. F., Louson, E., Blommel, C., & Green, A. R. (2021). Who coaches the coaches? The development of a coaching model for experiential learning. [springer.com]. *Innovative Higher Education*, *46*(3), 357–375. DOI: 10.1007/s10755-020-09537-3

Hellín, C. J., Calles-Esteban, F., Valledor, A., Gómez, J., Otón-Tortosa, S., & Tayebi, A. (2023). Enhancing student motivation and engagement through a gamified learning environment. [mdpi.com]. *Sustainability (Basel)*, *15*(19), 14119. DOI: 10.3390/su151914119

Herrera-Pavo, M. Á. (2021). Collaborative learning for virtual higher education. *Learning, Culture and Social Interaction*, *28*, 100437.

Holgado-Apaza, L. A., Ulloa-Gallardo, N. J., Aragon-Navarrete, R. N., Riva-Ruiz, R., Odagawa-Aragon, N. K., Castellon-Apaza, D. D., Carpio-Vargas, E. E., Villasante-Saravia, F. H., Alvarez-Rozas, T. P., & Quispe-Layme, M. (2024). The Exploration of Predictors for Peruvian Teachers' Life Satisfaction through an Ensemble of Feature Selection Methods and Machine Learning. *Sustainability (Basel)*, *16*(17), 7532. DOI: 10.3390/su16177532

Holmes, W., Bialik, M., & Fadel, C. (2019). *Artificial intelligence in education promises and implications for teaching and learning*. Center for Curriculum Redesign.

Holmes, W., Luckin, R., & Griffiths, M. (2021). The impact of AI on teacher effectiveness: Insights and implications. *AI & Society*, *36*(2), 89–101.

Huang, X., Li, H., Huang, L., & Jiang, T. (2023). Research on the development and innovation of online education based on digital knowledge sharing community. BMC psychology. springer.com

Huang, H., Hwang, G. J., & Chang, S. C. (2023). Facilitating decision making in authentic contexts: An SVVR-based experiential flipped learning approach for professional training. [HTML]. *Interactive Learning Environments, 31*(8), 5219–5235. DOI: 10.1080/10494820.2021.2000435

Huang, R., Liu, D., & Wang, Y. (2021). AI-enhanced virtual tutors: Redefining language education in immersive learning environments. *Computers & Education, 167*, 104187.

Huang, T. C., Chiang, M. H., & Li, H. C. (2020). AI-based education: The role of chatbots in enhancing student engagement and learning outcomes. *Computers & Education, 149*, 103795. DOI: 10.1016/j.compedu.2020.103795

Huang, T., Su, C., & Lin, Y. (2016). Application of augmented reality in language learning: A case study on Chinese language learning. *Computers & Education, 102*, 38–50. DOI: 10.1016/j.compedu.2016.06.001

Huang, X., Zou, D., Cheng, G., Chen, X., & Xie, H. (2023). Trends, research issues and applications of artificial intelligence in language education. *Journal of Educational Technology & Society, 26*(1), 112–131.

Hubbard, P. (2009). *Computer-assisted language learning: Critical concepts in linguistics*. Routledge.

Hubbard, P. (2018). Computer-assisted language learning and artificial intelligence. *ReCALL, 30*(1), 1–10.

Hutson, M. (2021). Robo-writers: The rise and risks of language generating AI. *Nature, 591*(7848), 22–25. DOI: 10.1038/d41586-021-00530-0 PMID: 33658699

Hwang, W. Y., Shadiev, R., & Lin, Y. T. (2022). Conversational AI for language learning: Trends, challenges, and future directions. *Computers & Education, 174*, 104335.

Hymes, D. (1972). On communicative competence. In Pride, J. B., & Holmes, J. (Eds.), *Sociolinguistics* (pp. 269–293). Penguin.

Imran, A. (2023). Why addressing digital inequality should be a priority. [wiley.com]. *The Electronic Journal on Information Systems in Developing Countries*, *89*(3), e12255. DOI: 10.1002/isd2.12255

Itoi, K., & Mizukura, R. (2024). Experience of Japanese exchange students in EMI programmes: Benefits and issues of translanguaging. [HTML]. *International Journal of Multilingualism, 21*(3), 1434–1453. DOI: 10.1080/14790718.2023.2177652

Jabali, O., Hamamra, B., & Ayyoub, A. (2024). Critical thinking, assessment, and educational policy in Palestinian universities. [springer.com]. *International Journal for Educational Integrity*, *20*(1), 12. DOI: 10.1007/s40979-024-00160-9

Jamil, S. (2021). From digital divide to digital inclusion: Challenges for wide-ranging digitalization in Pakistan. [HTML]. *Telecommunications Policy*, *45*(8), 102206. DOI: 10.1016/j.telpol.2021.102206

Javed, F. (2025). Preparing for Tomorrow: Evaluating and Innovating Educational Systems for Future Competence. In Fostering Teacher Skills and Critical Thinking in Modern Education (pp. 43-78). IGI Global Scientific Publishing. [HTML]

Jawhar, M., Bitar, Z., Miller, J. R., & Jawhar, S. (2024, May). AI-Powered Customized University and Career Guidance. In *2024 Intermountain Engineering, Technology and Computing (IETC)* (pp. 157-161). IEEE. DOI: 10.1109/IETC61393.2024.10564423

Jayanthi, K., Priya, M. S., Saranya, S., Gomathi, R., & Sam, D. (2023). E-Learning as a Desirable Form of Education in the Era of Society 5.0. In *Advances in Distance Learning in Times of Pandemic* (pp. 23–51). Chapman and Hall/CRC. DOI: 10.1201/9781003322252-2

Joachims, T. (2012). *Learning to classify text using support vector machines* (Vol. 668). Springer Science & Business Media.

Johri, A., Sayal, A., Chaithra, N., Jha, J., Aggarwal, N., Pawar, D., & Gupta, A. (2024). Crafting the techno-functional blocks for Metaverse-A review and research agenda. [sciencedirect.com]. *International Journal of Information Management Data Insights*, *4*(1), 100213. DOI: 10.1016/j.jjimei.2024.100213

Jones, B., & Flannigan, S. L. (2006). Connecting the digital dots: Literacy of the 21st century. *EDUCAUSE Quarterly*, *29*(2), 8–10.

Jones, R., & Hafner, C. (2012). Understanding digital literacies: A practical introduction. *Learning and Technology*, *19*(3), 1–7.

Jovanović, A. & Milosavljević, A. (2022). VoRtex Metaverse platform for gamified collaborative learning. Electronics. mdpi.com

Kamalov, F., Santandreu Calonge, D., & Gurrib, I. (2023). New era of artificial intelligence in education: Towards a sustainable multifaceted revolution. *Sustainability (Basel)*, *15*(16), 12451. DOI: 10.3390/su151612451

Kaur, S., Budhraja, K., Pahuja, A., Nayyar, V., & Saluja, S. (2024). Leveraging Artificial Intelligence in Education: Enhancing Learning Experience. In Ethical AI and Data Management Strategies in Marketing (pp. 125-140). IGI Global. [HTML]

Kayyali, M. (2024). Immersive Technologies: Virtual and Augmented Reality in Higher Education. In Reshaping Learning with Next Generation Educational Technologies (pp. 99-114). IGI Global. [HTML]

Khaiser, F. K., Saad, A., & Mason, C. (2023). Sentiment analysis of students' feedback on institutional facilities using text-based classification and natural language processing (NLP). *Journal of Language and Communication*, *10*(1), 101–111.

Kim, H., & Jeong, Y. S. (2019). Sentiment classification using convolutional neural networks. *Applied Sciences (Basel, Switzerland)*, *9*(11), 2347.

Kohnke, L., Moorhouse, B. L., & Zou, D. (2023). ChatGPT for language teaching and learning. *RELC Journal*, *54*(2), 537–550. DOI: 10.1177/00336882231162868

Kolluru, V., Mungara, S., & Chintakunta, A. N. (2018). Adaptive learning systems: Harnessing AI for customized educational experiences. [IJCSITY]. *International Journal of Computer Science and Information Technologies*, *6*(1), 2. DOI: 10.5121/ijcsity.2018.6302

Kukulska-Hulme, A. (2020). Mobile language learning. In *The Cambridge Handbook of Technology and Language* (pp. 391–409). Cambridge University Press., DOI: 10.1017/9781108330307.024

Kumar, A. (2024). Gamification in training with next generation AI-virtual reality, animation design and immersive technology. *Journal of Experimental & Theoretical Artificial Intelligence*, *36*(7), 1121–1134. DOI: 10.1080/0952813X.2022.2125080

Kumar, N., & Singh, P. (2022). Ethical implications of AI in education: Data privacy and bias considerations. *AI & Society*, *37*(1), 123–140.

Kye, A. (2023). *Comparative Analysis of Classification Performance for US College Enrollment Predictive Modeling Using Four Machine Learning Algorithms (Logistic Regression, Decision Tree, Support Vector Machine, Artificial Neural Network)* (Doctoral dissertation, Loyola University Chicago).

Κρυστάλλη, Π. (2023). Η ιστοεξερεύνηση στη διδασκαλία/εκμάθηση της ξένης γλώσσας ως εργαλείο για την ανάπτυξη γλωσσικών, επικοινωνιακών και ψηφιακών δεξιοτήτων. Στο Ε. Κανταρτζή & Αθ. Φουργκατσιώτης (Επιμ.), *8ο Πανελλήνιο Συνέδριο: Εκπαίδευση και Πολιτισμός στον 21ο αιώνα* (τ. Β'). Μουσείο Σχολικής Ζωής και Εκπαίδευσης του ΕΚΕΔΙΣΥ.

Lai, Y. H., Lin, Y. S., Chang, Y. C., & Chen, S. Y. (2024). Cyber-physical metaverse learning in cultural sustainable education. [HTML]. *Library Hi Tech.* Advance online publication. DOI: 10.1108/LHT-12-2023-0585

Lameras, P., & Arnab, S. (2021). Power to the teachers: An exploratory review on artificial intelligence in education. *Information (Basel)*, *13*(1), 14. DOI: 10.3390/info13010014

Lee, H. J. & Hwang, Y. (2022). Technology-enhanced education through VR-making and metaverse-linking to foster teacher readiness and sustainable learning. Sustainability. mdpi.com

Lee, J., & Kim, H. (2022). EduVerse: Leveraging AI for immersive K-12 learning. *International Journal of Virtual Learning*, *9*(3), 289–305.

Leu, D. J., Kinzer, C. K., Coiro, J., & Cammack, D. W. (2004). Toward a theory of new literacies emerging from the Internet and other information and communication technologies. *Theoretical models and processes of reading*, 5, 1570-1613.

Levy, M. (1997). *Computer-assisted language learning: Context and conceptualization.* Oxford University Press. DOI: 10.1093/oso/9780198236320.001.0001

Li, M. & Yu, Z. (2022). Teachers' satisfaction, role, and digital literacy during the COVID-19 pandemic. Sustainability. mdpi.com

Li, D., Ortegas, K. D., & White, M. (2023). Exploring the computational effects of advanced deep neural networks on logical and activity learning for enhanced thinking skills. *Systems*, *11*(7), 319.

Li, J., Zhang, X., & Liu, X. C. (2025). Exploring the motivational factors and learning outcomes of Virtual Reality educational games for middle school students: A unity 3D case study. [HTML]. *Interactive Learning Environments*, 1–21. DOI: 10.1080/10494820.2024.2446536

Lin, Y., Chen, H., Xia, W., Lin, F., Wang, Z., & Liu, Y. (2023). A comprehensive survey on deep learning techniques in educational data mining. *arXiv preprint arXiv:2309.04761*.

Li, X. (2023). Metaverse and foreign language learning: A review of emerging trends and pedagogical strategies. *Language Learning & Technology*, *27*(1), 1–15.

Li, Y., Wei, W., & Xu, J. (2022). The exploration on ethical problems of educational metaverse. *International Conference on Metaverse*. [HTML] DOI: 10.1007/978-3-031-23518-4_3

Lombardi, D., & Shipley, T. F., & Astronomy Team, Biology Team, Chemistry Team, Engineering Team, Geography Team, Geoscience Team, and Physics Team. (2021). The curious construct of active learning. *Psychological Science in the Public Interest, 22*(1), 8–43.

López-Jiménez, J. J., Fernández-Alemán, J. L., García-Berná, J. A., López González, L., González Sequeros, O., Nicolás Ros, J., Carrillo de Gea, J. M., Idri, A., & Toval, A. (2021). Effects of gamification on the benefits of student response systems in learning of human anatomy: Three experimental studies. [mdpi.com]. *International Journal of Environmental Research and Public Health, 18*(24), 13210. DOI: 10.3390/ijerph182413210 PMID: 34948818

Luckin, R. (2017). Towards artificial intelligence-based assessment systems. *Nature Human Behaviour, 1(3),* 0028.

Luckin, R., & Holmes, W. (2017). AI is the new TA in the classroom. How We Get To Next. January, 4.

Lu, X., Fang, Y., & He, J. (2022). AI-enhanced metaverse learning: Bridging virtual reality and language acquisition. *Interactive Learning Environments, 30*(4), 621–639.

Lythreatis, S., Singh, S. K., & El-Kassar, A. N. (2022). The digital divide: A review and future research agenda. [HTML]. *Technological Forecasting and Social Change, 175*, 121359. DOI: 10.1016/j.techfore.2021.121359

Mahindru, R., Kumar, A., Bapat, G., & Rroy, A. D., Kavita, & Sharma, N. (2024). Metaverse unleashed: Augmenting creativity and innovation in business education. *Engineering Proceedings, 59*(1), 207.

Malik, A., Onyema, E. M., Dalal, S., Lilhore, U. K., Anand, D., Sharma, A., & Simaiya, S. (2023). Forecasting students' adaptability in online entrepreneurship education using modified ensemble machine learning model. *Array (New York, N.Y.), 19*, 100303.

Mangenot, F. (2017). *Formation en ligne et MOOC: Apprendre et se former en langue avec le numérique*. Hachette.

Maqbool, M. A., Asif, M., Imran, M., Bibi, S., & Almusharraf, N. (2024). Emerging e-learning trends: A study of faculty perceptions and impact of collaborative techniques using fuzzy interface system. *Social Sciences & Humanities Open*, *10*, 101035.

Maqsoom, A., Zulqarnain, M., Irfan, M., Ullah, F., Alqahtani, F. K., & Khan, K. I. A. (2023). Drivers of, and barriers to, the adoption of mixed reality in the construction industry of developing countries. [mdpi.com]. *Buildings (Basel, Switzerland)*, *13*(4), 872. DOI: 10.3390/buildings13040872

March, T. (1998). Why webquests? An introduction. WebQuest for Learning. Retrieved https://tommarch.com/writings/why-webquests/

March, T. (2003). The learning power of WebQuests. Educational Leadership, 61(4), 40–44https://tommarch.com/writings/ascdwebquests/

Markauskaite, L., Marrone, R., Poquet, O., Knight, S., Martinez-Maldonado, R., Howard, S., Tondeur, J., De Laat, M., Buckingham Shum, S., Gašević, D., & Siemens, G. (2022). Rethinking the entwinement between artificial intelligence and human learning: What capabilities do learners need for a world with AI? *Computers and Education: Artificial Intelligence*, *3*, 100056. DOI: 10.1016/j.caeai.2022.100056

Marougkas, A., Troussas, C., Krouska, A., & Sgouropoulou, C. (2023). Virtual reality in education: a review of learning theories, approaches and methodologies for the last decade. Electronics. mdpi.com

Matsika, C., & Zhou, M. (2021). Factors affecting the adoption and use of AVR technology in higher and tertiary education. [HTML]. *Technology in Society*, *67*, 101694. DOI: 10.1016/j.techsoc.2021.101694

McClelland, D. C. (1961). *The achieving society*. Free Press. DOI: 10.1037/14359-000

Mendoza-Ramírez, C. E., Tudon-Martinez, J. C., Félix-Herrán, L. C., Lozoya-Santos, J. D. J., & Vargas-Martínez, A. (2023). Augmented reality: Survey. [mdpi.com]. *Applied Sciences (Basel, Switzerland)*, *13*(18), 10491. DOI: 10.3390/app131810491

Mikropoulos, T. A., & Natsis, A. (2011). Educational virtual environments: A ten-year review of empirical research (1999-2009). *Computers & Education*, *56*(3), 769–780. DOI: 10.1016/j.compedu.2010.10.020

Mirdad, K., Daeli, O. P. M., Septiani, N., Ekawati, A., & Rusilowati, U. (2024). Optimizing student engagement and performance usingai-enabled educational tools. *CORISINTA*, *1*(1), 53–60.

Mishra, D. R., & Varshney, D. (2024). Comprehensive analysis of human and AI task allocation in the education sector: Defining futuristic roles and responsibilities. *World Journal of Advanced Research and Reviews*, *22*(3), 10–30574. DOI: 10.30574/wjarr.2024.22.3.1949

Mishra, P., & Kereluik, K. (2011). What 21st-century learning means. *Educational Technology*, *51*(3), 22–25.

Molenaar, I., Chiu, M. M., & van der Maas, H. L. (2013). The role of adaptive learning in the design of interactive educational technologies: An evaluation of two types of interventions. *Journal of Educational Psychology*, *105*(4), 1043–1057. DOI: 10.1037/a0032412

Mourtzis, D., Panopoulos, N., Angelopoulos, J., Wang, B., & Wang, L. (2022). Human centric platforms for personalized value creation in metaverse. [HTML]. *Journal of Manufacturing Systems*, *65*, 653–659. DOI: 10.1016/j.jmsy.2022.11.004

Musarat, M. A., Irfan, M., Alaloul, W. S., Maqsoom, A., & Ghufran, M. (2023). A review on the way forward in construction through industrial revolution 5.0. [mdpi.com]. *Sustainability (Basel)*, *15*(18), 13862. DOI: 10.3390/su151813862

Muzata, A. R., Singh, G., Stepanov, M. S., & Musonda, I. (2024). Immersive Learning: A Systematic Literature Review on Transforming Engineering Education Through Virtual Reality. Virtual Worlds. mdpi.com

Mystakidis, S. (2021). *Motivation enhancement methods for community building in extended reality*. Augmented and Mixed Reality for Communities. [HTML] DOI: 10.1201/9781003052838-17

Nahi, A. A., Ghaib, A. A., & Ali, A. A. A. A. (2023, December). Metaverse Applications and Its Use in Education. In International Multi-Disciplinary Conference-Integrated Sciences and Technologies (pp. 61-80). Cham: Springer Nature Switzerland. [HTML] DOI: 10.1007/978-3-031-51716-7_5

Nakamura, Y., Takahashi, R., & Ito, M. (2023). Impact of AI tutors in metaverse classrooms: A case study from Japan. *Journal of Educational AI*, *18*(1), 45–63.

Naveed, H., Khan, A. U., Qiu, S., Saqib, M., Anwar, S., Usman, M., & Mian, A. (2023). A comprehensive overview of large language models. arXiv preprint arXiv:2307.06435.

Nawaz, G., & Nasreen, A. (2024). ICT Integration in Secondary Schools: Evaluating Ease of Use and Perceived Benefits for Effective Teaching and Learning. *Journal of Asian Development Studies*, *13*(3), 440–451. DOI: 10.62345/jads.2024.13.3.37

Nelson, W. & Luetz, J. M. (2021). The impact of short-term cross-cultural experience on the intercultural competence of participating students: A case study of Australian high school students. Social Sciences. mdpi.com

Nicolaou, C., Matsiola, M., Karypidou, C., Podara, A., Kotsakis, R., & Kalliris, G. (2021). Media studies, audiovisual media communications, and generations: The case of budding journalists in radio courses in Greece. [mdpi.com]. *Journalism and Media*, *2*(2), 155–192. DOI: 10.3390/journalmedia2020010

Nikou, S., De Reuver, M., & Mahboob Kanafi, M. (2022). Workplace literacy skills—How information and digital literacy affect adoption of digital technology. [emerald.com]. *The Journal of Documentation*, *78*(7), 371–391. DOI: 10.1108/JD-12-2021-0241

Niu, Y. (2023). Integrated physical education and medicine in general physical education at universities in the age of educational technologies. BMC Medical Education. springer.com

Nunan, D. (1989). *Designing Tasks for the Communicative Classroom.* Cambridge University Press.

O'Dowd, R. (2021). What do students learn in virtual exchange? A qualitative content analysis of learning outcomes across multiple exchanges. International Journal of Educational Research. sciencedirect.com

Omran, T. M., Sharef, B. T., Grosan, C., & Li, Y. (2023). Transfer learning and sentiment analysis of Bahraini dialects sequential text data using multilingual deep learning approach. *Data & Knowledge Engineering*, *143*, 102106. DOI: 10.1016/j.datak.2022.102106

Onu, P., Pradhan, A., & Mbohwa, C. (2024). Potential to use metaverse for future teaching and learning. Education and Information Technologies. springer.com

Orel, M. (2022). Collaboration Potential in Virtual Reality (VR) Office Space: Transforming the Workplace of Tomorrow. [HTML]

Othman, A., Chemnad, K., Hassanien, A. E., Tlili, A., Zhang, C. Y., Al-Thani, D., & Altınay, Z. (2024). Accessible Metaverse: A Theoretical Framework for Accessibility and Inclusion in the Metaverse. [mdpi.com]. *Multimodal Technologies and Interaction*, *8*(3), 21. DOI: 10.3390/mti8030021

Parmaxi, A., Athanasiou, A., & Demetriou, A. (2021). Introducing a student-led application of Google Expeditions: An exploratory study. [HTML]. *Educational Media International*, *58*(1), 37–59. DOI: 10.1080/09523987.2021.1908497

Patel, R., Singh, M., & Zhao, L. (2023). Assessing chatbot effectiveness in metaverse learning environments. *Educational Research Journal*, *20*(1), 78–95.

Pathak, S., & Malpani, D. (2025). Leveraging Virtual Reality to Improve Communication and Collaboration in Remote Work: Enhancing Team Dynamics and Engagement Through Immersive Technologies. In Optimizing Virtual Reality and Metaverse for Remote Work and Virtual Team Collaboration (pp. 191-224). IGI Global. [HTML]

Pedro, F., Subosa, M., Rivas, A., & Valverde, P. (2019). *Artificial intelligence in education: Challenges and opportunities for sustainable development*. UNESCO.

Pegrum, M. (2014). Mobile literacy: Navigating new learning opportunities and obligations. In W. C. C. Chu, H. C. Chao, & L. C. Jain (Eds.), Proceedings of International Computer Symposium (ICS) (pp. 660-667). Taichung: Dept of Computer Science, Tung Hai University.

Pegrum, M., Dudeney, G., & Hockly, N. (2018). Digital literacies revisited. *European Journal of Applied Linguistics and TEFL*, *7*(2), 3–24.

Pellas, N., Mystakidis, S., & Kazanidis, I. (2021). Immersive Virtual Reality in K-12 and Higher Education: A systematic review of the last decade scientific literature. [HTML]. *Virtual Reality (Waltham Cross)*, *25*(3), 835–861. DOI: 10.1007/s10055-020-00489-9

Pérez, M., & Murray, J. (2021). Personalized learning with AI: A framework for adaptive language instruction. *Journal of Educational Computing Research*, *59*(3), 487–505.

Perry, B. (2021). Gamified mobile collaborative location-based language learning. Frontiers in Education. frontiersin.org

Piccoli, G., Rodriguez, J., Palese, B., & Bartosiak, M. L. (2020). Feedback at scale: Designing for accurate and timely practical digital skills evaluation. *European Journal of Information Systems*, *29*(2), 114–133. DOI: 10.1080/0960085X.2019.1701955

Pregowska, A., Masztalerz, K., Garlińska, M., & Osial, M. (2021). A worldwide journey through distance education—from the post office to virtual, augmented and mixed realities, and education during the COVID-19 pandemic. Education Sciences. mdpi.com

Put, R., Xu, Q. S., Massart, D. L., & Vander Heyden, Y. (2004). Multivariate adaptive regression splines (MARS) in chromatographic quantitative structure–retention relationship studies. *Journal of Chromatography. A*, *1055*(1-2), 11–19. DOI: 10.1016/j.chroma.2004.07.112 PMID: 15560475

Pyae, A., Ravyse, W., Luimula, M., Pizarro-Lucas, E., Sanchez, P. L., Dorado-Diaz, I. P., & Thaw, A. K. (2023). Exploring User Experience and Usability in a Metaverse Learning Environment for Students: A Usability Study of the Artificial Intelligence, Innovation, and Society (AIIS). *Electronics (Basel)*, *12*(20), 4283.

Radanliev, P., De Roure, D., Novitzky, P., & Sluganovic, I. (2024). Accessibility and inclusiveness of new information and communication technologies for disabled users and content creators in the Metaverse. [tandfonline.com]. *Disability and Rehabilitation. Assistive Technology*, *19*(5), 1849–1863. DOI: 10.1080/17483107.2023.2241882 PMID: 37585705

Rahm, L. (2023). Educational imaginaries: Governance at the intersection of technology and education. Journal of Education Policy. tandfonline.com

Rajaram, K. (2023). Future of learning: Teaching and learning strategies. In *Learning Intelligence: Innovative and Digital Transformative Learning Strategies: Cultural and Social Engineering Perspectives* (pp. 3–53). Springer Nature Singapore.

Ramalingam, S. (2022). *Sentiment Analysis on Covid-19 Vaccination Reviews Using BERT and Comparative Study with LSTM, Vader, and Text blob Models* (Doctoral dissertation, Dublin, National College of Ireland).

Ramírez-Montoya, M. S., Andrade-Vargas, L., Rivera-Rogel, D., & Portuguez-Castro, M. (2021). Trends for the future of education programs for professional development. [mdpi.com]. *Sustainability (Basel)*, *13*(13), 7244. DOI: 10.3390/su13137244

Ramos, G., Meek, C., Simard, P., Suh, J., & Ghorashi, S. (2020). Interactive machine teaching: A human-centered approach to building machine-learned models. *Human-Computer Interaction*, *35*(5-6), 413–451. DOI: 10.1080/07370024.2020.1734931

Richards, J. C., & Rodgers, T. S. (2001). *Approaches and methods in language teaching*. Cambridge University Press. DOI: 10.1017/CBO9780511667305

Rizvi, Y. S., & Nabi, A. (2021). Transformation of learning from real to virtual: An exploratory-descriptive analysis of issues and challenges. [emerald.com]. *Journal of Research in Innovative Teaching & Learning*, *14*(1), 5–17. DOI: 10.1108/JRIT-10-2020-0052

Roa González, J., Sánchez Sánchez, N., Seoane Pujol, I., & Díaz Palencia, J. L. (2025). Challenges and perspectives in the evolution of distance and online education towards higher technological environments. [tandfonline.com]. *Cogent Education*, *12*(1), 2447168. DOI: 10.1080/2331186X.2024.2447168

Rodrigues, L., Pereira, F. D., Toda, A. M., Palomino, P. T., Pessoa, M., Carvalho, L. S. G., Fernandes, D., Oliveira, E. H. T., Cristea, A. I., & Isotani, S. (2022). Gamification suffers from the novelty effect but benefits from the familiarization effect: Findings from a longitudinal study. [springer.com]. *International Journal of Educational Technology in Higher Education*, *19*(1), 13. DOI: 10.1186/s41239-021-00314-6

Ryan, R. M., & Deci, E. L. (2000). Self-determination theory and the facilitation of intrinsic motivation, social development, and well-being. *The American Psychologist*, *55*(1), 68–78. DOI: 10.1037/0003-066X.55.1.68 PMID: 11392867

Safarov, F., Kutlimuratov, A., Abdusalomov, A. B., Nasimov, R., & Cho, Y. I. (2023). Deep learning recommendations of e-education based on clustering and sequence. *Electronics (Basel)*, *12*(4), 809.

Sailer, M., Hense, J. U., Mayr, S. K., & Mærkedahl, J. (2017). How gamification motivates: An experimental study of the effects of specific game design elements on psychological need satisfaction. *Computers in Human Behavior*, *69*, 10–17. DOI: 10.1016/j.chb.2016.12.033

Sajja, R., Sermet, Y., Cikmaz, M., Cwiertny, D., & Demir, I. (2024). Artificial intelligence-enabled intelligent assistant for personalized and adaptive learning in higher education. *Information (Basel)*, *15*(10), 596. DOI: 10.3390/info15100596

Schwienhorst, K. (2002). The state of VR-based language learning. *ReCALL*, *14*(2), 253–267.

Shao, A., Lu, Z., Zhong, B., Liu, S. Q., & Lu, W. (2024). Evaluating the adoption and effectiveness of human educators vs. AI tools in education. *Computers in Human Behavior*, •••, 108492.

Sharma, W., Lim, W. M., Kumar, S., Verma, A., & Kumra, R. (2024). Game on! A state-of-the-art overview of doing business with gamification. [sciencedirect.com]. *Technological Forecasting and Social Change*, *198*, 122988. DOI: 10.1016/j.techfore.2023.122988

Shawar, B. A., & Atwell, E. (2007). Chatbots: Are they really useful? *LNAI*, *4762*, 392–397. DOI: 10.1007/978-3-540-76314-9_48

Sidhu, M. S., Mousakhani, S., Lee, C. K., & Sidhu, K. K. (2024). Educational impact of Metaverse learning environment for engineering mechanics dynamics. [HTML]. *Computer Applications in Engineering Education*, *32*(5), e22772. DOI: 10.1002/cae.22772

Silitubun, E. (2023). The Relationship Between Student Self-confidence, AI Support, and Academic Achievement: A Study in the Psychology of Motivation and Learning. *Bulletin of Counseling and Psychotherapy*, *5*(3), 305–313.

Simelane-Mnisi, S. (2023). Effectiveness of LMS Digital Tools used by the academics to Foster Students' Engagement. Education Sciences. mdpi.com

Singh, M. (2024). Exploring the possibilities to implement metaverse in higher education institutions of India. Education and Information Technologies. springer.com

Skinner, B. F. (1953). *Science and human behavior*. Macmillan.

Skinner, B. F. (1957). *Verbal behavior*. Appleton-Century-Crofts. DOI: 10.1037/11256-000

Smith, S. L. (2024). The American Museum of Natural History. In Connecting with Our Ancestors: Human Evolution Museum Experiences (pp. 93-135). Cham: Springer Nature Switzerland. [HTML] DOI: 10.1007/978-3-031-69429-5_4

Smith, J., & Johnson, L. (2023). AI tutors in virtual reality classrooms: An empirical analysis. *Journal of Emerging Educational Technologies*, *14*(2), 321–340.

Smith, K. A., Sheppard, S. D., Johnson, D. W., & Johnson, R. T. (2005). Pedagogies of engagement: Classroom-based practices. *Journal of Engineering Education*, *94*(1), 87–101. DOI: 10.1002/j.2168-9830.2005.tb00831.x

Smith, R., & Jones, T. (2020). Virtual environments and second language acquisition: Insights from AI-driven learning models. *Language Teaching Research*, *24*(5), 678–693.

Šola, H. M., Qureshi, F. H., & Khawaja, S. (2024). AI Eye-Tracking Technology: A New Era in Managing Cognitive Loads for Online Learners. *Education Sciences*, *14*(9), 933. DOI: 10.3390/educsci14090933

Soliman, M., Pesyridis, A., Dalaymani-Zad, D., Gronfula, M., & Kourmpetis, M. (2021). The application of virtual reality in engineering education. [mdpi.com]. *Applied Sciences (Basel, Switzerland)*, *11*(6), 2879. DOI: 10.3390/app11062879

Soubrié, T. (2008). *Un nouveau cadre pour la conception d' activités TICE: la perspective actionnelle du CECR. Ensinar e aprender linguas e culturas estrangeiras hoje: que perspectivas?* Areal Editores.

Sousa-Vieira, M. E., Ferrero-Castro, D., & López-Ardao, J. C. (2021). Design, development and use of a digital badges system in higher education. Applied Sciences. mdpi.com

Speer, A. B., Perrotta, J., Tenbrink, A. P., Wegmeyer, L. J., Delacruz, A. Y., & Bowker, J. (2023). Turning words into numbers: Assessing work attitudes using natural language processing. *The Journal of Applied Psychology*, *108*(6), 1027–1045. DOI: 10.1037/apl0001061 PMID: 36455013

Steed, A., Waller, D., & Stott, L. (2021). Immersive environments and the Metaverse: Current research and emerging opportunities. *International Journal of Human-Computer Studies*, *144*, 102502. DOI: 10.1016/j.ijhcs.2020.102502

Strickland, J., & Nazzal, A. (2005). Using webquests to teach content: Comparing instructional strategies. *Contemporary Issues in Technology & Teacher Education*, *5*(2), 138–148.

Strielkowski, W., Grebennikova, V., Lisovskiy, A., Rakhimova, G., & Vasileva, T. (2024). AI-driven adaptive learning for sustainable educational transformation. Sustainable Development. wiley.com

Sweller, J. (1988). Cognitive load during problem solving: Effects on learning. *Cognitive Science*, *12*(2), 257–285. DOI: 10.1207/s15516709cog1202_4

Syed, T. A., Siddiqui, M. S., Abdullah, H. B., Jan, S., Namoun, A., Alzahrani, A., Nadeem, A., & Alkhodre, A. B. (2022). In-depth review of augmented reality: Tracking technologies, development tools, AR displays, collaborative AR, and security concerns. [mdpi.com]. *Sensors (Basel)*, *23*(1), 146. DOI: 10.3390/s23010146 PMID: 36616745

Tan, S. (2023). Harnessing immersive technologies for innovation in teaching and learnings. In *Learning intelligence: Innovative and digital transformative learning strategies: Cultural and social engineering perspectives* (pp. 305–334). Springer Nature Singapore. [HTML] DOI: 10.1007/978-981-19-9201-8_7

Tan, Y., Lo, L., Li, W., & Pang, G. (2023). Intellectual capital and student mobility. [HTML]. *Journal of Ethnic and Migration Studies*, *49*(18), 4641–4661. DOI: 10.1080/1369183X.2023.2270332

Thakkar, A., Mungra, D., Agrawal, A., & Chaudhari, K. (2022). Improving the performance of sentiment analysis using enhanced preprocessing technique and Artificial Neural Network. *IEEE Transactions on Affective Computing*, *13*(4), 1771–1782.

Tharp, R. G. (1993). *Teaching transformed: Achieving excellence, fairness, inclusion, and harmony*. Pergamon Press.

Timotheou, S., Miliou, O., Dimitriadis, Y., Sobrino, S. V., Giannoutsou, N., Cachia, R., Monés, A. M., & Ioannou, A. (2023). Impacts of digital technologies on education and factors influencing schools' digital capacity and transformation: A literature review. [springer.com]. *Education and Information Technologies*, *28*(6), 6695–6726. DOI: 10.1007/s10639-022-11431-8 PMID: 36465416

Tran, C. D. T. T. (2021). Cost efficiency–one size fits all? A university-level analysis of economies of scale and scope in Vietnamese higher education. [HTML]. *Asia Pacific Journal of Education*, *41*(2), 336–355. DOI: 10.1080/02188791.2020.1735996

Tripon, C., Gon a, I., & Bulgac, A. (2023). Nurturing minds and sustainability: an exploration of educational interactions and their impact on student well-being and assessment in a sustainable university. Sustainability. mdpi.com

TS, A., & Guddeti, R. M. R. (2020). Automatic detection of students' affective states in classroom environment using hybrid convolutional neural networks. *Education and Information Technologies*, *25*(2), 1387–1415. DOI: 10.1007/s10639-019-10004-6

Tyagi, S., Sibal, R., & Suri, B. (2022). Empirically developed framework for building trust in distributed agile teams. [HTML]. *Information and Software Technology*, *145*, 106828. DOI: 10.1016/j.infsof.2022.106828

Tzenios, N. (2020). Clustering students for personalized health education based on learning styles. *Sage Science Review of Educational Technology*, *3*(1), 22–36.

Vahed, A., & Rodriguez, K. (2021). Enriching students' engaged learning experiences through the collaborative online international learning project. [HTML]. *Innovations in Education and Teaching International*, *58*(5), 596–605. DOI: 10.1080/14703297.2020.1792331

Van der Burg, S., Wiseman, L., & Krkeljas, J. (2021). Trust in farm data sharing: Reflections on the EU code of conduct for agricultural data sharing. [springer.com]. *Ethics and Information Technology*, *23*(3), 185–198. DOI: 10.1007/s10676-020-09543-1

VanLehn, K. (2011). The relative effectiveness of human tutoring, intelligent tutoring systems, and other tutoring systems. *Educational Psychologist, 46*(4), 197–221. DOI: 10.1080/00461520.2011.611369

Vasalou, A., Joinson, A. N., Bänziger, T., & Kappas, A. (2020). Building and assessing virtual learning environments. *Computers & Education, 156*, 103939. DOI: 10.1016/j.compedu.2020.103939

Vaz, E. (2024). The Role of the Metaverse and the Geographical Dimension of Knowledge Management. In Regional Knowledge Economies: Exploring the Intersection of Technology, Geography, and Innovation in the Digital Era (pp. 23-40). Cham: Springer Nature Switzerland. [HTML] DOI: 10.1007/978-3-031-76906-1_3

Vázquez-Cano, E. (2020). *Language learning with technology: A practical guide for language educators*. Springer.

Veluvali, P. & Surisetti, J. (2022). Learning management system for greater learner engagement in higher education—A review. Higher Education for the Future. sagepub.com

Vesselinov, R., & Grego, J. (2012). *Duolingo effectiveness study*. City University of New York. Retrieved from https://www.duolingo.com

Vetrivel, S. C., Arun, V. P., Maheswari, R., & Saravanan, T. P. (2024). Technology integration in online learning platforms: Blended learning gamification. In Transdisciplinary Teaching and Technological Integration for Improved Learning: Case Studies and Practical Approaches (pp. 219-247). IGI Global. [HTML]

Vogel, J. J., Vogel, D. L., Cannon-Bowers, J. A., Bowers, C. A., Muse, K., & Wright, M. (2006). Computer gaming and interactive simulations for learning: A meta-analysis. *Journal of Educational Computing Research, 34*(3), 229–243. DOI: 10.2190/FLHV-K4WA-WPVQ-H0YM

Vygotsky, L. S. (1978). *Mind in society: The development of higher psychological processes*. Harvard University Press.

Wang, F., & Hannafin, M. J. (2008). Integrating WebQuests in preservice teacher education. *Educational Media International*, *45*(1), 59–73. DOI: 10.1080/09523980701847214

Wang, Y., & Vasquez, C. (2021). AI-driven adaptive learning: A game changer for second language acquisition? *Language Teaching Research*, *25*(6), 891–916.

Williamson, B. (2017). Big Data in Education: The digital future of learning, policy and practice. *Sage (Atlanta, Ga.)*. Advance online publication. DOI: 10.4135/9781529714920

Woolf, B. P. (2010). *Building intelligent interactive tutors: Student-centered strategies for learning*. Morgan Kaufmann.

Wu, S., Cao, Y., Cui, J., Li, R., Qian, H., Jiang, B., & Zhang, W. (2024). A Comprehensive Exploration of Personalized Learning in Smart Education: From Student Modeling to Personalized Recommendations. *arXiv preprint arXiv:2402.01666*.

Xiong, J., Hsiang, E. L., He, Z., Zhan, T., & Wu, S. T. (2021). Augmented reality and virtual reality displays: Emerging technologies and future perspectives. [nature.com]. *Light, Science & Applications*, *10*(1), 1–30. DOI: 10.1038/s41377-021-00658-8 PMID: 34697292

Yang, W., Fang, M., Xu, J., Zhang, X., & Pan, Y. (2024). Exploring the Mediating Role of Different Aspects of Learning Motivation between Metaverse Learning Experiences and Gamification. Electronics. mdpi.com

Yang, F., & Sun, Y. (2023). Artificial intelligence in immersive language learning: Real-time feedback and adaptive assessment. *Educational Review*, *75*(2), 311–330.

Yang, Q. F., Lian, L. W., & Zhao, J. H. (2023). Developing a gamified artificial intelligence educational robot to promote learning effectiveness and behavior in laboratory safety courses for undergraduate students. *International Journal of Educational Technology in Higher Education*, *20*(1), 18. DOI: 10.1186/s41239-023-00391-9

Yavuz, A. (2021). *Comparison of predictive performances of logistic regression and decision tree algorithms: An application of life satisfaction* (Master's thesis, Dokuz Eylul Universitesi (Turkey)).

Yu, H. (2023). Reflection on whether Chat GPT should be banned by academia from the perspective of education and teaching. Frontiers in Psychology. frontiersin.org

Zamiri, M. & Esmaeili, A. (2024). Methods and technologies for supporting knowledge sharing within learning communities: A systematic literature review. Administrative Sciences. mdpi.com

Zamiri, M. & Esmaeili, A. (2024). Strategies, methods, and supports for developing skills within learning communities: A systematic review of the literature. Administrative Sciences. mdpi.com

Zawacki-Richter, O., Marín, V. I., & Bond, M. (2022). Ethical dilemmas in AI-driven education. *Journal of Educational Ethics, 11*(1), 88–104.

Zhang, X., Chen, Y., Hu, L., & Wang, Y. (2022). The metaverse in education: Definition, framework, features, potential applications, challenges, and future research topics. Frontiers in Psychology. frontiersin.org

Zhang, W., Chen, L., & Xu, T. (2023). Metaverse-assisted language education: AI-driven personalization and adaptive learning models. *Computers in Human Behavior, 140*, 107583.

Zhang, Z., Wen, F., Sun, Z., Guo, X., He, T., & Lee, C. (2022). Artificial intelligence-enabled sensing technologies in the 5G/internet of things era: From virtual reality/augmented reality to the digital twin. *Advanced Intelligent Systems, 4*(7), 2100228. DOI: 10.1002/aisy.202100228

Zhao, K. & Guo, X. (2022). Analysis of the application of virtual reality technology in football training. Journal of Sensors. wiley.com

Zhao, Q., Mo, Z., & Fan, M. (2023). POS-ATAEPE-BiLSTM: An aspect-based sentiment analysis algorithm considering part-of-speech embedding. *Applied Intelligence, 53*(22), 27440–27458. DOI: 10.1007/s10489-023-04952-3

Zhao, Y. (2020). Emerging trends in virtual and augmented reality for language learning. *Journal of Educational Technology & Society*, *23*(4), 101–115. DOI: 10.2307/26834692

Zhou, K., Wang, L., & Chen, J. (2023). The future of AI and metaverse in education: Opportunities, challenges, and pedagogical shifts. *Computers in Human Behavior*, *139*, 107564.

Zufarjonovna, J. G. (2022). Benefits of using Web-Quest technology in English lessons as a foreign language. *International Journal of Social Science & Interdisciplinary Research*, *11*, 158–160.

Related References

To continue our tradition of advancing academic research, we have compiled a list of recommended IGI Global readings. These references will provide additional information and guidance to further enrich your knowledge and assist you with your own research and future publications.

Aburezeq, I. M., & Dweikat, F. F. (2017). Cloud Applications in Language Teaching: Examining Pre-Service Teachers' Expertise, Perceptions and Integration. *International Journal of Distance Education Technologies, 15*(4), 39–60. DOI: 10.4018/IJDET.2017100103

Acharjya, B., & Das, S. (2022). Adoption of E-Learning During the COVID-19 Pandemic: The Moderating Role of Age and Gender. *International Journal of Web-Based Learning and Teaching Technologies, 17*(2), 1–14. https://doi.org/10.4018/IJWLTT.20220301.oa4

Adams, J. L., & Thomas, S. K. (2022). Non-Linear Curriculum Experiences for Student Learning and Work Design: What Is the Maximum Potential of a Chat Bot? In Ramlall, S., Cross, T., & Love, M. (Eds.), *Handbook of Research on Future of Work and Education: Implications for Curriculum Delivery and Work Design* (pp. 299–306). IGI Global. https://doi.org/10.4018/978-1-7998-8275-6.ch018

Adera, B. (2017). Supporting Language and Literacy Development for English Language Learners. In Keengwe, J. (Ed.), *Handbook of Research on Promoting Cross-Cultural Competence and Social Justice in Teacher Education* (pp. 339–354). Hershey, PA: IGI Global. DOI: 10.4018/978-1-5225-0897-7.ch018

Ahamer, G. (2017). Quality Assurance for a Developmental "Global Studies" (GS) Curriculum. In I. Management Association (Ed.), *Educational Leadership and Administration: Concepts, Methodologies, Tools, and Applications* (pp. 438-477). Hershey, PA: IGI Global. https://doi.org/ DOI: 10.4018/978-1-5225-1624-8.ch023

Akayoğlu, S., & Seferoğlu, G. (2019). An Analysis of Negotiation of Meaning Functions of Advanced EFL Learners in Second Life: Negotiation of Meaning in Second Life. In Kruk, M. (Ed.), *Assessing the Effectiveness of Virtual Technologies in Foreign and Second Language Instruction* (pp. 61–85). IGI Global. https://doi.org/10.4018/978-1-5225-7286-2.ch003

Akella, N. R. (2022). Unravelling the Web of Qualitative Dissertation Writing!: A Student Reflects. In Zimmerman, A. (Ed.), *Methodological Innovations in Research and Academic Writing* (pp. 260–282). IGI Global. https://doi.org/10.4018/978-1-7998-8283-1.ch014

Alegre de la Rosa, O. M., & Angulo, L. M. (2017). Social Inclusion and Intercultural Values in a School of Education. In Mukerji, S., & Tripathi, P. (Eds.), *Handbook of Research on Administration, Policy, and Leadership in Higher Education* (pp. 518–531). Hershey, PA: IGI Global. DOI: 10.4018/978-1-5225-0672-0.ch020

Alexander, C. (2019). Using Gamification Strategies to Cultivate and Measure Professional Educator Dispositions. *International Journal of Game-Based Learning*, *9*(1), 15–29. https://doi.org/10.4018/IJGBL.2019010102

Anderson, K. M. (2017). Preparing Teachers in the Age of Equity and Inclusion. In I. Management Association (Ed.), *Medical Education and Ethics: Concepts, Methodologies, Tools, and Applications* (pp. 1532-1554). Hershey, PA: IGI Global. DOI: 10.4018/978-1-5225-0978-3.ch069

Awdziej, M. (2017). Case Study as a Teaching Method in Marketing. In Latusek, D. (Ed.), *Case Studies as a Teaching Tool in Management Education* (pp. 244–263). Hershey, PA: IGI Global. DOI: 10.4018/978-1-5225-0770-3.ch013

Bakos, J. (2019). Sociolinguistic Factors Influencing English Language Learning. In Erdogan, N., & Wei, M. (Eds.), *Applied Linguistics for Teachers of Culturally and Linguistically Diverse Learners* (pp. 403–424). IGI Global. https://doi.org/10.4018/978-1-5225-8467-4.ch017

Banas, J. R., & York, C. S. (2017). Pre-Service Teachers' Motivation to Use Technology and the Impact of Authentic Learning Exercises. In Tomei, L. (Ed.), *Exploring the New Era of Technology-Infused Education* (pp. 121–140). Hershey, PA: IGI Global. DOI: 10.4018/978-1-5225-1709-2.ch008

Barton, T. P. (2021). Empowering Educator Allyship by Exploring Racial Trauma and the Disengagement of Black Students. In Reneau, C., & Villarreal, M. (Eds.), *Handbook of Research on Leading Higher Education Transformation With Social Justice, Equity, and Inclusion* (pp. 186–197). IGI Global. https://doi.org/10.4018/978-1-7998-7152-1.ch013

Benhima, M. (2021). Moroccan English Department Student Attitudes Towards the Use of Distance Education During COVID-19: Moulay Ismail University as a Case Study. *International Journal of Information and Communication Technology Education, 17*(3), 105–122. https://doi.org/10.4018/IJICTE.20210701.oa7

Beycioglu, K., & Wildy, H. (2017). Principal Preparation: The Case of Novice Principals in Turkey. In I. Management Association (Ed.), *Educational Leadership and Administration: Concepts, Methodologies, Tools, and Applications* (pp. 1152-1169). Hershey, PA: IGI Global. https://doi.org/DOI: 10.4018/978-1-5225-1624-8.ch054

Bharwani, S., & Musunuri, D. (2018). Reflection as a Process From Theory to Practice. In M. Khosrow-Pour, D.B.A. (Ed.), *Encyclopedia of Information Science and Technology, Fourth Edition* (pp. 1529-1539). Hershey, PA: IGI Global. DOI: 10.4018/978-1-5225-2255-3.ch132

Bhushan, A., Garza, K. B., Perumal, O., Das, S. K., Feola, D. J., Farrell, D., & Birnbaum, A. (2022). Lessons Learned From the COVID-19 Pandemic and the Implications for Pharmaceutical Graduate Education and Research. In Ford, C., & Garza, K. (Eds.), *Handbook of Research on Updating and Innovating Health Professions Education: Post-Pandemic Perspectives* (pp. 324–345). IGI Global. https://doi.org/10.4018/978-1-7998-7623-6.ch014

Bintz, W., Ciecierski, L. M., & Royan, E. (2021). Using Picture Books With Instructional Strategies to Address New Challenges and Teach Literacy Skills in a Digital World. In Haas, L., & Tussey, J. (Eds.), *Connecting Disciplinary Literacy and Digital Storytelling in K-12 Education* (pp. 38–58). IGI Global. https://doi.org/10.4018/978-1-7998-5770-9.ch003

Bohjanen, S. L., Cameron-Standerford, A., & Meidl, T. D. (2018). Capacity Building Pedagogy for Diverse Learners. In Keengwe, J. (Ed.), *Handbook of Research on Pedagogical Models for Next-Generation Teaching and Learning* (pp. 195–212). Hershey, PA: IGI Global. DOI: 10.4018/978-1-5225-3873-8.ch011

Brewer, J. C. (2018). Measuring Text Readability Using Reading Level. In M. Khosrow-Pour, D.B.A. (Ed.), *Encyclopedia of Information Science and Technology, Fourth Edition* (pp. 1499-1507). Hershey, PA: IGI Global. DOI: 10.4018/978-1-5225-2255-3.ch129

Brookbanks, B. C. (2022). Student Perspectives on Business Education in the USA: Current Attitudes and Necessary Changes in an Age of Disruption. In Zhuplev, A., & Koepp, R. (Eds.), *Global Trends, Dynamics, and Imperatives for Strategic Development in Business Education in an Age of Disruption* (pp. 214–231). IGI Global. DOI: 10.4018/978-1-7998-7548-2.ch011

Brown, L. V., Dari, T., & Spencer, N. (2019). Addressing the Impact of Trauma in High Poverty Elementary Schools: An Ecological Model for School Counseling. In Daniels, K., & Billingsley, K. (Eds.), *Creating Caring and Supportive Educational Environments for Meaningful Learning* (pp. 135–153). IGI Global. https://doi.org/10.4018/978-1-5225-5748-7.ch008

Brown, S. L. (2017). A Case Study of Strategic Leadership and Research in Practice: Principal Preparation Programs that Work – An Educational Administration Perspective of Best Practices for Master's Degree Programs for Principal Preparation. In Wang, V. (Ed.), *Encyclopedia of Strategic Leadership and Management* (pp. 1226–1244). Hershey, PA: IGI Global. DOI: 10.4018/978-1-5225-1049-9.ch086

Brzozowski, M., & Ferster, I. (2017). Educational Management Leadership: High School Principal's Management Style and Parental Involvement in School Management in Israel. In Potocan, V., Üngan, M., & Nedelko, Z. (Eds.), *Handbook of Research on Managerial Solutions in Non-Profit Organizations* (pp. 55–74). Hershey, PA: IGI Global. DOI: 10.4018/978-1-5225-0731-4.ch003

Cahapay, M. B. (2020). Delphi Technique in the Development of Emerging Contents in High School Science Curriculum. *International Journal of Curriculum Development and Learning Measurement, 1*(2), 1–9. https://doi.org/10.4018/IJCDLM.2020070101

Camacho, L. F., & Leon Guerrero, A. E. (2022). Indigenous Student Experience in Higher Education: Implementation of Culturally Sensitive Support. In Pangelinan, P., & McVey, T. (Eds.), *Learning and Reconciliation Through Indigenous Education in Oceania* (pp. 254–266). IGI Global. https://doi.org/10.4018/978-1-7998-7736-3.ch016

Cannaday, J. (2017). The Masking Effect: Hidden Gifts and Disabilities of 2e Students. In Dickenson, P., Keough, P., & Courduff, J. (Eds.), *Preparing Pre-Service Teachers for the Inclusive Classroom* (pp. 220–231). Hershey, PA: IGI Global. DOI: 10.4018/978-1-5225-1753-5.ch011

Cederquist, S., Fishman, B., & Teasley, S. D. (2022). What's Missing From the College Transcript?: How Employers Make Sense of Student Skills. In Huang, Y. (Ed.), *Handbook of Research on Credential Innovations for Inclusive Pathways to Professions* (pp. 234–253). IGI Global. https://doi.org/10.4018/978-1-7998-3820-3.ch012

Cockrell, P., & Gibson, T. (2019). The Untold Stories of Black and Brown Student Experiences in Historically White Fraternities and Sororities. In Hoffman-Miller, P., James, M., & Hermond, D. (Eds.), *African American Suburbanization and the Consequential Loss of Identity* (pp. 153–171). IGI Global. https://doi.org/10.4018/978-1-5225-7835-2.ch009

Cohen, M. (2022). Leveraging Content Creation to Boost Student Engagement. In Driscoll, T.III, (Ed.), *Designing Effective Distance and Blended Learning Environments in K-12* (pp. 223–239). IGI Global. https://doi.org/10.4018/978-1-7998-6829-3.ch013

Contreras, E. C., & Contreras, I. I. (2018). Development of Communication Skills through Auditory Training Software in Special Education. In M. Khosrow-Pour, D.B.A. (Ed.), *Encyclopedia of Information Science and Technology, Fourth Edition* (pp. 2431-2441). Hershey, PA: IGI Global. DOI: 10.4018/978-1-5225-2255-3.ch212

Cooke, L., Schugar, J., Schugar, H., Penny, C., & Bruning, H. (2020). Can Everyone Code?: Preparing Teachers to Teach Computer Languages as a Literacy. In Mitchell, J., & Vaughn, E. (Eds.), *Participatory Literacy Practices for P-12 Classrooms in the Digital Age* (pp. 163–183). IGI Global. https://doi.org/10.4018/978-1-7998-0000-2.ch009

Cooley, D., & Whitten, E. (2017). Special Education Leadership and the Implementation of Response to Intervention. In Topor, F. (Ed.), *Handbook of Research on Individualism and Identity in the Globalized Digital Age* (pp. 265–286). Hershey, PA: IGI Global. DOI: 10.4018/978-1-5225-0522-8.ch012

Cosner, S., Tozer, S., & Zavitkovsky, P. (2017). Enacting a Cycle of Inquiry Capstone Research Project in Doctoral-Level Leadership Preparation. In I. Management Association (Ed.), *Educational Leadership and Administration: Concepts, Methodologies, Tools, and Applications* (pp. 1460-1481). Hershey, PA: IGI Global. DOI: 10.4018/978-1-5225-1624-8.ch067

Crawford, C. M. (2018). Instructional Real World Community Engagement. In M. Khosrow-Pour, D.B.A. (Ed.), *Encyclopedia of Information Science and Technology, Fourth Edition* (pp. 1474-1486). Hershey, PA: IGI Global. DOI: 10.4018/978-1-5225-2255-3.ch127

Crosby-Cooper, T., & Pacis, D. (2017). Implementing Effective Student Support Teams. In Dickenson, P., Keough, P., & Courduff, J. (Eds.), *Preparing Pre-Service Teachers for the Inclusive Classroom* (pp. 248–262). Hershey, PA: IGI Global. DOI: 10.4018/978-1-5225-1753-5.ch013

Curran, C. M., & Hawbaker, B. W. (2017). Cultivating Communities of Inclusive Practice: Professional Development for Educators – Research and Practice. In Curran, C., & Petersen, A. (Eds.), *Handbook of Research on Classroom Diversity and Inclusive Education Practice* (pp. 120–153). Hershey, PA: IGI Global. DOI: 10.4018/978-1-5225-2520-2.ch006

Dass, S., & Dabbagh, N. (2018). Faculty Adoption of 3D Avatar-Based Virtual World Learning Environments: An Exploratory Case Study. In I. Management Association (Ed.), *Technology Adoption and Social Issues: Concepts, Methodologies, Tools, and Applications* (pp. 1000-1033). Hershey, PA: IGI Global. https://doi.org/DOI: 10.4018/978-1-5225-5201-7.ch045

Davison, A. M., & Scholl, K. G. (2017). Inclusive Recreation as Part of the IEP Process. In Curran, C., & Petersen, A. (Eds.), *Handbook of Research on Classroom Diversity and Inclusive Education Practice* (pp. 311–330). Hershey, PA: IGI Global. DOI: 10.4018/978-1-5225-2520-2.ch013

DeCoito, I. (2018). Addressing Digital Competencies, Curriculum Development, and Instructional Design in Science Teacher Education. In M. Khosrow-Pour, D.B.A. (Ed.), *Encyclopedia of Information Science and Technology, Fourth Edition* (pp. 1420-1431). Hershey, PA: IGI Global. https://doi.org/DOI: 10.4018/978-1-5225-2255-3.ch122

DeCoito, I., & Richardson, T. (2017). Beyond Angry Birds™: Using Web-Based Tools to Engage Learners and Promote Inquiry in STEM Learning. In Levin, I., & Tsybulsky, D. (Eds.), *Digital Tools and Solutions for Inquiry-Based STEM Learning* (pp. 166–196). Hershey, PA: IGI Global. DOI: 10.4018/978-1-5225-2525-7.ch007

Delmas, P. M. (2017). Research-Based Leadership for Next-Generation Leaders. In Styron, R.Jr, & Styron, J. (Eds.), *Comprehensive Problem-Solving and Skill Development for Next-Generation Leaders* (pp. 1–39). Hershey, PA: IGI Global. DOI: 10.4018/978-1-5225-1968-3.ch001

Demiray, U., & Ekren, G. (2018). Administrative-Related Evaluation for Distance Education Institutions in Turkey. In Buyuk, K., Kocdar, S., & Bozkurt, A. (Eds.), *Administrative Leadership in Open and Distance Learning Programs* (pp. 263–288). Hershey, PA: IGI Global. DOI: 10.4018/978-1-5225-2645-2.ch011

Dickenson, P. (2017). What do we Know and Where Can We Grow?: Teachers Preparation for the Inclusive Classroom. In Dickenson, P., Keough, P., & Courduff, J. (Eds.), *Preparing Pre-Service Teachers for the Inclusive Classroom* (pp. 1–22). Hershey, PA: IGI Global. DOI: 10.4018/978-1-5225-1753-5.ch001

Ding, Q., & Zhu, H. (2021). Flipping the Classroom in STEM Education. In Keengwe, J. (Ed.), *Handbook of Research on Innovations in Non-Traditional Educational Practices* (pp. 155–173). IGI Global. https://doi.org/10.4018/978-1-7998-4360-3.ch008

Dixon, T., & Christison, M. (2021). Teaching English Grammar in a Hybrid Academic ESL Course: A Mixed Methods Study. In Kelch, K., Byun, P., Safavi, S., & Cervantes, S. (Eds.), *CALL Theory Applications for Online TESOL Education* (pp. 229–251). IGI Global. https://doi.org/10.4018/978-1-7998-6609-1.ch010

Donne, V., & Hansen, M. (2017). Teachers' Use of Assistive Technologies in Education. In Tomei, L. (Ed.), *Exploring the New Era of Technology-Infused Education* (pp. 86–101). Hershey, PA: IGI Global. DOI: 10.4018/978-1-5225-1709-2.ch006

Donne, V., & Hansen, M. A. (2018). Business and Technology Educators: Practices for Inclusion. In I. Management Association (Ed.), *Business Education and Ethics: Concepts, Methodologies, Tools, and Applications* (pp. 471-484). Hershey, PA: IGI Global. https://doi.org/DOI: 10.4018/978-1-5225-3153-1.ch026

Dos Santos, L. M. (2022). Completing Student-Teaching Internships Online: Instructional Changes During the COVID-19 Pandemic. In Alaali, M. (Ed.), *Assessing University Governance and Policies in Relation to the COVID-19 Pandemic* (pp. 106–127). IGI Global. https://doi.org/10.4018/978-1-7998-8279-4.ch007

Dreon, O., Shettel, J., & Bower, K. M. (2017). Preparing Next Generation Elementary Teachers for the Tools of Tomorrow. In Grassetti, M., & Brookby, S. (Eds.), *Advancing Next-Generation Teacher Education through Digital Tools and Applications* (pp. 143–159). Hershey, PA: IGI Global. DOI: 10.4018/978-1-5225-0965-3.ch008

Durak, H. Y., & Güyer, T. (2018). Design and Development of an Instructional Program for Teaching Programming Processes to Gifted Students Using Scratch. In Cannaday, J. (Ed.), *Curriculum Development for Gifted Education Programs* (pp. 61–99). Hershey, PA: IGI Global. DOI: 10.4018/978-1-5225-3041-1.ch004

Egorkina, E., Ivanov, M., & Valyavskiy, A. Y. (2018). Students' Research Competence Formation of the Quality of Open and Distance Learning. In Mkrttchian, V., & Belyanina, L. (Eds.), *Handbook of Research on Students' Research Competence in Modern Educational Contexts* (pp. 364–384). Hershey, PA: IGI Global. DOI: 10.4018/978-1-5225-3485-3.ch019

Ekren, G., Karataş, S., & Demiray, U. (2017). Understanding of Leadership in Distance Education Management. In I. Management Association (Ed.), *Educational Leadership and Administration: Concepts, Methodologies, Tools, and Applications* (pp. 34-50). Hershey, PA: IGI Global. https://doi.org/DOI: 10.4018/978-1-5225-1624-8.ch003

Elmore, W. M., Young, J. K., Harris, S., & Mason, D. (2017). The Relationship between Individual Student Attributes and Online Course Completion. In Shelton, K., & Pedersen, K. (Eds.), *Handbook of Research on Building, Growing, and Sustaining Quality E-Learning Programs* (pp. 151–173). Hershey, PA: IGI Global. DOI: 10.4018/978-1-5225-0877-9.ch008

Ercegovac, I. R., Alfirević, N., & Koludrović, M. (2017). School Principals' Communication and Co-Operation Assessment: The Croatian Experience. In I. Management Association (Ed.), *Educational Leadership and Administration: Concepts, Methodologies, Tools, and Applications* (pp. 1568-1589). Hershey, PA: IGI Global. https://doi.org/DOI: 10.4018/978-1-5225-1624-8.ch072

Everhart, D., & Seymour, D. M. (2017). Challenges and Opportunities in the Currency of Higher Education. In Rasmussen, K., Northrup, P., & Colson, R. (Eds.), *Handbook of Research on Competency-Based Education in University Settings* (pp. 41–65). Hershey, PA: IGI Global. DOI: 10.4018/978-1-5225-0932-5.ch003

Farmer, L. S. (2017). Managing Portable Technologies for Special Education. In Wang, V. (Ed.), *Encyclopedia of Strategic Leadership and Management* (pp. 977–987). Hershey, PA: IGI Global. DOI: 10.4018/978-1-5225-1049-9.ch068

Farmer, L. S. (2018). Optimizing OERs for Optimal ICT Literacy in Higher Education. In Keengwe, J. (Ed.), *Handbook of Research on Mobile Technology, Constructivism, and Meaningful Learning* (pp. 366–390). Hershey, PA: IGI Global. DOI: 10.4018/978-1-5225-3949-0.ch020

Ferguson, B. T. (2019). Supporting Affective Development of Children With Disabilities Through Moral Dilemmas. In Ikuta, S. (Ed.), *Handmade Teaching Materials for Students With Disabilities* (pp. 253–275). IGI Global. DOI: 10.4018/978-1-5225-6240-5.ch011

Fındık, L. Y. (2017). Self-Assessment of Principals Based on Leadership in Complexity. In I. Management Association (Ed.), *Educational Leadership and Administration: Concepts, Methodologies, Tools, and Applications* (pp. 978-991). Hershey, PA: IGI Global. https://doi.org/DOI: 10.4018/978-1-5225-1624-8.ch047

Flor, A. G., & Gonzalez-Flor, B. (2018). Dysfunctional Digital Demeanors: Tales From (and Policy Implications of) eLearning's Dark Side. In I. Management Association (Ed.), The Dark Web: Breakthroughs in Research and Practice (pp. 37-50). Hershey, PA: IGI Global. https://doi.org/DOI: 10.4018/978-1-5225-3163-0.ch003

Floyd, K. K., & Shambaugh, N. (2017). Instructional Design for Simulations in Special Education Virtual Learning Spaces. In Kidd, T., & Morris, L.Jr., (Eds.), *Handbook of Research on Instructional Systems and Educational Technology* (pp. 202–215). Hershey, PA: IGI Global. DOI: 10.4018/978-1-5225-2399-4.ch018

Freeland, S. F. (2020). Community Schools: Improving Academic Achievement Through Meaningful Engagement. In Kronick, R. (Ed.), *Emerging Perspectives on Community Schools and the Engaged University* (pp. 132–144). IGI Global. https://doi.org/10.4018/978-1-7998-0280-8.ch008

Ghanbarzadeh, R., & Ghapanchi, A. H. (2019). Applied Areas of Three Dimensional Virtual Worlds in Learning and Teaching: A Review of Higher Education. In I. Management Association (Ed.), *Virtual Reality in Education: Breakthroughs in Research and Practice* (pp. 172-192). IGI Global. https://doi.org/10.4018/978-1-5225-8179-6.ch008

Giovannini, J. M. (2017). Technology Integration in Preservice Teacher Education Programs: Research-based Recommendations. In Grassetti, M., & Brookby, S. (Eds.), *Advancing Next-Generation Teacher Education through Digital Tools and Applications* (pp. 82–102). Hershey, PA: IGI Global. DOI: 10.4018/978-1-5225-0965-3.ch005

Good, S., & Clarke, V. B. (2017). An Integral Analysis of One Urban School System's Efforts to Support Student-Centered Teaching. In Keengwe, J., & Onchwari, G. (Eds.), *Handbook of Research on Learner-Centered Pedagogy in Teacher Education and Professional Development* (pp. 45–68). Hershey, PA: IGI Global. DOI: 10.4018/978-1-5225-0892-2.ch003

Guetzoian, E. (2022). Gamification Strategies for Higher Education Student Worker Training. In Lane, C. (Ed.), *Handbook of Research on Acquiring 21st Century Literacy Skills Through Game-Based Learning* (pp. 164–179). IGI Global. https://doi.org/10.4018/978-1-7998-7271-9.ch009

Hamidi, F., Owuor, P. M., Hynie, M., Baljko, M., & McGrath, S. (2017). Potentials of Digital Assistive Technology and Special Education in Kenya. In Ayo, C., & Mbarika, V. (Eds.), *Sustainable ICT Adoption and Integration for Socio-Economic Development* (pp. 125–151). Hershey, PA: IGI Global. DOI: 10.4018/978-1-5225-2565-3.ch006

Hamim, T., Benabbou, F., & Sael, N. (2022). Student Profile Modeling Using Boosting Algorithms. *International Journal of Web-Based Learning and Teaching Technologies*, *17*(5), 1–13. https://doi.org/10.4018/IJWLTT.20220901.oa4

Henderson, L. K. (2017). Meltdown at Fukushima: Global Catastrophic Events, Visual Literacy, and Art Education. In Shin, R. (Ed.), *Convergence of Contemporary Art, Visual Culture, and Global Civic Engagement* (pp. 80–99). Hershey, PA: IGI Global. DOI: 10.4018/978-1-5225-1665-1.ch005

Hudgins, T., & Holland, J. L. (2018). Digital Badges: Tracking Knowledge Acquisition Within an Innovation Framework. In I. Management Association (Ed.), *Wearable Technologies: Concepts, Methodologies, Tools, and Applications* (pp. 1118-1132). Hershey, PA: IGI Global. https://doi.org/DOI: 10.4018/978-1-5225-5484-4.ch051

Hwang, R., Lin, H., Sun, J. C., & Wu, J. (2019). Improving Learning Achievement in Science Education for Elementary School Students via Blended Learning. *International Journal of Online Pedagogy and Course Design*, *9*(2), 44–62. https://doi.org/10.4018/IJOPCD.2019040104

Jančec, L., & Vodopivec, J. L. (2019). The Implicit Pedagogy and the Hidden Curriculum in Postmodern Education. In Vodopivec, J., Jančec, L., & Štemberger, T. (Eds.), *Implicit Pedagogy for Optimized Learning in Contemporary Education* (pp. 41–59). IGI Global. https://doi.org/10.4018/978-1-5225-5799-9.ch003

Janus, M., & Siddiqua, A. (2018). Challenges for Children With Special Health Needs at the Time of Transition to School. In I. Management Association (Ed.), *Autism Spectrum Disorders: Breakthroughs in Research and Practice* (pp. 339-371). Hershey, PA: IGI Global. DOI: 10.4018/978-1-5225-3827-1.ch018

Jesus, R. A. (2018). Screencasts and Learning Styles. In M. Khosrow-Pour, D.B.A. (Ed.), *Encyclopedia of Information Science and Technology, Fourth Edition* (pp. 1548-1558). Hershey, PA: IGI Global. DOI: 10.4018/978-1-5225-2255-3.ch134

John, G., Francis, N., & Santhakumar, A. B. (2022). Student Engagement: Past, Present, and Future. In Ramlall, S., Cross, T., & Love, M. (Eds.), *Handbook of Research on Future of Work and Education: Implications for Curriculum Delivery and Work Design* (pp. 329–341). IGI Global. https://doi.org/10.4018/978-1-7998-8275-6.ch020

Karpinski, A. C., D'Agostino, J. V., Williams, A. K., Highland, S. A., & Mellott, J. A. (2018). The Relationship Between Online Formative Assessment and State Test Scores Using Multilevel Modeling. In M. Khosrow-Pour, D.B.A. (Ed.), *Encyclopedia of Information Science and Technology, Fourth Edition* (pp. 5183-5192). Hershey, PA: IGI Global. DOI: 10.4018/978-1-5225-2255-3.ch450

Kats, Y. (2017). Educational Leadership and Integrated Support for Students with Autism Spectrum Disorders. In I. Management Association (Ed.), *Educational Leadership and Administration: Concepts, Methodologies, Tools, and Applications* (pp. 101-114). Hershey, PA: IGI Global. https://doi.org/DOI: 10.4018/978-1-5225-1624-8.ch007

Kaya, G., & Altun, A. (2018). Educational Ontology Development. In M. Khosrow-Pour, D.B.A. (Ed.), *Encyclopedia of Information Science and Technology, Fourth Edition* (pp. 1441-1450). Hershey, PA: IGI Global. DOI: 10.4018/978-1-5225-2255-3.ch124

Keough, P. D., & Pacis, D. (2017). Best Practices Implementing Special Education Curriculum and Common Core State Standards using UDL. In Dickenson, P., Keough, P., & Courduff, J. (Eds.), *Preparing Pre-Service Teachers for the Inclusive Classroom* (pp. 107–123). Hershey, PA: IGI Global. DOI: 10.4018/978-1-5225-1753-5.ch006

Kilburn, M., Henckell, M., & Starrett, D. (2018). Factors Contributing to the Effectiveness of Online Students and Instructors. In M. Khosrow-Pour, D.B.A. (Ed.), *Encyclopedia of Information Science and Technology, Fourth Edition* (pp. 1451-1462). Hershey, PA: IGI Global. DOI: 10.4018/978-1-5225-2255-3.ch125

Koban Koç, D. (2021). Gender and Language: A Sociolinguistic Analysis of Second Language Writing. In Hancı-Azizoglu, E., & Kavaklı, N. (Eds.), *Futuristic and Linguistic Perspectives on Teaching Writing to Second Language Students* (pp. 161–177). IGI Global. https://doi.org/10.4018/978-1-7998-6508-7.ch010

Konecny, L. T. (2017). Hybrid, Online, and Flipped Classrooms in Health Science: Enhanced Learning Environments. In I. Management Association (Ed.), *Flipped Instruction: Breakthroughs in Research and Practice* (pp. 355-370). Hershey, PA: IGI Global. https://doi.org/DOI: 10.4018/978-1-5225-1803-7.ch020

Kupietz, K. D. (2021). Gaming and Simulation in Public Education: Teaching Others to Help Themselves and Their Neighbors. In Drumhiller, N., Wilkin, T., & Srba, K. (Eds.), *Simulation and Game-Based Learning in Emergency and Disaster Management* (pp. 41–62). IGI Global. https://doi.org/10.4018/978-1-7998-4087-9.ch003

Kwee, C. T. (2022). Assessing the International Student Enrolment Strategies in Australian Universities: A Case Study During the COVID-19 Pandemic. In Alaali, M. (Ed.), *Assessing University Governance and Policies in Relation to the COVID-19 Pandemic* (pp. 162–188). IGI Global. https://doi.org/10.4018/978-1-7998-8279-4.ch010

Lauricella, S., & McArthur, F. A. (2022). Taking a Student-Centred Approach to Alternative Digital Credentials: Multiple Pathways Toward the Acquisition of Microcredentials. In Piedra, D. (Ed.), *Innovations in the Design and Application of Alternative Digital Credentials* (pp. 57–69). IGI Global. https://doi.org/10.4018/978-1-7998-7697-7.ch003

Llamas, M. F. (2019). Intercultural Awareness in Teaching English for Early Childhood: A Film-Based Approach. In Domínguez Romero, E., Bobkina, J., & Stefanova, S. (Eds.), *Teaching Literature and Language Through Multimodal Texts* (pp. 54–68). IGI Global. https://doi.org/10.4018/978-1-5225-5796-8.ch004

Lokhtina, I., & Kkese, E. T. (2022). Reflecting and Adapting to an Academic Workplace Before and After the Lockdown in Greek-Speaking Cyprus: Opportunities and Challenges. In Zhuplev, A., & Koepp, R. (Eds.), *Global Trends, Dynamics, and Imperatives for Strategic Development in Business Education in an Age of Disruption* (pp. 126–148). IGI Global. https://doi.org/10.4018/978-1-7998-7548-2.ch007

Lovell, K. L. (2017). Development and Evaluation of Neuroscience Computer-Based Modules for Medical Students: Instructional Design Principles and Effectiveness. In Stefaniak, J. (Ed.), *Advancing Medical Education Through Strategic Instructional Design* (pp. 262–276). Hershey, PA: IGI Global. DOI: 10.4018/978-1-5225-2098-6.ch013

Maher, D. (2019). The Use of Course Management Systems in Pre-Service Teacher Education. In Keengwe, J. (Ed.), *Handbook of Research on Blended Learning Pedagogies and Professional Development in Higher Education* (pp. 196–213). IGI Global. https://doi.org/10.4018/978-1-5225-5557-5.ch011

Makewa, L. N. (2019). Teacher Technology Competence Base. In Makewa, L., Ngussa, B., & Kuboja, J. (Eds.), *Technology-Supported Teaching and Research Methods for Educators* (pp. 247–267). IGI Global. https://doi.org/10.4018/978-1-5225-5915-3.ch014

Mallett, C. A. (2022). School Resource (Police) Officers in Schools: Impact on Campus Safety, Student Discipline, and Learning. In Crews, G. (Ed.), *Impact of School Shootings on Classroom Culture, Curriculum, and Learning* (pp. 53–70). IGI Global. https://doi.org/10.4018/978-1-7998-5200-1.ch004

Marinho, J. E., Freitas, I. R., Leão, I. B., Pacheco, L. O., Gonçalves, M. P., Castro, M. J., Silva, P. D., & Moreira, R. J. (2022). Project-Based Learning Application in Higher Education: Student Experiences and Perspectives. In Alves, A., & van Hattum-Janssen, N. (Eds.), *Training Engineering Students for Modern Technological Advancement* (pp. 146–164). IGI Global. https://doi.org/10.4018/978-1-7998-8816-1.ch007

McCleskey, J. A., & Melton, R. M. (2022). Rolling With the Flow: Online Faculty and Student Presence in a Post-COVID-19 World. In Ramlall, S., Cross, T., & Love, M. (Eds.), *Handbook of Research on Future of Work and Education: Implications for Curriculum Delivery and Work Design* (pp. 307–328). IGI Global. https://doi.org/10.4018/978-1-7998-8275-6.ch019

McCormack, V. F., Stauffer, M., Fishley, K., Hohenbrink, J., Mascazine, J. R., & Zigler, T. (2018). Designing a Dual Licensure Path for Middle Childhood and Special Education Teacher Candidates. In Polly, D., Putman, M., Petty, T., & Good, A. (Eds.), *Innovative Practices in Teacher Preparation and Graduate-Level Teacher Education Programs* (pp. 21–36). Hershey, PA: IGI Global. DOI: 10.4018/978-1-5225-3068-8.ch002

McDaniel, R. (2017). Strategic Leadership in Instructional Design: Applying the Principles of Instructional Design through the Lens of Strategic Leadership to Distance Education. In Wang, V. (Ed.), *Encyclopedia of Strategic Leadership and Management* (pp. 1570–1584). Hershey, PA: IGI Global. DOI: 10.4018/978-1-5225-1049-9.ch109

McKinney, R. E., Halli-Tierney, A. D., Gold, A. E., Allen, R. S., & Carroll, D. G. (2022). Interprofessional Education: Using Standardized Cases in Face-to-Face and Remote Learning Settings. In Ford, C., & Garza, K. (Eds.), *Handbook of Research on Updating and Innovating Health Professions Education: Post-Pandemic Perspectives* (pp. 24–42). IGI Global. https://doi.org/10.4018/978-1-7998-7623-6.ch002

Meintjes, H. H. (2021). Learner Views of a Facebook Page as a Supportive Digital Pedagogical Tool at a Public South African School in a Grade 12 Business Studies Class. *International Journal of Smart Education and Urban Society*, *12*(2), 32–45. https://doi.org/10.4018/IJSEUS.2021040104

Melero-García, F. (2022). Training Bilingual Interpreters in Healthcare Settings: Student Perceptions of Online Learning. In LeLoup, J., & Swanson, P. (Eds.), *Handbook of Research on Effective Online Language Teaching in a Disruptive Environment* (pp. 288–310). IGI Global. https://doi.org/10.4018/978-1-7998-7720-2.ch015

Meletiadou, E. (2022). The Use of Peer Assessment as an Inclusive Learning Strategy in Higher Education Institutions: Enhancing Student Writing Skills and Motivation. In Meletiadou, E. (Ed.), *Handbook of Research on Policies and Practices for Assessing Inclusive Teaching and Learning* (pp. 1–26). IGI Global. https://doi.org/10.4018/978-1-7998-8579-5.ch001

Memon, R. N., Ahmad, R., & Salim, S. S. (2018). Critical Issues in Requirements Engineering Education. In I. Management Association (Ed.), *Computer Systems and Software Engineering: Concepts, Methodologies, Tools, and Applications* (pp. 1953-1976). Hershey, PA: IGI Global. DOI: 10.4018/978-1-5225-3923-0.ch081

Mendenhall, R. (2017). Western Governors University: CBE Innovator and National Model. In Rasmussen, K., Northrup, P., & Colson, R. (Eds.), *Handbook of Research on Competency-Based Education in University Settings* (pp. 379–400). Hershey, PA: IGI Global. DOI: 10.4018/978-1-5225-0932-5.ch019

Mense, E. G., Griggs, D. M., & Shanks, J. N. (2018). School Leaders in a Time of Accountability and Data Use: Preparing Our Future School Leaders in Leadership Preparation Programs. In Mense, E., & Crain-Dorough, M. (Eds.), *Data Leadership for K-12 Schools in a Time of Accountability* (pp. 235–259). Hershey, PA: IGI Global. DOI: 10.4018/978-1-5225-3188-3.ch012

Mense, E. G., Griggs, D. M., & Shanks, J. N. (2018). School Leaders in a Time of Accountability and Data Use: Preparing Our Future School Leaders in Leadership Preparation Programs. In Mense, E., & Crain-Dorough, M. (Eds.), *Data Leadership for K-12 Schools in a Time of Accountability* (pp. 235–259). Hershey, PA: IGI Global. DOI: 10.4018/978-1-5225-3188-3.ch012

Mestry, R., & Naicker, S. R. (2017). Exploring Distributive Leadership in South African Public Primary Schools in the Soweto Region. In I. Management Association (Ed.), *Educational Leadership and Administration: Concepts, Methodologies, Tools, and Applications* (pp. 1041-1064). Hershey, PA: IGI Global. DOI: 10.4018/978-1-5225-1624-8.ch050

Monaghan, C. H., & Boboc, M. (2017). (Re) Defining Leadership in Higher Education in the U.S. In Wang, V. (Ed.), *Encyclopedia of Strategic Leadership and Management* (pp. 567–579). Hershey, PA: IGI Global. DOI: 10.4018/978-1-5225-1049-9.ch040

Morall, M. B. (2021). Reimagining Mobile Phones: Multiple Literacies and Digital Media Compositions. In C. Moran (Eds.), *Affordances and Constraints of Mobile Phone Use in English Language Arts Classrooms* (pp. 41-53). IGI Global. https://doi.org/10.4018/978-1-7998-5805-8.ch003

Mthethwa, V. (2022). Student Governance and the Academic Minefield During COVID-19 Lockdown in South Africa. In Alaali, M. (Ed.), *Assessing University Governance and Policies in Relation to the COVID-19 Pandemic* (pp. 255–276). IGI Global. https://doi.org/10.4018/978-1-7998-8279-4.ch015

Muthee, J. M., & Murungi, C. G. (2018). Relationship Among Intelligence, Achievement Motivation, Type of School, and Academic Performance of Kenyan Urban Primary School Pupils. In M. Khosrow-Pour, D.B.A. (Ed.), *Encyclopedia of Information Science and Technology, Fourth Edition* (pp. 1540-1547). Hershey, PA: IGI Global. https://doi.org/DOI: 10.4018/978-1-5225-2255-3.ch133

Naranjo, J. (2018). Meeting the Need for Inclusive Educators Online: Teacher Education in Inclusive Special Education and Dual-Certification. In Polly, D., Putman, M., Petty, T., & Good, A. (Eds.), *Innovative Practices in Teacher Preparation and Graduate-Level Teacher Education Programs* (pp. 106–122). Hershey, PA: IGI Global. DOI: 10.4018/978-1-5225-3068-8.ch007

Nkabinde, Z. P. (2017). Multiculturalism in Special Education: Perspectives of Minority Children in Urban Schools. In Keengwe, J. (Ed.), *Handbook of Research on Promoting Cross-Cultural Competence and Social Justice in Teacher Education* (pp. 382–397). Hershey, PA: IGI Global. DOI: 10.4018/978-1-5225-0897-7.ch020

Nkabinde, Z. P. (2018). Online Instruction: Is the Quality the Same as Face-to-Face Instruction? In Keengwe, J. (Ed.), *Handbook of Research on Digital Content, Mobile Learning, and Technology Integration Models in Teacher Education* (pp. 300–314). Hershey, PA: IGI Global. DOI: 10.4018/978-1-5225-2953-8.ch016

Nugroho, A., & Albusaidi, S. S. (2022). Internationalization of Higher Education: The Methodological Critiques on the Research Related to Study Overseas and International Experience. In Magd, H., & Kunjumuhammed, S. (Eds.), *Global Perspectives on Quality Assurance and Accreditation in Higher Education Institutions* (pp. 75–89). IGI Global. https://doi.org/10.4018/978-1-7998-8085-1.ch005

Nulty, Z., & West, S. G. (2022). Student Engagement and Supporting Students With Accommodations. In Bull, P., & Patterson, G. (Eds.), *Redefining Teacher Education and Teacher Preparation Programs in the Post-COVID-19 Era* (pp. 99–116). IGI Global. https://doi.org/10.4018/978-1-7998-8298-5.ch006

O'Connor, J. R.Jr, & Jackson, K. N. (2017). The Use of iPad® Devices and "Apps" for ASD Students in Special Education and Speech Therapy. In Kats, Y. (Ed.), *Supporting the Education of Children with Autism Spectrum Disorders* (pp. 267–283). Hershey, PA: IGI Global. DOI: 10.4018/978-1-5225-0816-8.ch014

Okolie, U. C., & Yasin, A. M. (2017). TVET in Developing Nations and Human Development. In Okolie, U., & Yasin, A. (Eds.), *Technical Education and Vocational Training in Developing Nations* (pp. 1–25). Hershey, PA: IGI Global. DOI: 10.4018/978-1-5225-1811-2.ch001

Pack, A., & Barrett, A. (2021). A Review of Virtual Reality and English for Academic Purposes: Understanding Where to Start. *International Journal of Computer-Assisted Language Learning and Teaching*, *11*(1), 72–80. https://doi.org/10.4018/IJCALLT.2021010105

Pashollari, E. (2019). Building Sustainability Through Environmental Education: Education for Sustainable Development. In L. Wilson, & C. Stevenson (Eds.), *Building Sustainability Through Environmental Education* (pp. 72-88). IGI Global. https://doi.org/10.4018/978-1-5225-7727-0.ch004

Paulson, E. N. (2017). Adapting and Advocating for an Online EdD Program in Changing Times and "Sacred" Cultures. In I. Management Association (Ed.), *Educational Leadership and Administration: Concepts, Methodologies, Tools, and Applications* (pp. 1849-1876). Hershey, PA: IGI Global. https://doi.org/DOI: 10.4018/978-1-5225-1624-8.ch085

Petersen, A. J., Elser, C. F., Al Nassir, M. N., Stakey, J., & Everson, K. (2017). The Year of Teaching Inclusively: Building an Elementary Classroom for All Students. In Curran, C., & Petersen, A. (Eds.), *Handbook of Research on Classroom Diversity and Inclusive Education Practice* (pp. 332–348). Hershey, PA: IGI Global. DOI: 10.4018/978-1-5225-2520-2.ch014

Pfannenstiel, K. H., & Sanders, J. (2017). Characteristics and Instructional Strategies for Students With Mathematical Difficulties: In the Inclusive Classroom. In Curran, C., & Petersen, A. (Eds.), *Handbook of Research on Classroom Diversity and Inclusive Education Practice* (pp. 250–281). Hershey, PA: IGI Global. DOI: 10.4018/978-1-5225-2520-2.ch011

Phan, A. N. (2022). Quality Assurance of Higher Education From the Glonacal Agency Heuristic: An Example From Vietnam. In Magd, H., & Kunjumuhammed, S. (Eds.), *Global Perspectives on Quality Assurance and Accreditation in Higher Education Institutions* (pp. 136–155). IGI Global. https://doi.org/10.4018/978-1-7998-8085-1.ch008

Preast, J. L., Bowman, N., & Rose, C. A. (2017). Creating Inclusive Classroom Communities Through Social and Emotional Learning to Reduce Social Marginalization Among Students. In Curran, C., & Petersen, A. (Eds.), *Handbook of Research on Classroom Diversity and Inclusive Education Practice* (pp. 183–200). Hershey, PA: IGI Global. DOI: 10.4018/978-1-5225-2520-2.ch008

Randolph, K. M., & Brady, M. P. (2018). Evolution of Covert Coaching as an Evidence-Based Practice in Professional Development and Preparation of Teachers. In Bryan, V., Musgrove, A., & Powers, J. (Eds.), *Handbook of Research on Human Development in the Digital Age* (pp. 281–299). Hershey, PA: IGI Global. DOI: 10.4018/978-1-5225-2838-8.ch013

Rell, A. B., Puig, R. A., Roll, F., Valles, V., Espinoza, M., & Duque, A. L. (2017). Addressing Cultural Diversity and Global Competence: The Dual Language Framework. In Leavitt, L., Wisdom, S., & Leavitt, K. (Eds.), *Cultural Awareness and Competency Development in Higher Education* (pp. 111–131). Hershey, PA: IGI Global. DOI: 10.4018/978-1-5225-2145-7.ch007

Richards, M., & Guzman, I. R. (2020). Academic Assessment of Critical Thinking in Distance Education Information Technology Programs. In I. Management Association (Ed.), *Learning and Performance Assessment: Concepts, Methodologies, Tools, and Applications* (pp. 1-19). IGI Global. https://doi.org/10.4018/978-1-7998-0420-8.ch001

Riel, J., Lawless, K. A., & Brown, S. W. (2017). Defining and Designing Responsive Online Professional Development (ROPD): A Framework to Support Curriculum Implementation. In Kidd, T., & Morris, L.Jr., (Eds.), *Handbook of Research on Instructional Systems and Educational Technology* (pp. 104–115). Hershey, PA: IGI Global. DOI: 10.4018/978-1-5225-2399-4.ch010

Roberts, C. (2017). Advancing Women Leaders in Academe: Creating a Culture of Inclusion. In Mukerji, S., & Tripathi, P. (Eds.), *Handbook of Research on Administration, Policy, and Leadership in Higher Education* (pp. 256–273). Hershey, PA: IGI Global. DOI: 10.4018/978-1-5225-0672-0.ch012

Rodgers, W. J., Kennedy, M. J., Alves, K. D., & Romig, J. E. (2017). A Multimedia Tool for Teacher Education and Professional Development. In Martin, C., & Polly, D. (Eds.), *Handbook of Research on Teacher Education and Professional Development* (pp. 285–296). Hershey, PA: IGI Global. DOI: 10.4018/978-1-5225-1067-3.ch015

Romanowski, M. H. (2017). Qatar's Educational Reform: Critical Issues Facing Principals. In I. Management Association (Ed.), *Educational Leadership and Administration: Concepts, Methodologies, Tools, and Applications* (pp. 1758-1773). Hershey, PA: IGI Global. https://doi.org/DOI: 10.4018/978-1-5225-1624-8.ch080

Ruffin, T. R., Hawkins, D. P., & Lee, D. I. (2018). Increasing Student Engagement and Participation Through Course Methodology. In M. Khosrow-Pour, D.B.A. (Ed.), *Encyclopedia of Information Science and Technology, Fourth Edition* (pp. 1463-1473). Hershey, PA: IGI Global. DOI: 10.4018/978-1-5225-2255-3.ch126

Sabina, L. L., Curry, K. A., Harris, E. L., Krumm, B. L., & Vencill, V. (2017). Assessing the Performance of a Cohort-Based Model Using Domestic and International Practices. In I. Management Association (Ed.), *Educational Leadership and Administration: Concepts, Methodologies, Tools, and Applications*(pp. 913-929). Hershey, PA: IGI Global. https://doi.org/DOI: 10.4018/978-1-5225-1624-8.ch044

Samkian, A., Pascarella, J., & Slayton, J. (2022). Towards an Anti-Racist, Culturally Responsive, and LGBTQ+ Inclusive Education: Developing Critically-Conscious Educational Leaders. In Cain-Sanschagrin, E., Filback, R., & Crawford, J. (Eds.), *Cases on Academic Program Redesign for Greater Racial and Social Justice* (pp. 150–175). IGI Global. https://doi.org/10.4018/978-1-7998-8463-7.ch007

Santamaría, A. P., Webber, M., & Santamaría, L. J. (2017). Effective School Leadership for Māori Achievement: Building Capacity through Indigenous, National, and International Cross-Cultural Collaboration. In I. Management Association (Ed.), *Educational Leadership and Administration: Concepts, Methodologies, Tools, and Applications* (pp. 1547-1567). Hershey, PA: IGI Global. https://doi.org/DOI: 10.4018/978-1-5225-1624-8.ch071

Santamaría, L. J. (2017). Culturally Responsive Educational Leadership in Cross-Cultural International Contexts. In I. Management Association (Ed.), *Educational Leadership and Administration: Concepts, Methodologies, Tools, and Applications* (pp. 1380-1400). Hershey, PA: IGI Global. https://doi.org/DOI: 10.4018/978-1-5225-1624-8.ch064

Segredo, M. R., Cistone, P. J., & Reio, T. G. (2017). Relationships Between Emotional Intelligence, Leadership Style, and School Culture. *International Journal of Adult Vocational Education and Technology*, *8*(3), 25–43. DOI: 10.4018/IJAVET.2017070103

Shalev, N. (2017). Empathy and Leadership From the Organizational Perspective. In Nedelko, Z., & Brzozowski, M. (Eds.), *Exploring the Influence of Personal Values and Cultures in the Workplace* (pp. 348–363). Hershey, PA: IGI Global. DOI: 10.4018/978-1-5225-2480-9.ch018

Siamak, M., Fathi, S., & Isfandyari-Moghaddam, A. (2018). Assessment and Measurement of Education Programs of Information Literacy. In Bhardwaj, R. (Ed.), *Digitizing the Modern Library and the Transition From Print to Electronic* (pp. 164–192). Hershey, PA: IGI Global. DOI: 10.4018/978-1-5225-2119-8.ch007

Siu, K. W., & García, G. J. (2017). Disruptive Technologies and Education: Is There Any Disruption After All? In I. Management Association (Ed.), *Educational Leadership and Administration: Concepts, Methodologies, Tools, and Applications* (pp. 757-778). Hershey, PA: IGI Global. https://doi.org/DOI: 10.4018/978-1-5225-1624-8.ch037

Slagter van Tryon, P. J. (2017). The Nurse Educator's Role in Designing Instruction and Instructional Strategies for Academic and Clinical Settings. In Stefaniak, J. (Ed.), *Advancing Medical Education Through Strategic Instructional Design* (pp. 133–149). Hershey, PA: IGI Global. DOI: 10.4018/978-1-5225-2098-6.ch006

Slattery, C. A. (2018). Literacy Intervention and the Differentiated Plan of Instruction. In *Developing Effective Literacy Intervention Strategies: Emerging Research and Opportunities* (pp. 41–62). Hershey, PA: IGI Global. DOI: 10.4018/978-1-5225-5007-5.ch003

Smith, A. R. (2017). Ensuring Quality: The Faculty Role in Online Higher Education. In Shelton, K., & Pedersen, K. (Eds.), *Handbook of Research on Building, Growing, and Sustaining Quality E-Learning Programs* (pp. 210–231). Hershey, PA: IGI Global. DOI: 10.4018/978-1-5225-0877-9.ch011

Souders, T. M. (2017). Understanding Your Learner: Conducting a Learner Analysis. In Stefaniak, J. (Ed.), *Advancing Medical Education Through Strategic Instructional Design* (pp. 1–29). Hershey, PA: IGI Global. DOI: 10.4018/978-1-5225-2098-6.ch001

Spring, K. J., Graham, C. R., & Ikahihifo, T. B. (2018). Learner Engagement in Blended Learning. In M. Khosrow-Pour, D.B.A. (Ed.), *Encyclopedia of Information Science and Technology, Fourth Edition* (pp. 1487-1498). Hershey, PA: IGI Global. DOI: 10.4018/978-1-5225-2255-3.ch128

Storey, V. A., Anthony, A. K., & Wahid, P. (2017). Gender-Based Leadership Barriers: Advancement of Female Faculty to Leadership Positions in Higher Education. In Wang, V. (Ed.), *Encyclopedia of Strategic Leadership and Management* (pp. 244–258). Hershey, PA: IGI Global. DOI: 10.4018/978-1-5225-1049-9.ch018

Stottlemyer, D. (2018). Develop a Teaching Model Plan for a Differentiated Learning Approach. In *Differentiated Instructional Design for Multicultural Environments: Emerging Research and Opportunities* (pp. 106–130). Hershey, PA: IGI Global. DOI: 10.4018/978-1-5225-5106-5.ch005

Stottlemyer, D. (2018). Developing a Multicultural Environment. In *Differentiated Instructional Design for Multicultural Environments: Emerging Research and Opportunities* (pp. 1–27). Hershey, PA: IGI Global. DOI: 10.4018/978-1-5225-5106-5.ch001

Swagerty, T. (2022). Digital Access to Culturally Relevant Curricula: The Impact on the Native and Indigenous Student. In Reeves, E., & McIntyre, C. (Eds.), *Multidisciplinary Perspectives on Diversity and Equity in a Virtual World* (pp. 99–113). IGI Global. https://doi.org/10.4018/978-1-7998-8028-8.ch006

Swami, B. N., Gobona, T., & Tsimako, J. J. (2017). Academic Leadership: A Case Study of the University of Botswana. In Baporikar, N. (Ed.), *Innovation and Shifting Perspectives in Management Education* (pp. 1–32). Hershey, PA: IGI Global. DOI: 10.4018/978-1-5225-1019-2.ch001

Swanson, K. W., & Collins, G. (2018). Designing Engaging Instruction for the Adult Learners. In M. Khosrow-Pour, D.B.A. (Ed.), *Encyclopedia of Information Science and Technology, Fourth Edition* (pp. 1432-1440). Hershey, PA: IGI Global. DOI: 10.4018/978-1-5225-2255-3.ch123

Swartz, B. A., Lynch, J. M., & Lynch, S. D. (2018). Embedding Elementary Teacher Education Coursework in Local Classrooms: Examples in Mathematics and Special Education. In Polly, D., Putman, M., Petty, T., & Good, A. (Eds.), *Innovative Practices in Teacher Preparation and Graduate-Level Teacher Education Programs* (pp. 262–292). Hershey, PA: IGI Global. DOI: 10.4018/978-1-5225-3068-8.ch015

Taliadorou, N., & Pashiardis, P. (2017). Emotional Intelligence and Political Skill Really Matter in Educational Leadership. In I. Management Association (Ed.), *Educational Leadership and Administration: Concepts, Methodologies, Tools, and Applications* (pp. 1274-1303). Hershey, PA: IGI Global. https://doi.org/DOI: 10.4018/978-1-5225-1624-8.ch060

Tandoh, K. A., & Ebe-Arthur, J. E. (2018). Effective Educational Leadership in the Digital Age: An Examination of Professional Qualities and Best Practices. In Keengwe, J. (Ed.), *Handbook of Research on Digital Content, Mobile Learning, and Technology Integration Models in Teacher Education* (pp. 244–265). Hershey, PA: IGI Global. DOI: 10.4018/978-1-5225-2953-8.ch013

Tobin, M. T. (2018). Multimodal Literacy. In M. Khosrow-Pour, D.B.A. (Ed.), *Encyclopedia of Information Science and Technology, Fourth Edition* (pp. 1508-1516). Hershey, PA: IGI Global. DOI: 10.4018/978-1-5225-2255-3.ch130

Torres, K. M., Arrastia-Chisholm, M. C., & Tackett, S. (2019). A Phenomenological Study of Pre-Service Teachers' Perceptions of Completing ESOL Field Placements. *International Journal of Teacher Education and Professional Development*, *2*(2), 85–101. https://doi.org/10.4018/IJTEPD.2019070106

Torres, M. C., Salamanca, Y. N., Cely, J. P., & Aguilar, J. L. (2020). All We Need is a Boost! Using Multimodal Tools and the Translanguaging Strategy: Strengthening Speaking in the EFL Classroom. *International Journal of Computer-Assisted Language Learning and Teaching*, *10*(3), 28–47. DOI: 10.4018/IJCALLT.2020070103

Torres, M. L., & Ramos, V. J. (2018). Music Therapy: A Pedagogical Alternative for ASD and ID Students in Regular Classrooms. In Epler, P. (Ed.), *Instructional Strategies in General Education and Putting the Individuals With Disabilities Act (IDEA) Into Practice* (pp. 222–244). Hershey, PA: IGI Global. DOI: 10.4018/978-1-5225-3111-1.ch008

Toulassi, B. (2017). Educational Administration and Leadership in Francophone Africa: 5 Dynamics to Change Education. In Mukerji, S., & Tripathi, P. (Eds.), *Handbook of Research on Administration, Policy, and Leadership in Higher Education* (pp. 20–45). Hershey, PA: IGI Global. DOI: 10.4018/978-1-5225-0672-0.ch002

Umair, S., & Sharif, M. M. (2018). Predicting Students Grades Using Artificial Neural Networks and Support Vector Machine. In M. Khosrow-Pour, D.B.A. (Ed.), *Encyclopedia of Information Science and Technology, Fourth Edition* (pp. 5169-5182). Hershey, PA: IGI Global. DOI: 10.4018/978-1-5225-2255-3.ch449

Vettraino, L., Castello, V., Guspini, M., & Guglielman, E. (2018). Self-Awareness and Motivation Contrasting ESL and NEET Using the SAVE System. In M. Khosrow-Pour, D.B.A. (Ed.), *Encyclopedia of Information Science and Technology, Fourth Edition* (pp. 1559-1568). Hershey, PA: IGI Global. DOI: 10.4018/978-1-5225-2255-3.ch135

Wiemelt, J. (2017). Critical Bilingual Leadership for Emergent Bilingual Students. In I. Management Association (Ed.), *Educational Leadership and Administration: Concepts, Methodologies, Tools, and Applications* (pp. 1606-1631). Hershey, PA: IGI Global. DOI: 10.4018/978-1-5225-1624-8.ch074

Wolf, F., Seyfarth, F. C., & Pflaum, E. (2018). Scalable Capacity-Building for Geographically Dispersed Learners: Designing the MOOC "Sustainable Energy in Small Island Developing States (SIDS)". In Pandey, U., & Indrakanti, V. (Eds.), *Open and Distance Learning Initiatives for Sustainable Development* (pp. 58–83). Hershey, PA: IGI Global. DOI: 10.4018/978-1-5225-2621-6.ch003

Woodley, X. M., Mucundanyi, G., & Lockard, M. (2017). Designing Counter-Narratives: Constructing Culturally Responsive Curriculum Online. *International Journal of Online Pedagogy and Course Design, 7*(1), 43–56. DOI: 10.4018/IJOPCD.2017010104

Yell, M. L., & Christle, C. A. (2017). The Foundation of Inclusion in Federal Legislation and Litigation. In Curran, C., & Petersen, A. (Eds.), *Handbook of Research on Classroom Diversity and Inclusive Education Practice* (pp. 27–52). Hershey, PA: IGI Global. DOI: 10.4018/978-1-5225-2520-2.ch002

Zinner, L. (2019). Fostering Academic Citizenship With a Shared Leadership Approach. In Zhu, C., & Zayim-Kurtay, M. (Eds.), *University Governance and Academic Leadership in the EU and China* (pp. 99–117). IGI Global. https://doi.org/10.4018/978-1-5225-7441-5.ch007

About the Contributors

Rubén González Vallejo holds a PhD from the University of Salamanca with a thesis entitled "Comparative Legal Language: Translation and Analysis of Environmental Crimes in the Italian Penal Code," he has focused his research on legal translation and the environment in the Italian-Spanish combination, as well as on new technologies (artificial intelligence) and language teaching. With a background in philology and translation and interpreting, he is a member of various national and international research groups and centers. He has taught undergraduate and master's courses in Italy and Ireland, and has participated in various Erasmus+ Teaching mobility programs, in addition to having been a visiting research fellow at University College Dublin for a year. His research has led him to coordinate monographs, supervise doctoral theses, participate in international teaching innovation projects, and participate in various transfer activities and projects. Finally, he serves on various scientific committees for journals and conferences, and has served as a member of the evaluation committee for international R&D projects.

***

Nurul Aini is a dedicated lecturer at the Faculty of Teacher Training and Education, specializing in English Education at Nahdlatul Ulama University, Indonesia. She holds a Doctorate in Linguistics from Sebelas Maret University, with a research focus on politeness strategies in media discourse. Her academic journey includes a Master's degree in Education from Muhammadiyah University of Surakarta and a Bachelor's degree in

English Education from STAIN Jurai Siwo Metro, Lampung. With years of experience in academia, she has served as the Head of the English Education Study Program and is currently the Head of the Language and Arts Centre. Her research interests include Language Education Sciences, Pragmatics, and Systemic Functional Linguistics. She has published multiple journal articles and books on language teaching and discourse analysis. Beyond academia, she actively participates in professional associations such as APSPBI and ADRI, contributing to English language education development. She is also involved in various academic committees, workshops, and seminars. Her expertise extends to instructional material development, innovative teaching strategies, and educational technology integration. Passionate about fostering student engagement and critical thinking, she continues to shape the future of language education in Indonesia.

Panagiotis Arvanitis is Professor at the Faculty of French Studies of the Aristotle University of Thessaloniki, in the field of Multimedia Databases, Information and Communication Technologies and New ICT Learning Environments, with a teaching and research experience. He has published several papers in the fields of New ICT Learning Environments, and the use of Multimedia Databases and Multimedia tools in Language Teaching and Learning. He is interested in online language learning, computer-supported collaborative language learning, web 2.0 and web 3.0 technologies, 3D virtual learning environments, mobile language learning tools and digital games based learning. He is especially interested in how language instructors can utilize Web 2.0 and Web 3.0 technologies to promote student collaboration and knowledge construction in both online and offline settings. Additionally, some of his articles encourage language teachers to carefully consider their selection and use of online educational technologies.

Andi Asrifan is an accomplished educator and academic leader with a Doctorate in Education, specializing in English Language Education from Universitas Negeri Makassar. With a strong academic foundation, he holds a Master's degree in the same field and a Bachelor's degree in Secondary Education. His dissertation focused on developing bilingual educational materials, reflecting his commitment to enhancing language education. Dr.

Asrifan has extensive experience in various educational roles, including serving as the Head of the International Affairs Office at Politeknik Negeri Nunukan and as the Head of the Institute for Student Development and Alumni at Universitas Muhammadiyah Sidenreng Rappang. He is also an active member of several professional organizations, including the Linguistics Society of Indonesia and TEFLIN. In addition to his administrative roles, Dr. Asrifan is a passionate advocate for educational innovation and has participated in numerous international conferences and webinars, sharing his insights on language teaching and curriculum development. His dedication to professional development is evident through his participation in various training programs.

Khristianto, S.S., M.Hum., is a senior lecturer at the Faculty of Cultural Sciences, Universitas Muhammadiyah Purwokerto. He completed his undergraduate studies in English Literature at UNS Surakarta and earned his master's degree in Applied Linguistics from UNY Yogyakarta. Currently serving as the Head of TPMF, Khristianto has a wealth of experience in both research and teaching. His research interests include gender ideology in women's writings, discourse analysis on multimodalities, and Javanese grammar. He has led numerous studies, such as analyzing gender ideology in online media and examining the concept of animacy in the Javanese language. He has also published extensively in national and international journals, with works focusing on topics such as cultural translation, multimodal meanings, and political discourse analysis. In addition to research, Khristianto has been actively involved in community service, focusing on language education for teachers. His dedication to both academia and community service has contributed significantly to advancing linguistic studies and education in Indonesia. His most recent publications explore contemporary issues in discourse, including modality in social media and linguistic landscapes in urban settings.

Pinelopi Krystalli is an Assistant Professor at Aristotle University of Thessaloniki School of French Language and Literature. She holds a PhD in Language and Communication Sciences, from the Faculty of Philosophy at the same university. Her research focuses on foreign language didactics and French language teaching, particularly emphasizing integrating technology in these fields. Her interests include mobile learning, gamification, serious games for language teaching, and distance education. She has contributed to several European research projects and has published numerous articles in international academic journals specializing in these fields.

Mohit Yadav is an Associate Professor in the area of Human Resource Management at Jindal Global Business School (JGBS). He has a rich blend of work experience from both Academics as well as Industry. Prof. Mohit holds a Ph.D. from Department of Management Studies, Indian Institute of Technology Roorkee (IIT Roorkee) and has completed Master of Human Resource and Organizational Development (MHROD) from prestigious Delhi School of Economics, University of Delhi. He also holds a B.Com (Hons.) degree from University of Delhi and UGC-JRF scholarship. He has published various research papers and book chapters with reputed publishers like Springer, Sage, Emerald, Elsevier, Inderscience etc. and presented research papers in national and International conferences both in India and abroad. He has many best paper awards on his credit too. He is reviewer of various international journals like Computers in Human Behavior, Policing etc. His areas of interest are Organizational Behavior, HRM, Recruitment and Selection, Organizational Citizenship Behavior, Quality of work life and role.

Rohit Yadav is an Associate Professor School of Management IILM University, Greater Noida

Index

A

B

C

D

E

F

G

R

S

T

U

V

W

www.ingramcontent.com/pod-product-compliance
Ingram Content Group UK Ltd.
Pitfield, Milton Keynes, MK11 3LW, UK
UKHW050946290926
15470UKWH00005B/1662

9 798369 399743